**Andy Thomas** is a leading [...] mysteries and cover-ups and [...] lecturers in this field. His [...] *Heretics, Conspiracies* and *The Truth* [...] author of *Vital Signs*, widely described as the definitive guide to the crop circle phenomenon and nominated for *Kindred Spirit* magazine's Best Book Award. Andy has also written books on folklore and history, including *Christmas: A Short History from Solstice to Santa*, and is a regular writer for *Nexus Magazine*.

Andy is co-organizer and MC for the renowned annual UK "Expand Your Horizons" conference, the Glastonbury Symposium, which has been running for three and a half decades, and is also founder of Changing Times, which holds events on free thinking and the unexplained.

Andy lectures extensively around the world and has made numerous TV appearances on channels such as NBC, History, National Geographic, Amazon Prime, Vice Media, the BBC and ITV. Andy has featured in countless radio programmes – mainstream and alternative – and is a frequent guest on internet podcasts.

More information on Andy, with news, articles to read, videos to watch and social media links, can be found at: *www.truthagenda.org*

# By the same author:

## On *Strange* ...

One of the most important things that can happen to us in this amazing world is for our minds to be opened to its mysteries, and Andy Thomas does just that in this exciting adventure of a book. *Strange* is really very strange, and that is exactly what is so marvellous about it.

**Whitley Strieber**, UFO/ET researcher and
contactee, and author of *Communion*

The thing that makes Andy Thomas stand out in his all his work is his unique clarity of thought and ability to communicate sometimes complex or unusual ideas in an accessible, down-to-earth style. He always retains a balance between the rational and seemingly irrational or inexplicable. I have been excited about reading this book for a while because these are the exact qualities needed to approach such a fascinating subject and document such surprisingly common experiences in people's lives.

We live in a strange world, and it's getting stranger. This is something that needs to be celebrated, as the less we think we know, the more potential for wonder and awe there is, which, in an age of cynicism and disenchantment, can only be a good thing. Andy guides the reader into this widening of perception with expertise and grace, thus contributing something essential to the world.

**Jez Hughes**, leading shaman and author of
*The Heart of Life* and *The Wisdom of Mental Illness*

Andy Thomas is the ideal author to guide you into, and through, the subjects contained in *Strange*. With his many published books, hundreds of interviews and thousands of hours of public presentations, Andy is well qualified to fully understand the subjects and also to write, comment on and describe what, to many people, just seem to be inexplicable mysteries. With Andy's accessible style and even-handed treatment, you will be well rewarded, better informed and more knowledgeable.

**Marcus Allen**, UK publisher of *Nexus Magazine*

## On Andy Thomas ...

I am delighted with Andy Thomas's endless pursuit of the unknown – an inspirational intellect that balances science and spirit in such an impartial, philosophical way. Over the years of knowing him, I have always celebrated his ability to find harmony and balance in opposing fields of thought, always respecting both, and bringing us new insights into the magic that is our unfolding multi-dimensional reality.

**Patricia Cori**, internationally acclaimed author, spiritual guide and public speaker

Andy Thomas makes complex and involved topics both entertaining and easy to understand and digest, while maintaining a high level of detail through his thorough investigations. He makes you want to experience the subject he writes about personally, as is the skill of a great raconteur. He lectures as he writes, with enthusiasm, warmth and knowledge.

**Ian Lynch**, writer, speaker, coach and guide on happiness and fortitude in life, and author of *Rites of Man*

Andy Thomas is an admirable writer with whom to explore paranormal experiences. He is an experienced researcher who offers integrity in carefully approaching the evidence, using the standards of "the reasonable man". I trust his judgement.

**Nick Kyle**, past President of the Scottish Society for Psychical Research, paranormal investigator and conference speaker

Andy's work as a researcher, author and speaker in the shadowy world of mysteries and conspiracies is second to none. He manages to combine a sense of wonder and open-mindedness with both a level-headed, forensic approach and an easy delivery that allow us to make up our own minds on some of life's most intriguing topics.

**Piers Adams**, world-renowned classical recorder player and truth seeker

I have known Andy Thomas for a number of years, and I find him to be an excellent author, researcher and conference organizer. He is also an interesting and informative speaker with a wealth of knowledge on many subjects from UFOs to the world's greatest mysteries.

**Gary Heseltine**, leading UFO researcher and editor of *UFO Truth Magazine* and author of *Non-Human*

Andy Thomas has comprehensive knowledge and experience in the field of crop circles and other related phenomena. He has been researching these for over thirty years. Having visited some crop circles myself, I've found his commentary and writings on this important subject have been valuable to me and given me a greater understanding of my own experience.

**Robert Salas**, former USAF officer and UFO whistleblower, author of *Faded Giant* and *UAPs and the Nuclear Puzzle*

## On Andy's *The New Heretics* ...

This is probably one of the most important and informative books you will ever read ... an extremely well written, valid and worrying insight ... I cannot recommend this new work highly enough; in fact, it's a ray of light and should be required reading in all secondary schools ... Buy it, read it and learn.

*Phenomena* magazine

Essential reading in our dangerously compromised times, *The New Heretics* is exceptionally well-informed and has that hard-to-put-down quality that confirms it as a must-read for anyone interested in the bewildering state of Western culture and society today. It's level-headed, wise and deeply insightful.

**Medium.com**

A rich, compelling and deeply timely book, one that should be on the must-read list of anyone interested in the underlying forces driving human society at this pivotal moment in history ... It explores in great detail, and with extensive research, changes in society, censorship and worrying losses of freedoms.

*Caduceus* magazine

Andy Thomas analyses polarization and tries to find ways to bridge the polarized divides and create a better way forward. It is a very thorough analysis ... the text is well written and testifies to an author with great insight in the field.

**Scandinavian UFO Information**

# ANDY THOMAS

# STRANGE

## PARANORMAL REALITIES IN THE EVERYDAY WORLD

WATKINS
1893

STRANGE
Andy Thomas

This edition first published in the UK and USA in 2025 by
Watkins, an imprint of Watkins Media Limited
Unit 11, Shepperton House,
89-93 Shepperton Road,
London
N1 3DF

enquiries@watkinspublishing.com

Design and typography copyright © Watkins Media 2025
Text copyright © Andy Thomas 2025

10 9 8 7 6 5 4 3 2 1

Printed and bound by CPI Group (UK) Ldt. Croydon, CRO 4YY

A CIP record for this book is available from the British Library

ISBN: 978-1-78678-937-2 (paperback)
ISBN: 978-1-78678-960-0 (ebook)

www.watkinspublishing.com

The manufacturer's authorised representative in the EU for product safety is
eucomply OÜ - Pärnu mnt 139b-14, 11317 Tallinn, Estonia,
hello@eucompliancepartner.com,www.eucompliancepartner.com

# CONTENTS

# ACKNOWLEDGEMENTS

This book would not exist without the many people who dared to share their experiences and memories with me over the years. So, firstly a thank you to all those nameless individuals for their part in inadvertently helping to reveal a whole other world to the one we are usually shown, and to the countless event organizers who have kindly asked me to speak over the years, thus facilitating those interactions.

Huge thanks also to those named in the text for taking the time to send me their fascinating written contributions – and to those whose stories sadly didn't make it in purely due to space and context. I would also like to thank all the generous contributors and reviewers for their humbling testimonials.

Additional thanks to my dearest wife Helen for her very appreciated patience, love and help; to Dick Alder and Martin Noakes; and to all at Watkins Publishing for their encouraging faith and excellent work, especially Fiona Robertson.

No artificial intelligence was used anywhere in the writing of this book, so any unintended oversights or omissions are due entirely to human error and will be happily corrected in future editions.

Extra special gratitude goes to my three moderators for *Strange* (see Introduction), Dr John Cole, Chris Connelly and Barry Reynolds, whose diligent checking and valuable observations were absorbed into the writing process and helped deepen its mission.

Here are their full biographies, in alphabetical order:

**Dr John Cole:** John studied Natural Science as an undergraduate at Cambridge and majored in Theoretical

Physics. He then spent two years travelling in Europe, Asia and the Middle East and learned several languages at a fundamental level. He has practised meditation for 51 years under the guidance of Prem Rawat and has four children and six grandchildren.

Qualifications:

1970: BA in Natural Science (1st Class Honours) from Cambridge University

1982: DPhil in Theoretical Physics from Sussex University with his thesis, "Renormalisation of the Electroweak Model"

1991: MA (with Distinction) in Linguistics with his thesis, "Iconicity in Verbal Morphosyntax"

2024: Publication in preparation: "On the Self-Organisation of Complex, Globally Interacting Systems"

**Chris Connelly MSc:** Chris has over 30 years' experience as a scientist and engineer in the space industry, developing imaging technologies and software used in scientific space missions. He is also an accomplished medium and educator, guiding countless individuals to delve into the intricacies of spiritual unfoldment and the scientific principles underpinning this profound practice. With a keen research interest in the altered states associated with Spiritualist trances, Chris integrates rigorous academic inquiry with experiential knowledge. He holds Master of Science degrees in both Applied Science and Psychology, reflecting his commitment to a comprehensive understanding of the mind and spirit.

Chris is an active contributor to the academic community, often collaborating with Spiritualist mediums and presenting his groundbreaking research at prestigious gatherings. His work is frequently published in respected academic journals, further establishing his reputation as a leading voice in the intersection of spirituality and science.

**Barry Reynolds:** Barry started writing computer programmes around 1977 when he astonished his teacher by instructing the school programmable calculator to calculate prime numbers, something no one knew was possible. From that moment forward his destiny was the world of computing, where he spent his entire career working his way up from a programmer to become Head of IT. He worked mostly in and around London in the banking and finance sector.

This "background of 1s and 0s, black and white" made him fiercely logical and encouraged him to seek sensible, rational explanations for all things unexplained, using the mantra "Data is everything". A lifetime of applying this approach has made him realize that actually "There are more things in heaven and earth, Horatio, than are dreamt of in your philosophy."

Barry retired a few years ago. He spends his spare time digitizing paper-based paranormal archives from the 1980s through to the early 2000s to ensure treasured, hard-to-come-by information is not lost for future generations.

Thank you all.

# INTRODUCTION

Sceptics are impossible to please. No matter what evidence is presented, for all their boasts of using scientific methods, if they have made up their minds not to believe in something then nothing will budge them. And they get very upset when confronted with things that do not fit their worldview. "Claims of the paranormal" or the "strange" are inevitably their main bugbear.

Here is a scenario I have experienced several times as a lecturer and author on the paranormal: I present my case in front of an audience, sharing images, evidence and anecdotes. I am careful not to tell anyone what to think, and merely point out that certain cases might be at least worthy of discussion. Most seem happy enough to listen. Nonetheless, one figure will sometimes stand out in the auditorium. Something in their body language disturbs the stillness with an unease, a shuffling, even a direct shaking of the head. These agitated souls feel the need to be seen, to communicate to those around them that something, in their view, has gone very wrong. And so I wait for the explosion in the Q&A session. The lights are raised, the figure stands, and the demolition of my character begins.

The accusations usually follow a set pattern: I am wrong about almost everything I have shared; there *is* no paranormal; all the eye-witnesses are naïve, mistaken or liars; these are subjects that should have been consigned to the trashcan of foolish superstitious history; worse, I am directly advocating a return to a world of dangerous "Dark Age" thinking that risks holding back the human race with wicked unscientific ways. Having delivered such a tirade, one gentleman once proffered this final assessment: "I put it to

1

you that there is only one explanation for your position: that you are a nutcase. A madman. Deranged." And so forth.

I am honoured to say that I have received this treatment from a variety of eminent people over the years, including two particularly incandescent physicists at the UK's National Physics Laboratory (which kindly invited me into the lion's den). I even feared they might resort to physical violence after the volatile public discussion, but thankfully I was surrounded by others when they approached the stage. There is little that can be done in such situations except to remain as polite as possible, let the aggressors have their say, and then beg to differ. And I do beg to differ, because it is plain to me that the paranormal – which shall be defined in Chapter 1 – definitely does exist.

It follows, therefore, that sceptics will not like this book and will probably throw it across the room within a few minutes. Try not to break anything if you do. Although these pages are not an exercise in blind belief against discernment and evidence – which *is* important – there will be no long chapters torturously addressing the minutiae of condemnation from cynics that can be found on any sceptic website.[1] Defences will be made as to why blanket scepticism, in this author's view, is misguided, but *Strange* mostly takes a different approach and assumes that particular instances of unexplained phenomena cannot always be put down to mundane causes. The title was chosen because it is becoming clear even to mainstream scientists that the universe is indeed a far stranger place than anyone previously thought. Simply dismissing the very odd experiences that people regularly encounter is no longer good enough; better explanations are required and the following chapters ask instead what *non*-mundane causes might explain them and help to identify the repeating patterns. The irony is that accounts of the strange are in fact so common that the very definition of "strange" may have to be rethought.

Over my three and a half decades of lecturing on cover-ups and the paranormal I have met or corresponded with thousands of apparently sane, reliable people with astonishing tales to tell that reveal a very different world to the materialistically limited one we are usually told we live in. Fearing ridicule, many of them have remained silent among friends and relatives, but frequently share their stories with me because they know that I will actually hear them out. This book exists to put those experiences – and a few of my own – on public record to make the case that the strange very definitely demands a new respect and an elevated profile. It is not another throwaway compendium of old stories but a fresh look at the subject using brand new material that will sometimes refer to famous cases to show correlations and give wider context.

In an era when even the US military has now accepted that, for example, Unexplained Anomalous Phenomena are indeed active in our airspace (see Chapter 6) and apparently contravening the known laws of physics – an extraordinary development, which officially acknowledges something scorned for so long, whatever the explanation – it remains a paradox that the mainstream still hesitates to report the paranormal seriously, despite the fact that a majority of people believe in such things. In a 2022 YouGov poll, 67 per cent of US citizens recorded having had at least one inexplicable encounter.[2] The signs are that something may be changing at last, but views are deeply polarized and far more change will be needed to undo the legacy of ingrained scepticism – and indeed *scientism*, effectively a religion in itself – that began in the supposed "Enlightenment" over three centuries ago.

Science is, of course, essential. We see its benefits (and sometimes hazards) all around us, but it can too often be closed-minded and refuse to see what is before our very eyes – the antithesis of a real scientific method. With this in mind, I have ensured that, alongside rebuttals of unreasonable scepticism, this book employs a scientific approach of its own. I am not a scientist and do not pretend to be – but I know people who are and I employed the knowledge of three rational but open-minded talents as moderators for this book. Throughout the writing process I have taken onboard their comments and suggestions, always starting from the assumption that paranormal events may have more complex causes than are usually allowed for. The panel, who occasionally feature directly in the narrative, are:

**Dr John Cole**, a physicist who studied Natural Science as an undergraduate at Cambridge and majored in Theoretical Physics. He also has an MA with Distinction in Linguistics.

**Chris Connelly MSc**, who holds Master of Science degrees in both Applied Science and Psychology, and works in space engineering. He is also a Spiritualist medium, taking a scientific approach.

**Barry Reynolds**, a retired computer programmer and former Head of IT working in the banking and finance sector. He is also a paranormal archivist and statistician.

Full biographies are featured in the Acknowledgements. Sceptics will complain that I have specifically chosen overseers who are flexible towards the paranormal and are therefore biased. And they are, which is the very reason I have selected them. If those sceptics believe that they themselves are not biased in their own way, they need to be more honest with themselves. All three of these candidates are considered trustworthy and reliable enough not to have shared anything other than their true opinions with me – and all are qualified in their fields and genuinely scientifically minded.

With this book, I hope to open the door to fresh thinking which might reveal that the universe does allow for bizarre phenomena after all. Ultimately, everything must have a scientific explanation: the supernatural is just the natural that we haven't yet understood.[3] If science isn't always looking in the right direction to find it, then a different approach is required.

Even for those who do already believe in the strange, we have been taught too often that the paranormal is a dark or "spooky" subject to be avoided. Although it can occasionally be threatening, we will discover through these pages that people's interactions with it can frequently be positive and life-affirming, sometimes even fun.

There is a powerful case to be made for a more innovative and open-minded attitude to the unexplained, not just for human understanding but also, perhaps, for human survival. Acknowledging our abilities to connect to realms beyond the physical may provide a way forward for civilization as the grip of artificial intelligence and technocracy tightens. Wherever we are headed, the world we thought we knew is looking less certain by the day and nurturing a new concept of it may help us ride the waves.

**Andy Thomas**, spring 2025

# CHAPTER 1

# THE EVERYDAY PARANORMAL

## Normal Paranormal

What do we mean by "the paranormal"? In its simplest form, *para* (Greek) means outside or beyond, while normal (from the Latin *normalis*) means ... normal. So, the term is used throughout these pages to describe things that appear to be beyond the normal. Dictionary definitions of the paranormal vary, but for clarity, I favour Brittanica.com's:

> *Strange events, abilities, etc., that cannot be explained by what is known about nature and the world.*[1]

This is good, because it does not imply that no explanation will ever be found for unusual phenomena but rather that something better than what is currently "known" needs to be established – and that is what this book explores. "Supernatural", which has a more directly esoteric meaning, is only employed where appropriate.

The fact is that a large number of very ordinary folk experience forms of the paranormal on a regular basis. How do I know this? Because, aside from all the other well-documented testimony, so many personal accounts are regularly shared with me at my lectures and live events, or by friends and relatives, while others are emailed from supporters around the world. I estimate that around one in ten people I talk to, maybe more, believe they have had an incredible experience that they just cannot explain. Even if we discount some of these as the mundane being mistaken for the paranormal – which sometimes happens – that still leaves a huge proportion of the human race that has encountered the *strange*. The paranormal is definitely more normal than is given credit for – and requires better recognition. Yet, too often those experiencing it are laughed at or dismissed as undiscerning cranks, which is unfair and foolish given the often high calibre of their characters and professional reliability.

## An Unexpected Journey

This is not, for the most part, a book about me, although I will share some of my own bizarre encounters, ones that compel me to be open to the experiences of others. From being physically shaken by a ghost, seeing a rock inexplicably illuminate itself in the Mojave Desert and encountering a violent unexplained drilling sound in my house, to observing glowing lights and dark shapes flying over fields and experiencing an uncanny premonition, I know for myself that strange things *do* happen. So, briefly explaining how I came into active paranormal research will help place things into context.

My early working life consisted of just about managing to hold down a grimly dull office job for nearly five years. One morning, I was struck with a crippling back problem resulting from a former childhood injury that left me unable to work for nearly nine months. This was perhaps an apt gestation period during which I discovered who I really was. To fill the time while lying flat and managing pain, and encouraged by friends to transcend my own difficulties, I came across books on the mystery realms. I had been brought up in a firmly Roman Catholic household and although I had decided that organized religion wasn't my path, an education in believing in miracles and holy enigmas does make one at least more open to *possibilities*. Now I found that perhaps the world was full of strange and wonderful things after all, but from a different perspective.

After undergoing spinal surgery, I returned to the daily grind but when I found myself "accidentally" dropping files out of the office window to pass the time, it became clear that mindless paperwork wasn't for me. Taking a chance, I embarked instead on a precarious career as an aspiring pop/rock keyboardist and composer, while working part-time in public relations.[2] And then I discovered crop circles and UFOs.

My adventures with crop circles have been well documented elsewhere, and my previous book *The New Heretics*, which makes its own stand against the persecution of "unorthodox" beliefs, has a long section on the fiery culture around circular investigation and the intense soul-searching it produced.[3] The circle phenomenon, which has not been treated kindly by the mainstream and even by some paranormal investigators, will be touched on in this book because, whether one believes these enigmatic but beautiful shapes that appear in fields are extra-terrestrial, extra-dimensional, the result of natural forces, psychic influences or human-made (or all of these and more), the profound questions they raise can be life-changing.

From the moment I saw my first crop formation emerge from the mist in the English meadows of Wiltshire in 1991, the deep, searching feeling it kindled in the pit of my stomach instantly told me that, somehow, things would never be the same again. I had been aware of crop circles, but not until that day had they imprinted themselves into my world.

Making contact with other researchers in my region of south-east England, I joined with them to form our own investigation team. The more we delved into the circle phenomenon, the more weird things happened to us, some of which will be explored in this book. We quickly realized these evocative shapes were a honeytrap, pulling us into a wider whirlpool of the paranormal. The regular public meetings we held (pre-proper internet, there was no faster way to discuss the latest news) became not only forums for entertainingly fierce debate but also a crucible in which I honed public-speaking skills. With experience of hacking out music reviews for a local magazine, I was the obvious choice to produce the group's news booklet, and thus my writing developed.[4]

One day my colleague Barry Reynolds, a moderator for this book, announced he was unable to attend the circle conference he was due to speak at. He handed me a carousel of slides and off I went instead. For all my nervousness, people seemed to appreciate the presentation and soon other speaking opportunities came my way. When my first humble book on Sussex crop circles was a surprising success, more doors opened and, without realizing it, I had embarked on a side career as an author and lecturer on the paranormal.[5]

From 1994 annual spots at the Glastonbury Symposium, a conference created to scrutinize such matters (an event I now help run), meant that I expanded my range further and found myself discussing all manner of unusual phenomena, intrigues and conspiracies.[6] Each person I met in a crop circle, on a UFO night watch, at an event or in a pub, introduced me to new ideas, new thinking and a broader view on life. And, of course, I also met and was interviewed by sceptics, who were forever dismissive. Yet I knew already from my own research that much of what was said in the mainstream was simply incorrect, or no more substantiated than the claims of those being attacked.

Most of all, though – providing the backbone to this book – at public talks I interacted with many ordinary people with very extraordinary tales to tell. I still meet them today. As far as I know, I am now one of the UK's most prolific lecturers giving several different presentations on "histories and mysteries". I have spoken in conference venues, community halls, hospitals, prisons, schools and many other places besides, and have come to realize, from all the witnesses I have met, that I have unexpectedly been granted a unique and broad perspective into people's paranormal lives that few others could ever have. I am grateful for it and these pages are an attempt to give something back.

My entirely unanticipated speaking journey has taken me around the United Kingdom and beyond, to the likes of the USA, Australia, Brazil, Peru and various European countries. Some events are huge and others modest but having now given several thousand lectures, wherever I go, I find the stories I am told are the same.

## The Power of Personal Testimony

Throughout my journey, I have come across an impressively broad body of folk whose frank and grounded testimony demonstrates that we live in a notably different world to the reductionist version we are fed. Most people with paranormal tales don't want fame or notoriety; they just want to tell *someone* about what they witnessed – to be heard. They have no reason to lie; indeed, they have every reason not to, risking ridicule, careers and reputations by saying anything. Many of them keep things to themselves for years or share them only with the closest friends and relatives – and even then they can be met with mockery. But, having heard me on a stage making clear I take such experiences seriously, it is almost as if a floodgate opens and they can contain themselves no further. They head cautiously up the aisles to speak to me after. When they do, the opening line is often: "I've never told anyone this before, but …" – and then they describe the previously indescribable and recount intriguing, sometimes astonishing, and occasionally shock-ing encounters with apparently paranormal forces they have never been able to explain.

Witnesses don't necessarily even want a response, but simply need the moment of release that comes with sharing. Mostly, I just listen, the priest in the confessional box. Some sound awestruck about their incredible encounters, but many – and this makes an important point – speak about them almost as if they were the most routine thing in the world. Ironically, it is often sceptics that make them *non*-routine by trying so fervently to denigrate this testimony. Think what we will about the cause of personal experiences – for those involved they are meaningful and, as far as they are concerned, simply *happened*.

It could be said that the kind of people likely to come to talks by someone like me will be biased towards the paranormal in the first place – but this is not so. The majority of my presentations are given to people from all walks of life who attend groups and organizations covering very normal subjects but which occasionally like to hear something out of the ordinary. Attendees frequently have little idea what they are letting themselves in for by coming along to hear me. I also address "alternative" events, of course, but many of the recorded anecdotes have come from the least probable places, which is what makes the repeating patterns so fascinating.

## Recording Strange Encounters

It is essential to describe how much of what follows has been recorded. Realizing that valuable testimony was slipping away, only over the last few years did I start keeping proper archives of the tales told to me. But this cache is rich enough. When faced with a string of faces wanting to share something special, it is mostly impossible to keep details of names and contacts (unless someone relates something very important), and people might clam up if they knew I wanted to do this. But I have developed a method of memorizing their descriptions.

As they speak, I take a mental snapshot of the person talking and plant key words in my mind's eye. So, if someone tells me of a ghost they saw in a bar in 1990s Santa Fe, I think "GHOST – BAR – 90s – SANTA FE". And so on. I then revolve these points around in my mind for as long as I can before the next person takes their place and the process begins again. The keywords provide the fundamentals and I am able to recall them as soon as I find a quiet space or return to my car. I then use the dictate-to-text facility to record the details of each encounter on my phone. If there is any doubt about detail I state this plainly to myself, noting it for further checking if possible (a place name, for example) – or I let that story go.

Although the minutiae cannot be guaranteed with subatomic precision, readers can be assured that the fundamentals of each story are correct (this has been verified when people have subsequently emailed me corroborative written accounts). My own friends and family are sometimes identified, but for narrative convenience or to protect privacy, I have created or changed names for those who have told me things in lecture conversations and left out identifying personal details, but the tellers are very real. Dates and places are omitted unless they are specifically relevant.

As cynics will not believe these stories anyway, or will dismiss a paranormal cause, I can offer no further assurance. It is clear from the demeanour of the tellers when something genuinely profound has occurred to them. Stories I suspect (from body language or their mental state) might be unreliable have not been included. Hopefully, those willing to take this journey will feel for themselves the authenticity of the experiences.

Written accounts are all first-hand and credited to the real people unless an alias has been requested. These have been compiled through contributions from kind supporters. Shrewd discernment has been applied equally here. Anecdotes gathered from live engagements or from personal relationships are featured as *Strange … Conversations*, while ones emailed to me are *Strange … Communications*. My own recollections are *Strange … Memories*.

## The Paranormal Top Ten

There are recurring patterns to the experiences people relate and I can usually guess within a few words which category they will fall into. Here are the top ten paranormal phenomena most reported to me, roughly in order:

1. Ghosts and poltergeists
2. UFO (UAP) sightings
3. Out-of-body and near-death experiences
4. Psychic phenomena of various kinds
5. Premonitions
6. Uncanny synchronicities and coincidences
7. Inexplicably bizarre events
8. Experiences in or around crop circles
9. Experiences at ancient sites
10. Sightings of unusual creatures

There is inevitably crossover between some of these. All, plus a few more areas, are explored in the following chapters. "Bizarre events" naturally cover a wide range; some really *are* bizarre but are also intriguing and deserve inclusion.

Although I can provide few definitive solutions to the mysteries described (if I could, I would be very famous or arrogant or both), along the way some fascinating hypotheses and their implications are explored, hopefully providing an overarching and useful insight into the too-often hidden world of the strange.

## A Micro-History of Modern Scepticism

The cynical will say that if the world were as full of weird encounters as this book implies then we would be hearing about them in the news and it would be impossible to cover them up. But sometimes paranormal stories *do* feature in the mainstream, as with the recent rise of high-level UFO whistleblowers, especially in the US. Without continual fresh evidence, though, attention wanes, the sceptics are given voice again and the subject returns to the backburner. Stories aren't necessarily erased from *public view* (although some plainly are, as explored in *The New Heretics*), especially when something is too high profile to do so, but a public with a short attention span is easily distracted, even as real evidence is quietly buried – something relied upon by those who would keep us in the dark.

This is not a history of paranormal investigation and scepticism (readers are directed to Terje G Simonsen's *A Short History of (Nearly) Everything Paranormal* for that).[7] But the polarization we see today has a long thread. When science declared it had liberated us from superstition and prowling phantoms, it threw a lot of babies out with the bathwater, effectively defining a very slender band of categories (of its own choosing) as "reality" and disregarding anything apparently falling outside of that. The thinking seems to be that if only "normal" is recognized to exist, there can *be* no paranormal. This flawed equation has led to an excess of presumptions and a failure to acknowledge phenomena that need proper examination.

Unfortunately, sceptics exercise undue influence over the media and the authorities, as the endless parade of undoubtedly skilled but narrow-minded celebrity scientists and alleged parapsychologists who shape our worldviews for us makes clear. Going by the polls, which demonstrate a high belief in the paranormal, more people disagree with the arch-reductionist and geneticist Richard Dawkins, for example, than agree – but it is Dawkins you will hear endlessly quoted rather than, say, the supposedly "maverick" evolutionary scientist Rupert Sheldrake (see page 154), whose ideas command a huge following. Social media and podcasts, along with populist movements' reshaping of who speaks for "us", are changing what people get exposed to and this may soon redefine what we see as "mainstream", but at the moment the old guard still fight to be the gatekeepers of what we are meant to believe in.

There have been brief periods in the last 150 years or so when fairer attitudes toward the paranormal looked possible. For example, there was a surge of interest in mediumship and séances thanks to the likes of Arthur Conan Doyle and the Society for Psychical Research in the late 1800s and early 1900s, especially when so many lives were lost in World War I and the yearning to discover whether there was anything beyond this realm took on more importance. Then there were the UFO flaps of the 1940s and 1950s, followed by the popular mysticism of the 1960s and 1970s (if boosted by psychedelics). These appeared to encourage a far more open-minded attitude to metaphysics, with the rise of popular speculators like "ancient aliens" researcher Erich von Däniken and the psychic Uri Geller, who were nevertheless often criticized; even rock stars and journalists openly courted such ideas. But then the self-elected "rationalists" seemed to get the upper hand and pushed such interests back to the fringes.

Make no mistake, there is an open war against paranormal beliefs from the likes of the Committee for Skeptical Inquiry (CSI), who count among their numbers famous scientists and academics of the kind referenced above. If you doubt their fervour, check out their concerted – and largely successful – attempts to cleanse Wikipedia of positive coverage of alternative views.[8] Their zealous achievements, which they openly crow about, are impressive – but this does not mean they are right. These extraordinarily arrogant warriors believe they are our rightful moral guardians and that their reality is the only reality. This needs to be challenged.

There *are* some researchers within genuinely scientific realms (although mostly those branded the "mavericks") who disagree with such savage methods and hold that any science that does not approach unconventional subjects with complete openness is not, by definition, truly scientific. Sadly, no matter what the sceptic warriors claim, that openness is all too often absent. Contrary to accusations, a belief in the paranormal does not equal an anti-scientific desire for a new Dark Age – how many people truly want that? Challengers are simply asking for a new honesty and a more open approach to unusual subjects.

We will from hereon, where possible, deal with the sceptics quickly and focus on examining the counter-evidence. What follows is an attempt to be truly open, daring to consider what might lie beyond modern barriers of disbelief to see if another, more illuminating worldview emerges from doing so.

# CHAPTER 2
# VISITS FROM THE AFTERLIFE

## An Established Phenomenon

Ghosts are all around us, and always have been it would seem. Every culture acknowledges the idea of spirits of the dead or beings from beyond crossing back into this world. They are embedded in the most ancient of texts, with the first clear description of ghosts, complete with an illustration, found on 3,500-year-old Mesopotamian clay tablets. Homer's *Odyssey* features them and even the gospels make direct references, clearly expecting the reader to know what a ghost is.[1] Entire Shakespeare plays and stories by Dickens pivot on our cultural acceptance of them.[2]

So, ghosts have an indelible place in our social and literary history. Yet, the tyranny of rational thinking says such things have no place in the modern world and that any personal experience that suggests otherwise can only be explained by malfunctioning minds, mistaken identification or outright trickery. Why, then, do so many people insist they have seen things that cannot be easily explained? Of all strange phenomena, ghosts and poltergeists are the most common themes I hear from witnesses. And they are *really* common.

Almost everyone has their own "spooky" anecdote or knows someone who does, to the degree that US writer and presenter David Sedaris lists hearing people's ghost stories as one of his pet hates, finding them "boring".[3] For me, they are far from boring, because if we even consider there might be a reality to conscious visitations from other realms or visual echoes from another era (or both and more), the implications for our understanding of space and time and our place within them are utterly profound. Ghosts constitute startling evidence that reveals a very different picture to the mundane world we are sold by reductionists – which is probably why they have no choice but to scoff: their careers would be destabilized by showing the slightest chink in their supposedly scientific armour.

There are different kinds of ghosts and spirits and varying definitions. In Spiritualist circles, "ghost" refers to an apparition of a "living person indelibly left in the space of where the person may have lived and generally do not show an awareness of their situation" (according to one of this book's consultants, Chris Connelly), whereas "spirit" is seen as a discarnate personality that "refers to the consciousness of a living person after bodily death that shows a form of intelligence and has an awareness of their surroundings". More widely, the terms are often interchangeable and I sometimes follow the more populist approach, but make the distinction where appropriate.

Although laying out the basics for what constitutes a ghost, this chapter focuses on one particular aspect – apparently conscious visitations from spirits frequently known or related to those who see them, crossing back from what we nebulously call "the afterlife". Other spectral experiences are also available and will be discussed in the next chapter.

## Ghost Protocols

I came across a perfect example of the usual sceptic position on ghosts, perhaps unexpectedly, in a health journal.[4] This well-meaning but ultimately presumptuous article written by a medical doctor addresses the not insignificant number of people who claim to have visitations from recently deceased relatives. Their experiences are explained as "post-bereavement hallucinations". Taking the example of just one patient (who claimed his recently dead wife came to sit with him most nights), never once does the article consider that perhaps, even very occasionally, there could be a level of reality to such meetings. Instead, because ghosts simply do not exist in the academic world, we are told they are "easily explained by neurochemical reactions". As usual, precisely *how* is never outlined.

But is it so easy to explain all the many sightings and even reported full conversations with dead friends and relations this way? Not from what I have heard from witnesses. "Hallucinations" is a usefully snappy term, used often by reductionists (and, by default, the media) to dismiss ghosts and psychic visions, as if hallucinations are fully understood in themselves. In fact, there are many unanswered questions around this subject and how we should tell the difference between a hallucination and something actually happening in front of our eyes.

For the record, here are the standard sceptic explanations for ghost encounters:

• **Waking dreams:** A state of consciousness, usually experienced between falling into sleep or when awakening, where the person sees things that seem ostensibly "real" but can in fact be artefacts of the brain already having entered or retaining levels of a semi-dream state.

• **Sleep paralysis:** A disquieting occurrence (that I have had) in which the person's mind becomes fully awake, usually in the middle of the night, but is unable to send any signals to the body, making movement impossible. This is seen as a phenomenon related to waking dreams. Visions sometimes witnessed in that condition are again treated as hallucinatory.

• **Infrasound:** Consisting of low-frequency sound waves that fall below the hearing threshold of the human ear, infrasound can reportedly generate feelings of fear and anxiety. This can cause people to misinterpret the mundane as supernatural.

• **Electromagnetism:** A key force of nature (basically, an interaction of electrically charged particles) responsible for much of the universe around us, it is both simple and deeply complex, capable of many remarkable things and mostly beyond the scope of this book. Laboratory experiments in which varying electromagnetic fields have been applied to the human brain have reportedly produced dream-like visions and personality changes.[5]

The brain is a very mysterious and often peculiar thing and some seemingly supernatural experiences might indeed be explained by organic malfunction or electromagnetic influence under certain circumstances. But all? Many ghost encounters do not occur in the above circumstances but in everyday waking states. Also, how do these options explain sightings of the *same ghost* made by more than one person, sometimes at the same time? Can everyone be sharing the same hallucination, or having identical ones at completely different times? And how do they explain the more convincing videos and photos, many documented long before the advent of today's deep-fake technology, including footage captured on multiple security cameras?

As for the things we see in vision states (and by those who have experimented with psychedelics), are these just stray electrical impulses triggering random images in the mind's eye – as sceptics argue – or are we in actuality "shifting our frequency", as a New Ager might put it, thus *enabling* us to view things that are usually (sometimes thankfully) beyond normal perception? Experiments with psychoactive plants that produce the likes of DMT (dimethyltryptamine), psilocybin and mescaline, which are often employed by shamans, have suggested so to some researchers. As for electromagnetism, this may well be involved in paranormal manifestations, based on readings picked up by ghost-hunters, but sometimes as an external force and not simply something natural messing with our brains.

Other "rational" explanations have been put forward, including draughts of air being mistaken for non-corporeal presences or flickers of light being inflated in a person's mind into a "ghost", and yes, there are a few fanciful types who might trick themselves this way. But with the following cases, something more must be at work than imagination or illusions of the mind.

### *Strange ... Memories*: Ghostly Children

My easier acceptance of the experiences of others has been aided by my own encounters with the strange, and what appear to have been ghosts have featured (directly) twice in my life.

Before the world of mysteries and cover-ups filled my time, music was my first calling. Among various projects, the most ongoing musical partnership was with my friend Phil. With him on vocals and guitar and me on keyboards, we shook the walls of pubs, clubs and halls for more than 30 years.[6] Eager audiences were to be found in the West Country of England. On one such expedition, in the mid-1990s, we booked accommodation in a cheap static trailer in a holiday park near the village of Looe in Cornwall.

Arriving after a long drive, Phil made himself comfortable on the sofa at the sunny end of the trailer. Our peace was quickly disturbed by the sounds of a young boy and girl beyond the partition door. It was clear they had come through the entrance at the other end and were running around inside. We could feel their footsteps vibrating through the floor and hear their playful voices. Deciding I had better shoo them out, I walked to the door and pulled it open. Instantly, silence fell. There were no children and no further sounds. I checked everywhere; the back door where we thought the children must have come in was firmly bolted from the inside and the gaps in the open windows in the small bunk cabins were too small even for children to have squeezed through. In the way that people rationalize peculiarity, I shrugged and figured there must be *some* easy explanation.

A short while later, I headed for the sleeping cabins to get some rest. These had simple entrances with no doors and I lay face up on the bunk with my feet by the open end. Within a minute or so, with me still wide awake but trying to relax with eyes closed, something took my right foot and *shook* it. Not nastily, but firmly; a mischievous joke. Despite the earlier events, it didn't occur to me then that this was anything other than Phil playing a trick. I instantly arose to try to catch him walking back through but heard no footsteps or felt any shaking except that caused by me (every movement was registered in this trailer). I opened the partition door and there was Phil, asleep. He forever swore he didn't walk through that afternoon. But the force that had gripped my foot was very real. I realized then that it had felt playful – the kind of thing a child would do as a prank – perhaps carried out by the very "children" we had heard? I felt a little odd as I realized something genuinely mysterious had occurred. It didn't seem hostile, and there was no sudden supernatural temperature drop, and yet I knew then that I had just experienced my first ghost.

I related this encounter to a few locals and some regaled me with tales that others had had visitations from invisible children in that same trailer park. But whether or not they were mocking me, I was never entirely sure. It didn't happen again, but neither did we find any explanation.

### Strange ... Communications: Child of the Liner

Mary Helen Hensley, whose own experiences of the strange appeared to be triggered by a near-death experience resulting from a serious car crash (see pages 111–12), relates the following tale of another childish presence. Visiting the ocean liner the *Queen Mary*, today berthed as a floating hotel off Long Beach in Los Angeles and reputed to be one of the most haunted ships, Mary Helen had a series of paranormal encounters, including the following one:

> I wasn't sure which way to go to get back to the lobby of the colossal ship. I eventually went left and found myself walking past door after door of infinite cabins and hidden

*walkways. I took another turn and suddenly realized I wasn't by myself. You know that feeling when you know you're not alone? When you can actually feel someone in your space? Not only could I feel it, but I heard giggling, just as I turned around to see a little girl following me down the hall. She wore a drop-waist white dress with pleats at the bottom and a very large bow in her hair. She laughed because she* knew *I could see her; I joined in her merriment because* I knew that she knew I could see her, too![7]

Meeting a child in a corridor might not seem particularly unusual. Except that this child, who vanished as mysteriously as she appeared, precisely matched the description of a girl who had tragically drowned in the ship's swimming pool around 50 years before. At least she seemed happy enough with her spectral existence, whereas some appear weighed down by the trauma of their demise, as we shall see.

This not to suggest that what I had a brush with had died in the trailer park (if so, it is not recorded); as will become clear, there are many scenarios that might generate or attract ghosts.

### *Strange ... Memories*: Night Chaos

Long after the trailer events, with researching the strange now an everyday part of my life, I was invited to speak at 25 Palmerston Place in Edinburgh, Scotland, home to what is now known as the Sir Arthur Conan Doyle Centre.[8] Then full of towering shelves holding books and papers on the psychical research and Spiritualism that Doyle (better known for his Sherlock Holmes novels) was a key advocate for, this imposing Victorian building boasts a huge spiral staircase reaching to its upper floors – classic "haunted house" territory. At the top, rooms had been converted into a self-contained flat where my wife Helen and I stayed the night after the talk.

We were perturbed to learn we would be the sole people in the building. We ascended the darkly atmospheric stairs and gratefully shut ourselves away in the flat. But as we lay there, attempts at slumber were thwarted by constant shouting heard through the walls, seemingly from an adjacent dwelling. We couldn't hear the words, but it sounded like a man's voice, angry and aggressive. This was punctuated by bangs and crashes, as if furniture was being moved or even thrown around. We hoped all this would subside, but the sounds persisted into the early hours until in the end weariness blotted them out.

Next morning, we related the incident to our hosts and asked about the difficult people living next door. But there weren't any. No one lived either side of the flat; what we had heard, we were assured, were the same belligerent terrors heard by several others who had stayed there. We were informed that we were lucky not to have been kicked down the staircase … another indignity occasionally inflicted there.

Was this "myth-making"? It didn't seem so. Perhaps the years of opening doorways to other realms had left the building energetically leaky? Creating portals is a serious business – what may quietly sneak in after benevolent channelled entities have come and gone may not be so welcome. Presences beyond this dimension can be both light *and* dark, as some of the experiences in disturbed locations such as Skinwalker Ranch in Utah suggest (see Chapter 7).

The easiest way to navigate the many different kinds of ghost encounters and explore their implications is to present them here in approximate order of the examples most often related to me. Although some interactions can be scary or unsettling, the majority tend to be peaceful and offer a strange kind of comfort to the living.

## Visits from Friends and Relatives

We saw above how the medical world treats those who believe they have interactions with deceased relatives. But if all the multiple cases I have heard are hallucinatory, then much of the human race must suffer from a recurring mass psychosis – and the absence of a proper medical model to explain this is problematic. If we only "see what we want to see" because the brain is responding to grief, then I personally feel short-changed. I have lost relatives and friends (some younger than they deserved) who I would have very much liked to have had visitations from, even just the smallest sign from the beyond. But, for me, nothing – and that's as a *believer in ghosts*. So, mere wishful thinking is not enough to trigger an apparition.

Certain people seem more tuned in to the paranormal than others; again, it may be a frequency thing. But it doesn't follow that those prone to the strange have any particular interest in it. Indeed, most who encounter recently lost loved ones (and other ghosts) tend to be very normal, down-to-earth folk, sometimes even former sceptics. I have lost count of the personal stories I have heard introduced with the words, "Well, I don't really believe in these things, but …", followed by a description of something quite astonishing that they cannot rationalize away. Society's conditioning towards denial, fortified with the fear of ridicule, is strong and frequently creates paradoxical thinking.

Witnesses of lost loved ones usually describe them standing and smiling, looking healthy or as they were in the prime of life. Sometimes they speak, generally giving short messages that they are "alright now", or words to that effect. This may sound trite, but perhaps this is all a departing being is permitted to say, or capable of, in such a transition state. Guitarist Phil's mother, whom I knew, was one of the most "real-world" characters you could meet, but she swore she saw her *own* dead mother three times shortly after she passed, standing in the house, dressed as normal, each time giving the above reassuring statement. Such encounters occur usually in the hours or days following the deceased's passing. After a few moments, consolation conveyed, the apparition fades away. Entire conversations *are* reported but these would appear to be rarer and occur in particular circumstances that raise interesting questions (see below). Spiritualists and mediums, of course, believe they can conduct full and regular conversations with those "in spirit" long after they have passed, but we will focus primarily on more spontaneous paranormal events.

Visitations *after* death make contextual sense if we believe that some kind of echo of our earthly consciousness does transform into a new state when we exit this physical realm. But another recurring experience is when people unexpectedly bump into – and have completely normal conversations with – friends or relatives, only to find later that the person they were happily chatting to actually died elsewhere *around the very moment that the interaction took place.* This is known as After Death Communication (and can include electronic exchanges). The dead conversationalist might make some oblique reference about coming to "say goodbye", to the puzzlement of the living, but mostly nothing out of the ordinary is said, almost as if even the ghost isn't aware of anything strange. Those who experience this then usually look around to find the loved one mysteriously gone. Later, they learn the shocking truth – and realize the apparent impossibility of what they witnessed.

Deaths in these instances usually appear to have been quick – for example, in nasty accidents. Does a ghost that turns up for such meetings even know it is dead yet? Is the spirit released so suddenly in these instances that it is automatically pulled toward those it has a close connection to, through some kind of quantum entanglement process that forever binds things that have previously been connected?[9] Ghosts do seem to result more (although not exclusively) from fast and unexpected deaths, than from people who pass peacefully with expectation.

Shortly before my godmother Brenda died of cancer (in her 50s), she had voiced disappointment that, due to her illness, she had been unable to visit her friend, an elderly lady who lived nearby. Brenda used to regularly spend time with her but this had inevitably fallen away. On the day Brenda died, the lady, sound of mind, said to her visiting carers (according to them) words to the effect of, "Brenda came to see me this morning. It was so nice to see her again." Having already been informed of Brenda's passing, the disconcerted carers assured her this could not have happened and gently broke the news as to why. But the lady was adamant that it *had* happened. When they established the time of Brenda's claimed visit, it took place at almost the exact moment she had died.

Final visitation scenarios of this kind are oft-reported, where the deceased appear to come back briefly to tie up unfinished personal business. Do spirits take on actual physical form at such times or do witnesses experience this in some kind of visionary state indistinguishable from everyday reality? We are assured they are just hallucinations, after all ... Yet in the above case the lady had not been informed that Brenda was ill, let alone dying. Was it really a coincidence that such a hallucination occurred that day and at that very moment?

From these and numerous other examples recorded around the world, it seems that at least a few of us are graced with a very limited time to make some last social calls when we pass, almost as if there is a momentary bridge between worlds where this is possible (see also Jonathan Cainer's story on page 33). For most, it would seem to be a brief window indeed. With the exception of specifically repeating ghost appearances, which we will explore, meetings with loved ones predominantly cease after a few days. Are we given a "choice" about this when we pass or is the phenomenon random?

We have all seen spooky movies with mystics telling entities to "move toward the light" and heard tales of near-death experiences where tunnels of light between existences are described, but the clichés are based on reported phenomena. It is not for these pages to decide whether some kind of archetypal Heaven (or indeed Hell, though let's hope not) exists. There are innumerable other beliefs about halls of gods, "Summerlands" or reincarnation zones (core of the famous *Tibetan Book of the Dead*) that might lie on the other side of this life, and readers will have their own views.[10] But it is strongly suggestive from the evidence I have heard that *something* survives when we leave this world. Whether it retains our full personality or is just a lingering essence that eventually subsumes into something more nebulous is unknown. An afterlife may not explain every ghost in any case; there are kinds that may be better put down to glitches in time and space, as we shall see.

## Wilful Visitations

Notwithstanding the above observations, ghosts of relatives *can* occasionally come back seemingly at will – sometimes to the embarrassment of those who survive them.

### *Strange ... Conversations*: Awkward Relatives

Thelma and Michael lived in an old house with a narrow staircase. One day, Michael was alarmed to find a strange man sitting halfway down the stairs, wearing a straw hat and smoking a pipe. When Michael gently asked him who he was, the figure stood up – and faded away. Terrified, Michael rushed to tell Thelma. The description he gave made clear to her that the man was almost certainly her first husband, long deceased. She broke down and admitted that she had never properly been able to let him go. Indeed, in quiet moments she would talk to him and sometimes (presumably when Michael was not there ...) set out a place at the table for him when she ate. And so her former husband had quietly continued to accompany her. Knowing the game was up, Thelma got out her old photo albums and showed Michael his predecessor, who he confirmed was the man he had seen. Happily, their marriage survived and no further visitations were recorded – or at least admitted to.

Such tales raise the slightly disquieting possibility that deceased loved ones can shadow their former partners' continuing earthly lives; inspiration, perhaps, for the 1990 film *Truly, Madly, Deeply*, in which persistent appearances from a woman's recently dead boyfriend become more trouble than they are worth.[11]

Even the above film doesn't go quite so far as the following experience, though. Hannah, whose husband had died some years before, would regularly see him as a ghost and could openly converse with him. This became difficult when she remarried – and she would see her dead husband defiantly lying in the bed between her and the new husband … The fact there was a space between them large enough for the ghost to fill perhaps says something about the distance this unresolved situation was creating. In the end, Hannah had a heart-to-heart with the dead husband, imploring him with some sadness to leave her alone to live her new life in full. There were no further visits.

Deceased partners, then, are not always welcome. Indeed, shortly after losing her husband Lucas, Mary moved to a new home but became acutely aware of his "presence", often in the corner of her new lounge. She couldn't see him but knew he was there. Although she sensed only good intentions and felt that Lucas was merely checking that she was coping on her own, eventually, as anyone under 24/7 home surveillance might, Mary became annoyed about it. Sharing her feelings vocally, albeit to an apparently empty room, she finally told Lucas she was fine and that he should no longer worry. She detected him just one more time but, after this, he apparently took the hint and didn't return.

In fact, Mary had a history of being irritated by spirits. Years before, she was shopping in a hardware store shortly after her father died, when she heard him calling to her in a ghostly Hollywood voice from over her shoulder. No one was visible. Feeling this to be inappropriate, she angrily voiced her protest and her father didn't bother trying again. I have heard from others prone to hearing "spirit voices", where the spirits sometimes just call their names but on occasion speak more complex sentences. Some experiencers would clearly prefer it didn't happen, so psychic gifts can be a blessing and a curse.

Critics will cite possible schizophrenia in cases such as this, but disembodied voices have sometimes been caught on audio recordings. Electronic Voice Phenomena, in which celestial conversations are channelled through specifically designed electrical equipment is a whole art beyond exploration here, although since the development of digital communications, there has been a spate of claims that the dead have messaged through emails, texts and social media. This is easy to scorn, but if beings can converse through human larynxes and "automatic writing" (handwritten channellings), why not also electronics?[12]

Readers may spot a trend here; this is, of course, only a selection of accounts, and women do seem more comfortable with sharing anecdotes of the strange than men, but it nonetheless appears that dead male partners (or fathers) visit their surviving women more than the other way around. Men will feature more in these pages soon but this tendency makes sense as, statistically, women outlive them by about seven years in old age, while unfortunately men are also far more prone to dying earlier in accidents, homicides or suicides.[13] It might also be noted that men seem less good at coping without women in their lives than the other way around; perhaps this longing extends beyond the grave?

*How* people experience their dear departed can plainly differ, from full-body sightings to unseen presences – but it can be just facial features that intrude into this world.

### *Strange ... Conversations*: **Faces from Beyond**

Shortly after her mother died, Carolyn was in bed, fully awake, when she unexpectedly saw the gently glowing face of her mother "in the corner of the room", high up near the ceiling. The face seemed at peace. No words were spoken. Carolyn wasn't frightened by this but felt comforted. The face then quietly vanished. She felt this intervention was a sign from her mother that she was now happy and safe. When Carolyn spoke to me, she seemed very grounded and almost matter-of-fact about it. When it happens to us, the strange can no longer feel quite so strange. Carolyn hadn't thought about her experience for years until she heard me speak on such phenomena and felt moved to share it.

Note that the face in Carolyn's room was glowing; a large number of witnesses describe a radiance from ghosts, presumably through their being energetic presences rather than physical. This luminosity may also explain why ghosts are often seen at night (although far from always) – simply because they show up more. Another reason may be because normal human activity is lessened at night, with many people asleep, perhaps allowing a clearer spectrum for psychic activity to thrive.

Ethereal faces don't always have family connections. Adelaide once kept a Chesterfield sofa in her bedroom. One night, with the lights on, she looked up and there, in the region of one arm of the sofa, was the face of a young girl staring out from it. At first Adelaide thought it must be her daughter but realized that the face was unfamiliar – and was coming partway *through* the sofa with no protruding body on the other side. Startled, she rushed toward the sofa but the girl melted away.

Sceptics will say, naturally, that these people must have fallen asleep or passed into the waking dream stage, but both the above witnesses claimed these instances occurred in fully conscious states.

\* \* \*

The late and famous astrologer Jonathan Cainer told of his own experience of seeing the face of his first wife, Melanie, *with* spoken conversation, at the very moment she was dying in an operating theatre. It is a tale he told to doubting journalists over the years, but he also recounted it personally to my wife Helen in much more detail.[14] (The very mention of astrology will have cynics tearing their hair out but most critiques of the ancient art are based on fundamental and often wilful misunderstandings about how it actually works, something that I deal with in *The New Heretics* and won't repeat here.)[15]

In 1992, Melanie had a serious car crash involving a lorry. With seven young children (including two seven-month-old twins) to care for, Jonathan was unable to be at the hospital while she underwent serious surgery. As he was serving tea to his children, anxiously awaiting news, a bizarre apparition opened up in the corner of the kitchen a few feet above the floor. Described to Helen as being like "a television screen materializing in the air", he saw Melanie's face hovering in a shimmering blue light, serene but telling him she was "going". Despite Jonathan's protestations that he still needed her in this realm, her image and voice dissipated. He later discovered she had died at almost that exact moment.

On occasion, fuller embodiments occur. A similar encounter to the hovering face in Carolyn's bedroom was related by Debra – as a young woman, while in bed, she saw the complete bodily form of her dead grandfather. Again, he was nonchalantly floating in the corner near the ceiling, looking down on her benevolently. Debra felt consoled by this, not scared. Having established that it was him, she didn't feel compelled to speak or shout but instead, knowing she was being watched over, turned over and went to sleep soundly.

Why some people have full-body sightings and others see only faces (or even just limbs – see page 64), while some have conversations and others don't, is beyond our current understanding. Just as they are passing away, dying people will often say to loved ones (as did Melanie above, and my maternal grandfather) that they are "going". Going quite where takes us back to personal beliefs but, encouragingly, it does suggest a sensation of leaving this realm for another destination, rather than fading to nothing.

It seems there may also be ambassadors from the other side waiting to help make that journey a smoother ride, if the multiple reports of perfectly lucid but dying people hearing or seeing already-passed loved ones even days before their own deaths is anything to go by. My maternal grandmother, hospitalized but not necessarily expected to die, said that she heard her own mother "calling" to her in the days before she slipped away.

## Other Kinds of Visitations

Drop-ins from deceased family members, or at least signs of their presence, can also occur in other ways.

*Strange ... Conversations*: **Postcards from the Edge**
Shortly after her husband Peter died, for a while Barbara frequently had the disconcerting feeling of him still being next to her *physically* in bed, even when she wasn't asleep. She could feel the mattress bending in toward the presence. Later, Barbara went on a cruise as part of her bereavement process. One day a bright ball of light appeared in her cabin, just for a few seconds. As it hovered, just a few inches across, she felt instinctively that it was Peter again, now in more ethereal form. Yet seemingly he still had influence over the physical world, because at home Barbara would leave her slippers around in an untidy manner, only to find them placed neatly side by side when she came back to them. Peter, she said, was always a tidy man.

* * *

Experiencing loved ones as balls of light (the latter a phenomenon in its own right, explored in Chapter 6) is more common than one might think. A friend, traumatized by the recent loss of her father, looked out her window at the nearby hills one night to see a bright orb hovering just beyond the garden. While UFO-hunters or earth mysteries aficionados would immediately become excited for other reasons, for her the timing of the light's arrival (never having witnessed such a thing before) was a reassuring sign of her father's presence, felt in her heart beyond any cold rationalization.

Another lady, Patricia, said that shortly after her mother passed away, she was looking down from the top of her staircase through the balustrades when she spotted a small white light flying through the hallway. The light came up toward her and then dived right past, not threatening or mischievous, but almost affectionate. Patricia felt strongly that this was her mother, manifested as light. Again, she found it comforting and took it as evidence that the essence of her mother still existed and that she was happy. It cannot be ruled out that the lights just coincided with these bereavements but, if so, they remain meaningfully synchronistic.

Similarly, Audrey recounted that from the time her husband died some years before, small white orbs appeared in the house they once shared. They would manifest mainly in her bedroom but sometimes in other rooms, notably the lounge. This might be dismissed as a trick of the mind were it not for the fact that Audrey's best friend, whom I also spoke to, said she had seen the lights *herself* when visiting and described them as very bright, pure white. Audrey finds this continuing phenomenon inherently reassuring and remains convinced it is the spirit of her husband in some way still there for her. She accepts the lights as a part of everyday life, believing they will continue to visit for as long as she lives.

These cases are very direct materializations, but possible signs from the beyond can be more subtle. I have heard of personal objects belonging to recently passed loved ones appearing out of the blue in prominent places around the home, even things long thought lost (see also page 218), or photos of the deceased being left in the middle of a floor, prominently moved or falling off walls, as if to make a point. Some might be coincidence, but the recurrent reports and appropriateness of *where* the mementoes are often found can suggest something else at work.

When "coincidence" seems to stretch credulity even for sceptics, they doubtless prefer to imagine that family members are placing such objects in plain sight, perhaps to offer well-meaning comfort to the bereaved. But the thought that people would play such disturbing mind games with their own relatives on so many occasions seems more incredible than paranormal explanations. In any event, some who describe these happenings live alone. Mediums may see the appearance of relevant objects as "apports", a phenomenon where items are openly materialized in front of psychic groups.

Some signs of this kind are symbolic rather than physical; these, along with other extraordinary synchronicities, are discussed in Chapter 7.

## Ancestral Visits

Fascinatingly, there is evidence that spirits of deceased family members sometimes visit children and grandchildren whom they didn't actually meet in their lifetimes. I have heard several such anecdotes.

### Strange ... Conversations: Visits to Children

Tom had been sceptical about the supernatural, but events in his own home changed this. When his son was young, the boy claimed that an elderly gentleman with a hat and an old-fashioned white clay pipe would come into his bedroom at night, always carrying a large scythe-like instrument over his shoulder. The man would sit on the end of the bed and talk to him. Despite the Grim Reaper connotations, the child found the old gentleman kindly and was unafraid. The recurring stories became impossible to ignore; when his son gave details, Tom realized it was a perfect description of the boy's great-grandfather, dead long before the son was born. He had been a farmer and would often carry an agricultural scythe.

A similar tale was recounted by Muriel. When her grandfather died, his old rocking chair was brought into their house. They weren't sure what to do with it, so they placed it in the bedroom of their five-year-old daughter. From then on, each morning the daughter would describe seeing an old man in the chair in the night, rocking gently. When this became a little disquieting, they took the chair out of her room. No one else witnessed anything, but one day, looking through old family photographs, Muriel's daughter pointed and said, "That's the man I saw in my bedroom." The photo was of her deceased grandfather. Still somehow bonded to his favourite chair, he was apparently continuing to enjoy it – and had the ability to physically move it. Whether he was aware of where he now was is unclear but some spirits maintain strong connections with physical objects, as we shall see, as opposed to "auric residue" cases (see below), which seem to be unconscious energetic echoes.

A very physical component features in this account. When Roland was a boy, his mother still used a hefty old-fashioned washing mangle to squeeze water from wet clothes. One day, she asked if he could bring it up the stairs. It looked far too heavy and Roland was worried about trying. Serendipitously, at that moment a man appeared at the foot of the stairs and said, "Don't worry son, I'll give you a hand." Roland was grateful for this new helper and the two of them managed to get the mangle up the stairs. But when he turned around at the top, he was alone again.

When he asked his mother who her friend was, she didn't know what he meant. The house doors were locked and no one could have come in. Suspecting that something odd had occurred, his mother realized from Roland's details that it was a perfect description of his uncle, who had died ten years earlier. It seems the uncle was keeping a watchful eye on the child – a very practical guardian angel to have.

I have heard many comparable stories: young children nonchalantly report to parents folk who appear and sit there benevolently or interact with them. Not knowing this kind of thing isn't normal, they take it in their stride and often accurately describe a dead relative. Some knew the children before passing on, but others never met them and appear to be checking in with their descendants, either through an ongoing ancestral duty or simple curiosity.

Not all visitors are identifiable and merely seem to be spirits coming by to say hello. Perhaps ghosts get lonely and just enjoy the company; the majority of these types of visitations do appear to be from friendly presences. Negative experiences *are* sometimes reported, though, when dark entities appear to latch on to willing hosts. Some researchers argue that specific ghosts are indeed lonely, alienated and keen to get attention by any means. Happily, such instances appear to be rarer, but here is one cautionary tale.

Priscilla told me of her daughter's first baby, who tragically was stillborn. Two years later, more happily, she gave birth to a healthy girl, Eva. Around the age of three, Eva began to describe nightly visits from a girl, floating above her bed. Far from being a guardian angel, the girl was spiteful, saying, "Your mummy is not your mummy; she's *my* mummy." Concerned, the family made the reasonable presumption that this must be the spirit of the dead baby, displeased at having been usurped; even more remarkably, from Eva's descriptions, it seemed to grow older as the years went by, as if living out its denied earthly years in some other realm.

Things began to feel more dangerous. A box of trinkets connected with the stillborn baby that the mother couldn't bear to part with, radiated a bad feeling – the family's cats and dogs wouldn't go near it. Moreover, the visitations were affecting Eva's childhood. Despite moving house several times, the ghost followed them (a phenomenon discussed more on pages 95–6), plainly attached to Eva.

Finally, the parents decided to hold a ceremony, celebrating the stillborn's life but imploring its spirit to leave its sister alone, to now let her live without fear and interference. Thankfully, after this, the message was apparently understood and the ethereal sister was seen no more. One can only wonder what might have happened had she continued the haranguing into adulthood. We have seen that some spirits just seem to need a good talking to and appear to respond to firm words. Others require a little more persuasion (see next chapter).

For balance, it should be said that some parents have described sensing *positive* presences of the spirits of lost or stillborn children throughout their lives. This darker haunting involving a child is, thankfully, very much the exception. Despite chilling movies like *The Exorcist*, the reality is usually gentler, as my own family discovered.

### *Strange ... Memories*: Home Visitors?
One morning, one of our grandsons, only three years old, unconcernedly mentioned that "ghosts" had walked into his bedroom the previous night. His descriptions were oddly particular: there was a boy, accompanied by a lady with "a baby in her tummy". They said, "What are you doing here?", before getting into bed with him ... When he awoke later, they were gone. He wasn't frightened and said that he "liked ghosts".

Easy, then, to presume nothing more than an infant's fantastic dream. Except curiously, his mother, sleeping in a nearby bedroom, had been awoken at 4:30am by the sound of footsteps on the landing outside – but none of us had been out there. At that very moment, the *baby monitor activated*, as they do when detecting significant movement – yet the image just showed our grandson fast asleep and unmoving. The door to his room was also ajar in the morning, when it was firmly shut the night before, as always. Although our house appears to be perfectly "happy", my wife Helen and guests staying have heard mysterious footsteps there before now, and an inexplicable light was once seen floating up the stairwell.

This proves nothing – but I have learned through our own experiences not to dismiss similar tales. It is easy to assume that nightly visitors are merely the invisible friends children invent for themselves, but perhaps not always. Children, often charmingly unflinching at benign strangeness, are probably the perfect conduits for ethereal ambassadors (and, notably, often witnesses to ostensibly religious apparitions, as with the extraordinary events at Fatima, Portugal in 1917). It is perhaps disappointing that as we grow older our access to other realms becomes more selective, not helped by conditioning that deals only with material realities and tells children not to be silly when they believe the strange has occurred. It may also be that changes to the body during adolescence alter psychic faculties and that this is part of our natural development. Curiously, there is increasing evidence that autistic children, especially non-verbal ones, have stronger telepathic abilities and retain them longer, but on the whole maybe we are not yet ready as a species for daily chats with the ancestors, which could become intimidating as we try to get on with our own lives.[16]

There is an entire phenomenon around anomalous objects being recorded on infra-red baby monitors and security cameras (and, increasingly, doorbells with cameras), with apparent faces, entities and flying "orbs" having created much discussion since these devices became ubiquitous. I have been sent several videos of such footage. Some of it is almost certainly explainable, insects and dust being the main culprits, but occasional clips deserve more scrutiny, as the shifted spectrums pick up things our eyes cannot see. On our own family baby monitors, we have observed spots of light abruptly accelerating and/or turning right angles in the air, when there are no fans or draughts to move them and no bugs around, especially in winter. Comparing these movements with dust highlighted in sunlight coming into the same room by day, I have seen nothing that replicates them.[17]

It is, of course, an uncomfortable thought that our children – and all of us – might be surrounded by anomalous phenomena with uncertain origins, but it has probably always been this way. Now we have gadgets that can detect them, in the same way that some children can hear electronic cat scarers but adults can't. Maybe it is simply time to accept that we might be harmlessly interacting with multi-dimensional forces on a daily basis – one of the key points of this book.

Reports of deceased relatives appearing in photographs of *current* family gatherings or turning up in images of everyday activities are also rife. Some are vague and open to interpretation, but others are more convincing. In this age of deep-fake manipulation it is almost impossible to be sure of anything's veracity, but many earlier pictures taken on emulsion film remain unexplained. Again, we must ask why there would be so many people willing to freak out their own families for the sake of a cheap thrill or a brief, and likely contested, moment in the limelight.[18]

Numerous ghosts seem to have direct connections with the people they appear to, then. But sightings can take us by surprise in a wide variety of circumstances, raising questions about the very fabric of reality, as we will now explore.

# CHAPTER 3
# OTHER GHOSTS AND POLTERGEISTS

## Primal Fears

There is a certain comfort factor to encountering ghosts of loved ones because even if they are initially unsettling, they imply hearteningly that the essence of that person somehow survives, maintaining a gentle watch on those who remain. Experiencing the ghost of someone you don't know has a very different flavour. Not only is there the shock of the apparition itself and the sheer alienness of something that doesn't fit everyday parameters, but primal fears immediately arise: is the entity dangerous or welcoming? These are instincts we employ about the *living* in unfamiliar circumstances, so it is perfectly natural and not unwise to feel such apprehension towards spectral company.

However, we should note that in the last few centuries we have been conditioned to fear ghosts as inherently disruptive and untrustworthy anomalies, hence the "spooky" context they are mostly dramatized in, moaning in old gloomy houses, with thunder, lightning and lashing rain outside. The human race loves to scare itself. In fact, most ghosts appear in perfectly normal surroundings and often when people least expect them, which can be perturbing in itself.

In the West, at least, before the Protestant Reformation in the 1500s, there had been an assumption that ghosts were glimpsed visions of souls in purgatory (a punitive waiting room between Heaven and Hell where, if lucky and with enough prayers of intercession from the living, those with a greyer legacy might eventually be allowed through the pearly gates). But when Protestants declared purgatory a Catholic falsity not mentioned anywhere in the Bible, ghosts suddenly needed explaining. As nothing so unsettling could surely come from the realms of light, which were now believed unreachable in this world anyway, it was declared by certain devout factions that ghosts could only be demonic forces from Hell. Opinions have softened a little since but the legacy of that black-and-white thinking weighs heavily today, as anything seemingly paranormal (even UFOs and aliens) that does not obviously emanate from God is still assumed by some to be associated with the Devil or evil spirits.[1]

Christian exorcisms *have* been known to have expelled dubious presences on occasion but whether that is through the sheer force of human psychic will or the gifts of God is up for discussion. Entities may just get fed up with all the shouting and bells and leave for a quieter afterlife. Charismatic evangelical preachers have turned the practice into a dramatic entertainment in more recent times. Either way, some ghost hunters believe that exorcism wielded by "deliverance ministers" to address more harmless cases is a spiritual sledgehammer being used to crack a nut. Employing exorcism to clear demons from "possessed" people may also not be the most sensible approach where treatment for mental health issues or brain impairment should be considered first. This is not to say that people are never possessed by dark forces, but inept or inappropriate attempts to dispel them can do more harm than good.[2]

While acknowledging some more sinister cases, and without disavowing anyone of their religious convictions, the following exploration will try to sap some of the fear, and indeed demonization, out of an area that is more often than not neutral, if not benevolent. Our inevitable fear of the unknown does not make negativity an inherent element of the supernatural.

# Ghost Indicators

Before surveying some common sightings, the peripheral phenomena surrounding ghosts should be explored a little. Sometimes, there are clear indications that something odd is occurring, even without a full manifestation.

Many people report the ability to sense "presences". These are harder to pin down than specific ghost encounters – with sceptics forever sniffing for any hint of vagueness, it can be tempting to put these claims aside as the work of vibrant imaginations. But reports of presences are rife and, as science itself has revealed, there is more to the world around us than what we see within our own limited spectrum. When our less-used but more subtle senses suddenly activate, we should probably take more notice than we do.

Animals seem to have less problems with this: anyone who has owned a dog will know that they often react to things that remain invisible to human eyes. Our dear departed golden retriever Selena was fascinating to observe on these occasions. She could be lying peacefully when her head would abruptly go up, alert, and, with no insects around nor any other motion, we could follow her eyes as she plainly observed *something* moving across the room. She wouldn't react as urgently as she might, say, if a stranger were to enter the room, but she wasn't looking at nothing.

Sometimes, Selena would stand suddenly and bark loudly in an agitated stance, her stare fixed on one spot (usually in our kitchen), a couple of feet or so above the ground. We would reassure Selena, although frankly, without knowing what she saw, that might have been hollow to her ears. Was she just picking up on stray electromagnetic pulses swimming into her visual range (rather like the baby monitor orbs), random sound frequencies from electronic cat-scarers and the like or something else? Entities, maybe? Dogs appear to be the most sensitive creatures, but cats can also show unusual reactions to things plainly beyond our vision.

Of course, it could be argued that when humans see ghosts, this is exactly what is going on with us; something usually invisible temporarily dips into our frequency – or we briefly cross the other way. That, or a "dimensional gateway" momentarily opens. Such sci-fi terms can induce scoffing, but sci-fi has turned out to be right about a number of things. Whichever, we return to the realization that far more may be going on around us than we typically see, perhaps thankfully. Some specific places, branded "haunted", appear to act as portals, but certain individuals appear to attract presences to *them*, wherever they are.

For those able to detect presences with a "sixth sense", knowing that something abnormal has arrived in the room with them is a powerful (if not always welcome) ability, although some take it in their stride as we have seen, especially if they feel the presences are safe and familiar. Random unseen arrivals can be more unsettling. Here follows a typical tale, which includes another classic phenomenon associated with ghosts.

### *Strange ... Conversations*: A Cold Holiday

Penny once stayed in a country holiday cottage in a row converted from old alms-houses (homes once maintained by charities). One afternoon, there was a sudden power outage and the main room became dramatically cold. When they complained to central reception, they learned that no other cottage had reported problems. The staff gave them heaters but the temperature had mysteriously normalized when they returned with them. Later that evening, both Penny and her husband felt a strong sense of "presence" in the room. She found herself spontaneously speaking aloud with consoling words to whoever was there, at which point the feeling subsided and didn't return.

Abrupt temperature drops into near freezing conditions within seconds, even in the warmest conditions, are habitual in ghost-lore, often accompanying visual sightings. It has been likened to someone opening a door to an extraordinarily cold environment and then closing it again. Does this mean spirits in other realms sit there with chattering teeth and icicles? Probably not, but either there is a temperature differential between "there" and here, or transitions between dimensions momentarily drain warmth away before it is quickly restored, raising the question of whether the "there" gets a blast of heat in exchange?

It is believed by some that entities make the exchange into our world by absorbing the energy around them to power their appearance. Whether this is done knowingly or is an inescapable part of the process is unknown. In this hypothesis, heat, which is a form of energy, is absorbed, while cold, essentially the *absence* of heat, is what we are left with, along with power outages (as related by Penny above) and flickering lights. Some researchers argue that ghosts enter through natural vortices that disturb the air, hence perhaps the sputtering flames and unexpected breezes connected with hauntings.

Mediums who facilitate communication with spirits – probably opening doors to other dimensions through psychic forces – have themselves described falling temperatures, especially when a strong presence comes through. Thermal imaging monitors and sensitive gauges have therefore become key tools for ghost hunters, with not uninteresting results. If nothing is seen optically, air pressure changes can be registered, while heat anomalies (sometimes human-shaped) can be caught on camera using infrared devices.[3] The adventures of dedicated ghost hunters, with their arrays of detection equipment, are beyond the scope of this book but readers are encouraged to find out more. They have become a jokey reality-TV staple in recent decades, but that is not a fair representation of all of them. Their accumulated data, albeit habitually attacked as "unscientific" by critics, should be considered more seriously.[4]

However, none of these effects are universal and ghosts can happily appear without any notable change in the environment or the need to call an emergency heating engineer. Some mediums claim they feel *warmer* when channelling.

# Lingering Trauma

Indications of ghosts can extend to other senses. We have seen how disembodied voices are sometimes heard, but sounds of actual events, usually past traumas, battles or tragedies, are also reported in the areas where they occurred. Although often disdained as stories concocted for tourists, I have myself heard convincing first-hand accounts.

### *Strange ... Conversations*: Unending Battles
By coincidence, the following experience took place near to where I once lived, although I knew nothing of the phenomenon at the time. James told me that some years ago he was walking down the aptly named Deadmantree Hill, a rural road between the English villages of Barcombe and Cooksbridge in East Sussex. It was night, but in the darkness he unexpectedly heard thundering horses' hooves and men's voices, shouting, aggressive. Disturbed, and expecting to be ridden down by a mounted mob, James anxiously looked around but could see nothing. He was frozen to the spot as the clamour continued until eventually a car approached; this seemed to break the spell and the sounds were gone.

There may be good reasons why James experienced this where he did. In 1264, a bloody battle took place at the town of Lewes, just two miles or so to the south. A confrontation between powerful barons led by the rebel Simon de Montfort against King Henry III initially came to a head there, resulting in the deaths of around 2,000 men and the king's (temporary) defeat. However, the battle spread into the surrounding areas as fleeing troops were pursued and slaughtered – and

Deadmantree Hill was the scene of one of these skirmishes. James later heard a local legend that "blood ran down the hill" there.[5]

After hearing this story, I investigated the area more and discovered that others had for many years reported hearing this extraordinary breaking through of medieval carnage into the modern world – or an echo of it at least.

This is not a one-off. Residents near significant battle sites around the world have reported the same phenomenon. Famous examples include the site of the Battle of Gettysburg, where Confederates and Unionists clashed in 1863 during the American Civil War. It was a decisive victory for the Unionists and Gettysburg would turn the fortunes of the remaining conflict in their direction, but around 50,000 men died there during three days of horror. This may explain why the site is considered to be one of the most haunted in the USA, with some remaining buildings encountering a higher than usual level of paranormal activity. Not only have sounds of battle, groans of the wounded and other traumatic noises been reported but also sightings of spectral fighters and dying men, still resonating into the now.[6]

Other American Civil War locations and the numerous bloodied conflict zones of England have attracted similar claims, while battle locations such as Passchendaele in Belgium (World War I), Stalingrad in Russia (World War II) and Culloden in Scotland (1746) are other hotspots for hauntings.[7] Major air and train crash sites, where many people were lost in one incident, also generate tales of repeating "loops" where sounds from the disaster and uncanny happenings persist. Some accounts may be myth-making but the fact that this is a recurring mystery around the world suggests that perhaps there is no smoke without at least a little battle fire.

We have established that many ghosts seem tranquil, but the more troubled spirits do frequently appear to have been energetically stranded by unexpected and often painful deaths, through conflict, murder or accidents. Something about being ripped from this world in terror and/or too rapidly seems to tear through reality in a way that passing peacefully (with seeming guidance and preparation from both sides if we accept some of the accounts in Chapter 2) does not. The trauma may leave a psychic rift that allows or compels those spirits to pass back and forth through time. The need to manifest as a ghost may also sometimes be a yearning for company or a cry for help from entities "trapped between worlds". Otherwise, a radiated energy forcefully produced by the original trauma may somehow electromagnetically imprint itself onto physical surroundings, allowing traces of certain events (the sounds and/or the sights) to be mindlessly replayed like a recording when something activates it or when someone sensitive is there to accidentally press "play".[8]

John G Fuller's bestselling 1976 non-fiction book *The Ghost of Flight 401* asserted that items recovered from the fatal crash of a Lockheed TriStar airliner over the Florida Everglades in 1972 and then re-used in other airplanes had to be removed when people on those later flights experienced apparitions of deceased crew members from the crash, most frequently its pilot. It was as if the physical items and the dead crew were indelibly linked by the catastrophe. Denied by sceptics, naturally, and indeed the Eastern Air Lines company, it remains curious that when the widow of the dead pilot attempted to sue Fuller, her lawsuit was dismissed by the courts and so the book's assertions were never officially debunked.[9]

Exactly how this ghostly imprinting works is one of the big mysteries of paranormal phenomena, but it should make us think when we get angry or fearful; we never know what we might be embossing into the environment around us. Hence the classic observation that you can sometimes pick up the "vibes" in a room where a nasty argument has taken place, even when all is still and the people have left.

This has profound implications for much human activity. We leave psychic trails we cannot see, but they may interfere with wider existence more than we know, especially when fascinating experiments with collective consciousness are taken into account.[10]

The fact that extrasensory "recordings" are commonly triggered at places with difficult histories implies an interesting likelihood that physical matter can be transmuted by consciousness itself, an effect made stronger when melded with bodily and emotional suffering. Weirdly, *physical* objects are sometimes witnessed in spectral form, such as entire "ghost trains" or cars associated with past disasters – meaning that crossings from one dimension to another are not necessarily restricted to sentient beings. For example, rumours persist of continued sightings of the funeral train that took the body of assassinated president Abraham Lincoln across America in 1865.[11]

Ghost and poltergeist activity frequently arise when rebuilding or construction work begins, either on an old house or a patch of ground that might once have been inhabited. The act of disruption seems to disturb the energetic environment; either it hits "play" on the psychic recordings or it snaps the spirits associated with the original structure back through portals like elastic, willingly or unwillingly. Here follow two examples where these factors may have been involved.

### *Strange ... Conversations*: A Poltergeist Protests?

When Lynne's daughter was only four, they moved into an old farmhouse and decided to convert the adjoining barn into a lounge. On the day the builders started to knock down one of the walls, Lynne and her husband found that the daughter's bed had been thrown up against the bedroom window on its end. One of its legs had been removed and placed carefully on top of a glass of water that had been next to the bed ... They could not see how a small girl could possibly have achieved this, and she always denied doing it. Other objects were found placed in peculiar places around the house that day, with "things falling down" in an alarming fashion that were nothing to do with the builders. Lynne felt sure the disruption to the barn had somehow triggered this.

Poltergeists are discussed more fully below, but although some researchers see them as a separate psychokinetic mystery, often associated with adolescent girls (rather than four-year-olds), I have found there is frequently a crossover that *does* suggest the direct involvement of entities. Lynne felt the poltergeist or spirit must have approved of the barn conversion in the end, because the strange activity occurred only on the day the wall was demolished.

### *Strange ... Conversations*: The Memory of Wood?

Marjorie used to live in a house that was not particularly old but did incorporate wooden beams that had been salvaged from an earlier house lost in a fire. Marjorie's daughter and her daughter's boyfriend would often sense a presence there and hear a distinctive sound, almost like the rustling of a long dress. One night, Marjorie's son, around 16 at the time, started screaming from his bedroom. When they rushed to investigate, he said that he had seen a tall lady in a "Victorian dress" standing at the foot of his bed, though he had been unable to see her face. Although Marjorie and her husband never personally experienced anything, they did believe the family's claims and the son was deeply unnerved by what he witnessed. They all felt that the wooden beams from the burned house, which had been Victorian, had some connection with the ghostly lady, almost as if her presence was attached to the beams themselves.

Links between objects and paranormal activity are also supported by the art of "psychometry", whereby psychics can learn the identity and history of an item's owner by handling it and "reading" the impressions they receive (see page 141).

**Strange … Communications: A Soldierly Presence?**
Following the subject of battle sites and emotional residue, it seems pertinent to record an encounter with a possible victim of war in Hong Kong, as shared by Mike Waller:

*My family and I were living in a flat of HK Government Quarters, located near the summit of a steep hill on Hong Kong island. One could mount a footpath which led up to the inclined summit and beyond to other hills. One evening in the 1970s, I set out with my dog "Queen Queen" for an evening walk. As we neared the summit I noted, in the distance, a strange light in the shape of a human! We continued along the path and drew near, about 20ft [6m] distance from it, when I stopped and watched to see what it could be. Overhead was a new moon and dark sky. No buildings, cars or people were anywhere near us. It was totally dark, so the strange light stood out. I noted it swayed gently from side to side. Suddenly, Queen Queen made a terrible noise. I saw all the hairs on her back were stood up and her teeth were bared. With a scream, she left me and ran for her life down the footpath.*

*I so wanted to solve this mystery, so I edged forward to about 6ft [2m] distance. I was able to see the form was made up of many small circles of light, adjacent to each other. I wondered if I should try to touch it? A thought entered my mind: "It has not interfered with you. Should you now interfere with it, that situation could change with horrific circumstances." Instead, I collected two or three large, distinctive stones and placed them where I had stood, then slowly went back down the footpath. I turned to see if it would follow me, but it did not. I felt a great feeling of sadness, as if it wanted me to stay. The next day, I retraced my footsteps to the stones: there was nothing where the light had stood. Only smooth sand covered the ground.*

*A few days later, I enquired about this site at the HKG Land Registry. This showed that during World War II there had been a terrible battle with the Japanese Army, covering this area, with many fatalities on both sides. [British, Canadian and Indian army regiments fought the Japanese invasion of Hong Kong in December 1941.*[12]*] There were no burials in this area. It seemed possible that a soldier could have been shot while retreating up the footpath toward the hill summit, then may have died on the spot where I had seen the strange light? Much later, the corpse would have been removed with others for cremation elsewhere, without leaving any kind of memorial. As time passed by, I often thought of this incident and felt strangely moved to want to do something for whatever this strange object may have been. I could have simply read some Sutras at the site, but alas did not. Maybe a lost opportunity?*

It is interesting to note the granulated circles of light making up the figure, and once again a dog's stark response to something it knew was an anomaly. The sadness around the figure and Mike's lingering sense of regret around not knowing what to do for it is an aspect I have picked up from a number of ghost witnesses. There are emotional layers often not acknowledged beneath all the spooky trappings we place on such cases. Are we just projecting our own imaginings of an entity's loneliness? We are assured by reductionists that neural and chemical reactions alone create our feelings, but if traces of emotion *are* somehow retained within fields of consciousness, this may be why they appear to persist when the flesh is long gone.

## Smells and Smoke

If feelings of presences and sounds from past events are more subtle pointers to the paranormal, there is another sense that can come into play: smell. Emotional memories can be dramatically sparked by the briefest waft of a particular perfume or aftershave – but less welcome odours can also be the gateway to the strange when they seem to come from nowhere.

### Strange ... Conversations: The Perfumed Poltergeist, the Cook and the Smoker

Adelaide, who saw the child's face in the sofa, had other encounters in an old Victorian house she lived in earlier. There, she and her family would frequently scent an unusual and unexplained perfume. She never saw anything but when the perfume came, their dog would always act peculiarly. In particular, it did not like the main staircase and they all felt some kind of presence there. When a builder was working in the house, he smelled the perfume for himself. Clearly tuned into such things, he actually saw a woman descending the staircase in a long old-fashioned dress and experienced electrical plugs being pulled in and out of the wall and other poltergeist activity. He persisted with the project, but it is no surprise that he did not like working in the house.

Another lady, Daphne, used to live with her family in an old flint cottage built in the 1700s, where they had regular poltergeist activity. Drawers were observed opening and closing by themselves and the bedroom door would never stay closed; even when firmly latched, it would always reopen. In the end, as is often the way when people live with ghosts, they got used to it and gave up closing the door. Although they could sometimes feel a presence, the most overwhelming sign it was there was when a strong smell of cooked onions would pervade the house – even when nothing was on the hob, nor was coming from neighbours' homes.

Perfume and cooking aromas are at least mostly pleasant, but one of the most reported spectral smells is smoke from cigarettes, cigars and pipes (vaping is still to come, one assumes), usually associated with a specific person and coming directly from the spot where the now deceased smoker once sat.

Pauline told me that in the months after her father (who lived with them) died, the living room in which he would regularly sit puffing away would still mysteriously fill with cigarette smoke each day. Thinking that the father's favourite chair, plus the carpets and curtains, imbued as they were with years of nicotine, might be the problem, they threw them all out – but the smoke still returned. Eventually, it stopped; perhaps her father's transitional period had ended or he had finally decided to "kick the habit" at last. This may sound humorous but mediums have related many times that a continued yearning for earthly addictions can be one of the very problems some spirits have with moving on from this realm.

We can never truly know (in our dimension, at least) what is over the "other side" but the general impression from those who believe they have had glimpses is of something far more ethereal (but perhaps more fulfilling) than the temporary stimulations we all too often seek here. Yet, drink, drugs and sex (see page 142) are powerful holds for some people and the desire for them may not entirely fade when we exit. In the same way there seems to be some emotional hangover from this world into the next, the legacy of an addiction may last longer than we know. Those who claim to have "astrally travelled" (see Chapter 4) into different layers of existence have described certain lower realms that are probably best avoided by spiritual tourists, filled as they reportedly are with dark souls still warped by worldly obsessions. Perhaps Hell does exist after all.[13] If you are just about to light up a cigarette as you read this, smoking is almost certainly not a ticket to that place, although it can be the death of us here, but this makes the point that what we latch onto in one world may take a few future lifetimes or scaling of karmic levels to let go of.

\* \* \*

The apparent entanglement of consciousness with inanimate objects (smoke-stained chairs, for instance) and locations (houses, battlefields and so on) tells us that it is not space–time coordinates that spirits are attached to, but physicality itself. The world may look essentially still, but with the motion of the Earth around the sun, its daily spin and the fact that the solar system and galaxy that it exists within are moving at even faster speeds, the reality is that we are moving with incomprehensible rapidity every second of our lives. The space–time coordinates you were sitting in when you read the previous line have already shot off thousands of miles away: you just didn't notice because everything around you was travelling at the same rate. For this reason, nitpickers of time travel stories point out that moving in time without also moving in space would never bring us back to the same location in the way they usually depict. Doctor Who's TARDIS (being a space–time machine) might get away with it, but H G Wells's *Time Machine* traveller would in reality have found himself floating in space asphyxiated rather than on a future Earth.

In other words, places must be haunted through a fundamental bond between the mind/discarnate spirit and the corporeal world of everyday objects and substances. Exactly how the ghostly smells manifest, and whether this means that dead uncle Joe is still smoking away somewhere in a higher dimension is another matter. Presuming the afterlife to be a smokeless zone (Hell aside), do spirits deliberately conjure up smoke and other scents as a sign of their presence or does something imprinted in their innate energy fields stimulate the olfactory nerves of the living? And yet spectral smoke is sometimes *seen* as well as sniffed, which suggests it can have a real presence.

### *Strange ... Conversations*: Impossible Smoke
Margaret lived in a row of old terraced stone cottages, each with its own chimney. Their fireplaces had long ago been

closed off, the rooms heated by modern radiators. Margaret was alarmed to see, then, when returning to her house one day, smoke pouring out of her chimney. She dashed into the house, fearful that fire had broken out in the rafters. But there were no signs of either smoke or flames inside.

Margaret called a workman in to investigate. Doubtful about her sighting, he was able to confirm that nothing could have produced smoke; the fireplaces and chimney were firmly blocked, as was the case with the adjoining cottages. There was no residue of a fire in the attic. Margaret was embarrassed. She kept seeing smoke from the chimney but had to keep this odd secret to herself. If the neighbours ever saw anything, they didn't report it.

However, fortuitously one day the workman was driving past Margaret's house when he saw the smoke for himself, puffing out of the chimney. Pulling over, he ran to the cottage, anxious to investigate. Once again, there was nothing visible inside, nor any possibility that the smoke could have come from the fireplaces, chimney or elsewhere. Bamboozled, the workman apologized for his earlier dismissal but they were never able to solve the mystery.

Having established that sounds, objects, smokes and smells all play their part in the wider fabric of supernatural experiences, it is time to explore some common types of visual sightings – and physical contact with ghosts.

# Walking Through Walls

A widely reported phenomenon is that of ghosts walking into or out of walls. Observers may not realize they are seeing one until they unexpectedly disappear into a seemingly solid surface. Presuming there hasn't been an unreported outbreak of teleportation, it can be safely assumed that if this happens we are looking at a ghost. Despite their apparent entanglement with physical reality, walls, doors and structures seem to present no meaningful boundaries for them. But sometimes entities can emerge from the strangest places – like the face in the sofa – and it seems appropriate, given the discussion of fireplaces, to recount the following story.

### *Strange ... Conversations*: The Lady in the Fireplace

A challenge to the sceptical position that ghosts are a hallucinatory anomaly in a single brain are the significant numbers of occasions where two or more people see the same ghost at the same time.

Roger and Joan (who related this story to me together) owned a grand old house, with a large ornate fireplace. The fire was a favourite spot for them, armchairs placed either side; a perfect retreat in winter. But one afternoon, the coziness was disrupted. As they sat with hot drinks and newspapers, they became aware of a glow that seemed different to the flames from the logs. A shape of light began to grow before their eyes. It expanded from the fireplace until, to their astonishment, it became the full-sized figure of a woman in "period dress".

Unusually, this spectral figure stopped and acknowledged Roger and Joan, turning her head to look specifically at one and then the other. Apparently unperturbed to find herself standing in a fireplace observing people dressed in what must have looked to her like futuristic garb, she turned her gaze forward, strode across the room and vanished into the wall opposite.

The woman was not seen again, but Roger and Joan discovered later, by examining old plans, that long before the room was substantially reconstructed and the fireplace installed, a passageway once followed precisely the course the woman took from the fire into the wall. Did she once upon a time stroll through her house and have a momentary vision of an unexpected fireplace with two shocked people sitting either side of it? Or was this her spirit, knowingly visiting our present to see what things were like now? If so, for her, the old passageway clearly remained a legitimate through-way she wasn't prepared to deviate from, the new fire and walls providing no obstacle.

Cases like this, where the witnesses are acknowledged, imply that the spirits have some kind of spatial awareness of our here and now – but it doesn't impede them, as if there is a dimensional crossover in which boundaries are fluid.

Joint experiences like Roger and Joan's are important. Their tale was told credibly and without sensationalism and it was plain they had shared something profound. I have also met tour guides (usually working at old buildings or historical sites) who have described entire groups of astonished tourists witnessing the same apparition striding into or out of walls in the time-honoured fashion. If we consider the standard sceptic explanation, how can lots of people be having the same hallucination? It is obvious that better explanations are sometimes required.

Here is another account of a ghost walking through a now-removed entrance, and where, again, both partners were witnesses.

### Strange ... Conversations: Man from the Corner/ Vanishing Figures

Susan and David would frequently see a male figure walking into their lounge as if from nowhere through the narrow wall between a window and a door in a corner. He would always advance toward them, as if preparing to say something. At first they were fearful but his arrivals became so frequent that eventually they would just say "hello" to him. He never responded and would just dematerialize in front of them. Later, when having work done on the house, they discovered there was once a doorway in exactly the space where the man routinely entered the room. They guessed that he was still following the course he knew in his time. If a spirit (as his apparent attempts to approach Susan and David suggested) rather than a timeslip, perhaps he was forever perplexed to find people and sofas in his way.

Mildred, meanwhile – in yet another joint experience – said that she and her husband were exploring timeworn maritime buildings at the foot of a funicular railway (steep lines that ascend cliffs) in an old English coastal town. They noticed a knot of people walking along the street before them, all wearing Victorian-style clothes. Assuming them to be some kind of tourist attraction, they were stunned when, as one, the group suddenly turned to walk directly *through* a heavy closed door that fronted an under-cellar, melting into it as if it wasn't there. Mildred and her husband were astounded, though they found it odd rather than frightening. [Alert readers might have noticed that the word "Victorian" keeps popping up in these sightings; there is an interesting observation to be made around this, which we will examine soon.]

It has been noted that some people are more prone to the strange than others: Mildred also told me that she once lived in an old house that a century or so ago employed servants, who would sleep in separate upstairs quarters. One day she went into one of the upper rooms – and stumbled across a group of phantom staff, standing there before her, as if ready for inspection. One of them stepped forward and said, "We are looking after this place." At this, Mildred hurriedly left the room. She did not have such a direct encounter again, but would sometimes feel their presence and, in the end, felt oddly reassured by their statement of intent.

### Strange ... Communications: Walls Are No Barriers
In Chapter 2 we met Mary Helen Hensley aboard the *Queen Mary*, berthed near Los Angeles. Following her encounter with the mysterious playful girl, it seems she had become attuned to other presences there, capable of coming and going

through solid matter as they wished. As we saw with the long-dead servants or the lady in the fireplace, it is particularly fascinating when ghosts are fully aware of *our* presence. Mary Helen adds:

> *My friend and I made our way up to the Observatory Bar, a beautiful example of classic art-deco design. We settled down for a bite to eat and a chat … when a man behind her in the far corner of the bar caught my eye. It wasn't his dashing good looks that commanded my attention, but the look of sheer surprise on his face that I had noticed him. I couldn't help but stare, as he stared right back. Dressed in a tan-coloured maintenance man's uniform and as in-the-flesh as every other live person in the bar, I nearly choked on a tortilla chip as he stepped left and went straight through the wall and out to the observation deck. Before I could tell my friend what was happening, the man leaned back through the wall with only the upper half of his body, as if to let me know that I wasn't just "seeing things".*[14]

### Strange … Conversations: The Gentle Quaker

For all the ghosts that adhere to layouts they once knew, they can also haunt buildings that were *not* there in their day, suggesting a more conscious presence than is sometimes acknowledged – and this story is another example of a ghost making direct eye contact.

Rebecca lived in another old Victorian house. It had a long upstairs corridor that linked many rooms. One day, as she entered one of them, she was startled to see a gentleman sitting at the desk, looking like the "Quaker Oats man", the friendly looking gentleman with the 17th-century wig and trademark of the Chicago-based food company. As she stopped in her tracks, bemused, he looked straight at her – and smiled. Something in his expression made her feel unafraid.

Rebecca met the gentleman one more time when he physically brushed shoulders with her when delicately pushing past her from the corridor into a room. Steeling herself, she followed him in. He turned around and again looked her in the eye, not unkindly, but with evident consciousness that she was there. He regarded her for a while without speaking, before dissolving into invisibility.

The anomaly here is why the man's dress was plainly 17th century, even though the house was 19th century. Rebecca could not explain this, but thought that perhaps an older house once stood on the site. Ghosts can inhabit buildings later than their own time, strongly implying that some are able to navigate physical structures they never knew, *choosing* to be somewhere rather than tied to one dwelling. There are numerous tales of people moving out of haunted houses, only to find that the ghosts they thought they were leaving behind have moved with them, as with the stillborn phantom (see pages 38–9). This suggests that spirits can make a direct attachment to an individual, or at least that some individuals act as living, breathing portals to the strange wherever they go.

## Hospital Visits

For ghosts that *do* linger in the places they personally knew, locations with a longer history are more likely, by simple probability, to host both these and time echoes. This may explain why hospitals, especially older ones, are another common source of ghost encounters. The death and suffering that unavoidably accompanies the healing in them can leave imprints.

*Strange ... Conversations*: **Weirdness on the Wards**
Rosemary used to work in a large hospital in South Africa, where she trained as a nurse in the 1960s. One particular ward, although more recently constructed, retained walls

from the original building at either end. Each evening, at midnight precisely, the door in one wall would open and close, and there would be a strong feeling of a presence, if invisible, passing through the room. The door in the opposite wall would then also open and close, and that would be that until it would do it all again the next night. It was so routine that staff, none of whom liked working in the troubling ward, would be ready to distract any patients still awake while the crossing was occurring.

This clockwork schedule, the same in any weather condition, meant that the opening and closing of the doors were not due to air currents. The door through which the presence would exit led to a surgical theatre in the old part of the hospital but no one was ever there when staff (bravely) went to look. There was a strong sense that the ghost was female. Rosemary knew of a rumour that a depressed nurse had once taken her own life in the theatre long ago.

It is of note that this ghost saw the need to physically open the doors, rather than pass through them, carefully closing them again after. It is also a notable case of a repeating pattern, which we will explore further below, its predictability suggesting that time can get "stuck in a groove".

Visible spectral sightings also occur in medical units, if not always full-body ones. Joanna was once a nurse at a key London hospital. While on night shift, ward staff would sometimes see a shadowy male figure creeping down one of the aisles but they were never able to identify him. Eventually, a nurse at the far end of the room saw him at the same time as Joanna and the two of them moved in on the figure from both sides, thinking they now had their man – but he simply vanished as they came together.

Joanna added that a number of dying patients in the same hospital claimed that a *female* figure would on occasion come to comfort them. This was inevitably put down to hallucinatory effects – that is, until staff actually witnessed the patients talking to a mostly invisible something. "Mostly" invisible because, looking down, they would see a ghostly pair of shoed feet standing next to the bed, with nothing more to be seen above the ankles. Sightings of – or touches from – apparently disconnected limbs and body parts are another recorded phenomenon explored below.

Tales of resident hospital ghosts are rife. Another woman told me that when she was training as a young nurse, staff would quietly talk about the "grey lady" who could often be found on a chair in the reception area before mysteriously vanishing. Thinking this was a joke told to new recruits, although she never saw the lady for herself, she came to realize that it was taken perfectly seriously by those who had.

It is an unavoidable fact that many hospital beds will have hosted dying people. As such, we try to forget this if we unfortunately find ourselves in one of those beds. While most of us seem to leave no trace as we leave this world, the exceptions can be dramatic.

Christine worked as a nurse in a hospital known to be particularly prone to the paranormal by those who worked there. Poltergeist activity and "odd" things would regularly occur. One night, Christine and the other nurses saw an unknown lady sitting on one of the beds. When they walked over to investigate, she vanished before their eyes. Later, in the same ward, patients were disturbed by a repeating, groaning, snoring-like sound clearly coming from the bed opposite – but the bed was empty. Christine knew that an elderly nun had died in it about a week before and had been making exactly the same noises.

## Auric Residue

As some ghosts appear indelibly linked to objects they have been associated with, especially if trauma has occurred, it can be understood that a bed someone may have been in for a long time before passing or whose occupant died with regrettable discomfort might bear a strong consciousness imprint. However, sometimes insubstantial glowing impressions of the recently departed in their dead form (rather than an animated "conscious" ghost) are seen hovering over the beds in which they passed, and these may have a different explanation. Those who believe in auras – energetic fields that radiate from the body but are only visible to certain people (or devices) with the gift of seeing into that spectrum – have argued that the "auric body" can take up to several weeks to fade even when the spirit has gone – which may explain such sightings.[15]

The spirit appears to be a separate component from our auric fields – people keeping vigil with dying loved ones have described seeing translucent clouds or heat-like shimmers rising from the body at the moment of death. My wife Helen, present with her sisters, watched this occur as their mother passed. Interestingly, the spirit appeared to rapidly stream upward from the diaphragm. Whatever is visibly "leaving" seems to be nicely on its way to wherever fairly quickly, but auric presences may still be energetically tethered to the beds. (Is an "out-of-body experience" a part-projection of one of our *living* auric fields? – see Chapter 4.)

### Strange … Conversations: Bedtime Stories

In yet another haunted hospital, yet another nurse, Phillipa, reported many peculiar happenings, including full ghost sightings and hysterical patients seeing the auric bodies of former (dead) occupants of the beds floating just inches above their faces … This happened so often that it became impossible to hide, but patient–staff relations were, to put it mildly, poor; Phillipa witnessed patients being treated as "mentally disturbed", when the reality was that they were seeing something they had no context for and were understandably terrified. In extreme cases, some claimed to have been beaten to ensure their silence.

Why did this particular hospital attract such a rash of auric traces, when presumably this could be expected in every healthcare establishment dealing with death? Was there something in the design of the beds or in the general environment that triggered auric residue to this degree? As the hospital exhibited paranormal phenomena of several kinds, it may be that something about it and its location (perhaps it was on an earth energy hotspot) made it a wider portal for the strange.

Auric echoes are not restricted to medical environs. The following account was told to me by a close friend of Jonathan, whose grandfather died when the friend was just a boy. Two weeks later, the family moved the bed on which his grandfather had passed into Jonathan's room to provide a sleeping place for visiting friends and cousins. That night, he looked across the room – and saw a softly glowing image of his grandfather's body suspended above his old bed. He screamed in terror, bringing his mother into the room to see what was wrong – to her distress, but to his later satisfaction (for the verification), she saw the same apparition.

Beds can carry more than just auric memories, as we saw with some of the stories in the previous chapter. Ellen had moved into her deceased parents' old house, taking on their antique bed. Her husband would usually stay up later than her, so she would begin the night sleeping by herself. Despite this, she could often feel the weight and movement of somebody lying next to her, the bed responding as if someone were turning over in it (see also page 34). No figure was visible but the mattress would visibly compress downward. Certain that this was the spirit of one of her parents (she was not sure which), Ellen felt oddly soothed by it. Whether this continued when her husband joined her is not recorded; presumably it did not, as it would not make for a good night's sleep.

# Stitches in Time

The regular midnight visitor to the South African hospital above makes the noteworthy point that some ghosts follow clockwork routines synchronous with our 24-hour cycles, performing the same routine over and again. We don't know how time passes in other realms and it may be that the *appearance* of a regular routine is an illusory stitch in time somehow entangled with the Earth's natural phases and the electromagnetic changes that come with that. Others follow *annual* patterns – one lady told me that, without fail, she would always see a spectral "gardening man" with an old-fashioned wheelbarrow coming up the path of her garden each 7 October, only to vanish again. Let us hope for the ghosts' sakes that they *aren't* aware of being stuck in these loops.

Here are more cases of repeating cycles.

### *Strange ... Conversations*: Eternal Footsteps

Duncan and his wife lived in an English house that was around 600 years old. Uncanny things would occur there, the most obvious being that they would hear footsteps on the wooden boards in the room above almost every night at the same time. Without fail, the unknown prowler would walk across the floor to the same spot, where scratching noises would then be heard in the wall, as if someone was trying to claw their way through it. Duncan tried many times to dash upstairs and catch it in the act, but all would be still, nor could any scratches be seen. On other occasions, they would hear a mysterious baby crying in one of the rooms.

When this became wearing, Duncan did some research and discovered that a "labourer" had once lived in the house in an earlier stage of its development. Concerned that some vestige of its old occupant might be trapped there, he decided to take the exorcism route. The exorcist told them he sensed that the man had somehow lost his mother but was continually looking for her in the house. The baby remained unexplained (unless this was a projection of the man as a young child, whose mother had died?). Compelling the spirit to move on and assuring the ghostly labourer that his mother was long gone, the exorcist was successful on this occasion and the noises stopped.

This story bears similarities to an experience my wife Helen and her sister's family had while staying in northern Spain. Renting the lower floor of a town house – the upper floor was disused – on the night they arrived they were perturbed to hear sounds of stomping footsteps from the supposedly empty level above. Footfalls would cross the floorboards, followed by the sound of a heavy chair being dragged toward the window side of the house. A squeaking window would then be heard, as if being pushed upward. Then, the cycle would start all over again. What was especially disturbing was that the sounds were *exactly the same* every time, repeating *ad infinitum* in a continual loop for the entire night, as if a vinyl record's "needle" kept jumping back to the beginning. Helen and family in their beds below were unable to sleep, petrified by the unending sequence.

At the crack of dawn, they piled their belongings into the cars and checked out, happy to put miles between them and this place of wrongness. The owners had assured them no one was on the upstairs level, but even if a squatter had somehow got in, who would or could perform the same actions in such an obsessive pattern for hours on end so perfectly that each cycle was identical? The chair was never heard being dragged back to its starting point, in any case.

Did someone once drag a chair to the window to help throw themselves out of it, thus imprinting their trauma into the villa? Or was it a meaningless moment that time and space accidentally swept into a loop because, well, sometimes it does. Could my footsteps going to the kitchen to make coffee right now become a similar repeating meme for future occupants of the house, without me ever knowing? These are layers of reality that we don't yet understand, but perhaps one day we will and so recording such anecdotes is important.

Not all repeated sightings occur at precisely the same time or quite so regularly. Many appear to trigger at random, even if the apparition performs the same actions seen by others. Good examples of this can be found in cases of ghosts seen crossing roads, another common trope. These are not hikers mistaken for something odd, but often floating, radiating figures of the classic variety. For example, there is one busy road in the English county of Kent where several completely unconnected witnesses have described to me seeing the same "white lady" in a period dress, passing across without any physical effect from the vehicles going by and always vanishing before reaching the opposite side. This is compelling evidence that these are not delusional liars but everyday drivers sharing something real and inexplicable.

Here are some other related tales of the road.

### Strange ... Conversations: Road Apparitions
Olivia and Don were driving one night when they saw a white glowing humanoid form abruptly coming straight toward them on the road. Don slammed on the brakes, but it was too late – this was surely going to be a terrible pedestrian death. But, instead, the shape passed straight through the car and vanished into the darkness. They looked at each other in fright. Don said, "Did you just see what I saw?" She had. Neither of them had believed in ghosts until then, but after this Olivia, at least, changed her mind on the subject.

In a comparable incident, guitarist Phil was on his way in a van to a gig with his rock band in the 1970s. On a country road, in full daylight, a strange but very localized patch of bright "thick cloud" suddenly materialized and appeared to deliberately wait in the van's path. There was no way to avoid it – but, again, they passed harmlessly through and the cloud was gone. The band members in the front seats who witnessed this were so shocked by what they had seen that no one said anything in the moment, as if all were afraid to admit to something so overtly weird. Only later did they discuss it and confirmed what they had all observed.

It goes without saying that the internet is full of claims of "haunted highways", particularly in the USA, with tales of sightings and even direct meetings with the apparent spirits of those who died in tragedy, either having been knocked down by cars, died in nasty crashes or having thrown themselves from bridges and so on.[16] With road accidents being one of the leading modern causes of deaths around the world it is inevitable that ghosts and roads will always go together.[17] But the cases I have come across seem mostly more passive – and can be descriptions of people from the pre-car era. Perhaps these spectres are using long-lost pathways that, as with altered houses, are now crossed by tarmac.

Phil's late father, another claimed sceptic (but who, by definition, wasn't), on a number of separate occasions observed a lady in – once again – a "Victorian" dress in the street near their home. She would stand for a short while beneath the old-fashioned streetlamp there and then literally float across the road, with no sign of a walking motion, before fading away. I knew Phil's father and can testify that, as he of all people said this, it must have occurred.

This floating quality, oft-described, is notable, because if this was a timeslip ghost one would presumably observe leg movements. Not many of us float around in our daily lives, so this suggests such entities *choose* to propel themselves this way. That, or a spirit is unconsciously visiting old places, again on a repeat setting, but in a manner that reflects its current ethereal existence, not its former bodily form.

Sometimes, however, spectral figures seen walking across or actually *on* existing roads show signs of being echoes rather than sentient – because they can be waist-deep (or lower) in the ground, moving along quite contentedly on the level that clearly existed in their time, not ours. Sightings of entire Roman legions have been described as exhibiting this phenomenon, or are witnessed in deep places like cellars. It is easy to forget how much physical material has been overlaid onto surfaces over the centuries and that the levels we live at today are significantly higher than those our ancestors knew.

## Ghost Time Limits?

The subject of Roman ghosts brings us usefully to a point alluded to above, and one with intriguing implications. As readers will have noted, the majority of ghost encounters I personally hear about describe either recently passed relatives, people from the last century or so, or characters dressed in "Victorian" clothes. Let us examine this a little.

"Victorian" is used to denote the people and fashions from the era in which Queen Victoria reigned over Britain and its Empire between 1837 to 1901. Although primarily a term used in those territories and less popular now because of the colonial inferences, it is still sometimes employed more globally to denote the 19th century in general. But I have noticed that many people's understanding of history hazily merges events of entirely disparate centuries into one general cauldron known as "the past", and "Victorian" is often applied simply to mean any previous age where people wore fancier costumes. Some descriptions of Victorian ghosts, therefore, should be treated with caution, as they might refer to anything from Medieval to Edwardian apparitions.

Some costumes are more clearly identifiable, as with a lady who described seeing a very distinctive and tall "cavalier" (the Royalist faction in the English Civil Wars of the 1640s) in an old house, dressed in blue with a feather in his hat. Eerily, he was visible only in the large mirror she was using to adjust her make-up, standing behind her looking right into her reflected eyes – but when she turned, the room was empty. Francis, who we will meet properly in Chapter 8, was also once staying in an old house when he was awoken by the screaming face of a bearded man just inches above him, clearly displaying the styles of the same century; the lady who owned the house had also witnessed the same unsettling apparition.

So, occasionally descriptions seem clear even if modern comprehension of historical dress is notoriously vague. Nonetheless, it is curious that accounts of ghosts who do genuinely appear to come from much earlier centuries are notably fewer. Sightings of ape men are notable by their absence, but I hear little, for example, even of phantoms that might hail from the so-called Dark Ages of the Anglo-Saxon and Viking eras (between the fifth and tenth centuries in Europe). They *do* sometimes occur, and monks, peasants, warriors, Native Americans, tribal peoples from around the world and others who might be projections from earlier periods have been reported – and see more about Roman ghosts below – but they are exceptions to what seems to be a rule: that most ghosts have a limited lifespan.

It stands to reason that as ghosts are particularly bonded to physicality (perhaps explaining why most retain or generate an ethereal version of their clothes and aren't naked), old houses that have stood for several hundred years will bear their energetic imprint the longest, even if some spectres insist on navigating the original routes of a building. As for spirits that occupy newer houses, they still mostly appear to be of the "Victorian" variety.

If energetic imprints explain some ghosts, we know that energy eventually weakens or transforms (look up "entropy", which defines the slow degradation of matter and energy). It makes sense, then, that whatever fuels their appearances is likely to lose its influence in the end, like a battery running down or when electromagnetic particles in a tape recording lose their coherency. The further back in time it is, perhaps the less chance the ghost has of maintaining its manifestations, unless there are exceptional circumstances to keep it "powered up".

The other reason ghosts might vanish is that conscious spirits still wandering around in our dimension may finally sort themselves out and find their way through to their ultimate destination.

# Roman Ghosts

What of the Roman ghosts that *have* been seen? The spectral legions (reported even marching near a building where we used to hold crop circle lecture meetings, through which the course of an old Roman road passed) are reportedly oblivious to the fact they are being observed, suggesting more basic timeslips at work. For them, it was probably just another day of drudgery, the soldiers never knowing that the fabric of space–time had decided to loop their image for centuries after. But why would those loops survive when most phantoms, well, give up the ghost after a while? The Romans flourished (and occupied much of Europe for a time) mainly between 753 BC and the early 5th century AD, so this was a long way back. Perhaps the weight of numbers plays a role. With energy unwittingly imprinted on the environment by whole legions rather than individuals, this might have provided longer-lasting "battery" strength.

But a few Roman entities, it seems, can appear without their legions, demonstrating that, although rare, figures from earlier times can break through occasionally.

### Strange ... Conversations: Roaming Romans
While staying in a traditional English hotel, Marcella was sitting in bed reading while Dominic was in the bathroom,

when a movement caught her eye. She looked up and saw, to her shock, what she described as a "Roman nobleman", walking out of the wall into the room. He was dressed in a toga and finery, as we see depictions of Roman officials. He was also "glowing brightly". She observed his face in detail as he walked forward; he looked impassive and unresponsive to where he was. Somehow, this seemed all the more frightening and at last she screamed, bringing Dominic dashing into the room. Both of them watched the figure vanish through the opposite wall (another shared sighting). Wondering if they were indeed having some bizarre joint hallucination, they realized they weren't when they heard a scream from the adjacent room – where presumably their neighbouring hotel guests were witnessing the nobleman coming through their side of the wall.

The fact that the figure was walking straight through, in an unwavering line that ignored walls and took him into other rooms, may suggest another example of an entity following an old course. The ghost's seeming unawareness suggests a timeslip rather than a conscious spirit, but what was powering his solo materialization is unknown, unless there was something special about the location itself. Perhaps the hotel was built on a former Roman site of some importance?

Curiously, some years after my conversation with Marcella, I heard a parallel tale from a completely separate source. Whether or not this occurred in the same hotel I never discovered, but there are similarities. Josephine and her husband were staying in an English hotel when, one evening, a strange light unexpectedly appeared in their room. It began as a ball of light that hovered in the air and then gradually grew longer to take on the shape of a man, its legs extending to the floor. Josephine described him as wearing classic Roman soldier gear. He then proceeded to walk out of the room through the wall.

★　★　★

It is curious that Roman ghosts should be more ubiquitous than those from other earlier eras in European countries but, in fairness, the Romans were around for a very long period of time and we should consider that it may be that "Roman" is sometimes used to describe a variety of more ancient peoples because of many people's inability to distinguish other distinct historical periods. It would be interesting to make a detailed study comparing ghosts and their apparent eras from around the world to see if distinct cultural patterns emerge.

# Hotel Hauntings

Hostelries are, perhaps inevitably, rich locations for strange encounters. The "haunted hotel" has become a stereotype in ghost-lore. Many lodgings have stood for centuries, or been converted from buildings that had an earlier use, and huge numbers of humans, with all their loves, laughs, dramas and tragedies, pass through them every year, relentlessly imprinting as they go – and maybe opening portals too.

*Strange ... Conversations*: **Unwelcome Guests**
Terence and his wife were staying in a bed and breakfast while travelling across Canada. Despite believing he was not tuned into such things, as they sat in the lounge that night he became aware of the presence and then slow materialization of a tall man standing in the corner, wearing an old-fashioned coat and a stovepipe hat. When the man became fully visible, Terence, with trepidation, finally pointed him out to his wife. Clearly being rather more tuned into such things and at peace with them, she simply remarked "Oh yes, he's been here all evening. I was wondering if you would notice him!"

Robert received a bolder and more knowing visitor in his accommodation. Staying with his wife Betty in a hotel in

Zimbabwe, she was in the bathroom when he became aware of a woman coming up behind him. She very deliberately touched him on the back of his head, and then, somewhat cheekily, walked *through* him. Robert felt nothing as she did so. The lady then swung around to face him, smiling at him. He could see she was a white woman wearing, as ever, a "Victorian or Edwardian" dress with a high neck collar. Seemingly satisfied she had made her point, the lady turned on her heel and walked across the room, vanishing into the wall.

Taken aback by this, Robert was enlightened when, later on during their stay, he and Betty noticed a painting on the hotel wall – of the very same lady he had seen, who had lived there in colonial times. They also learned there was once a doorway precisely where she vanished into the wall.

Robert and Betty found their room had other oddities, not least the fact that the ceiling fan would go on and off by itself despite having no time switch. When they complained, the staff came to investigate … and discovered for the first time that when the fan had been installed it had never actually been connected to the mains – and yet it worked; perhaps courtesy of the mischievous lady?

These ethereal visitors were at least rather more benevolent than those in some lodgings. The case has been made that the "scary" associations continually attached to ghosts are not a fair reflection of their general reality, disquieting though some can be. But more disturbing events do occur too, and we must darken the tone for a short while to address this.

Hotel staff must know the paranormal realities of where they work, even if their experiences are wisely kept from guests. Caroline was a staff member in a hotel converted from a large house originally used as a brothel. The place had a very "strange feeling" and a man had reputedly been murdered in one of the rooms years before. Objects would fly around and peculiar and unpleasant sounds would be heard. Worse,

Caroline would sometimes hear a threatening voice coming out of nowhere, saying, "I am going to get you next."

Just as the hotel was having a refit to move it on further from its former associations, a major fire broke out among building materials. Caroline was there when they all had to evacuate. After flames had gutted many of the rooms and the hotel was completely renovated, the supernatural activity stopped, almost as if the fire had swept away not only the fixings and furnishings but also the energy imprints, mercifully taking the malign entity with them.

### *Strange ... Communications*: Hotel California

Malevolent beings are sometimes said to group together, perhaps originating from the lower astral realms (see page 55). Maybe because of the cocktail of energies held within them, hotels can act as assembly points. Emmanuelle had a disturbing experience while travelling with her partner near California's spectacular Death Valley, which on this occasion perhaps lived up to its name.

> We were staying in the strangest casino right on the border of California and Nevada, with deserts sweeping off into shimmering distances. The huge expansiveness of the desert was rather at odds with the flashing neon signs and life-sized Betty Boop figurines of this singular building in the middle of nowhere.
>
> As I slept that night in our gold-plated, gold-leafed, chandeliered bedroom, I was facing downward with my face pushed up against the pillow when I felt a hand slip into mine. It was so real I awoke from my dreams – and assumed it was my partner's hand. I gave it a stroke but had the sense that something wasn't quite right ... it felt too small to be his.
>
> Several moments later, I felt a hand slip into mine on the other side. I immediately reacted by clawing at the hands, which I now knew did not belong to my partner.

*Almost in immediate response to my change of sentiment, I suddenly felt a huge weight on my back from above. I could feel dozens and dozens of hands pushing down on my spine all at once with so much force that I couldn't move at all. The physicality of it was terrifying. I fought with all of my energy to push this immense force off me, but it wouldn't seem to shift. I then immediately called to perhaps what some might call God, or what I simply refer to as "the light". There were a few moments of nothing and then I felt a very strong source of white light come from nowhere – it was so powerful it blasted all of the ghostly presences away at once. I sat bolt upright, quite shaken and also rather cross. Safe to say, I was happy to leave the next day.*

It might be argued that Emmanuelle's experience has as much in common with some claimed alien abduction descriptions (see Chapter 6) as with spirits but, as we shall see, it is increasingly believed that ETs and ghosts can sometimes occupy the same realms.

## Touched by Ghosts

The above account, and others before it, reinforce the point that some entities, as with poltergeists, are able to apply a physical influence in our world rather than just being insubstantial phantasms. The feeling of hands being slipped into our own is not unique. Here is a gentler expression of that phenomenon, and some other examples of physical contact.

### *Strange ... Conversations*: Hands of Friendship
Laura told me that her (adult) daughter Jane was by herself in Scotland on a guided group tour to Edinburgh's famous catacombs beneath the South Bridge. Built in the 1700s, they became fetid shelters for the poor and homeless for long years

and housed illegal distilleries and other murky enterprises. Their reputation for hauntings may be well founded.[18]

During the tour, the guide turned off the lights to demonstrate just how dark it was down there. In the blackness, Jane felt a small hand slip itself into hers, like a child's grasp, seeking comfort; yet she knew there had been no children in the group. Feeling oddly unafraid and sensing strongly that she should not shake it off, Jane stood holding the hand for two to three minutes while the guide spoke. When the lights went back on, there was nobody there and the grip released instantly. It is likely that a number of children died in the vaults; their spirits are still seeking love and reassurance, it would seem.

There is a tenderness to some reports of ghostly touching. Jill remembered a bedroom in her aunt's house where guests would describe feeling their foreheads being gently stroked. It seemed kind and well-meaning. Jill had been a nurse decades ago and said that back then (when such things were permissible) they would stroke the foreheads of patients who needed to be calmed or reassured.

Dorothy felt an invisible touch of a much stronger kind, but one that again felt friendly, albeit slightly invasive. She was cynical about ghosts until she found herself organizing a big event at the horse-racing stables where she worked. While making sandwiches at a table, she felt a very strong arm take her around the waist – so strong that it physically lifted her up into the air and held her there for a few moments. At first she thought it a prank by one of the stable hands, but she could see no one was there. The grip was firm, though not unpleasant. She was then placed down and the sensation ended. Dorothy instinctively sensed this was the spirit of an elderly man who she had helped tend to in his dying months a short while before. In his prime he had been tall and physically robust and would have been able to lift her easily.

\* \* \*

The majority of ghosts seem to pass through without corporeal interaction, but some plainly have the ability to touch or intervene – and things aren't always so friendly, as Emmanuelle discovered above. We will come to more traditional poltergeists shortly, but as well as all the gentle spirits, I have unfortunately also heard of shaking, hitting and even strangling occurring from unseen but very present forces.

Others have reported a pressing sensation on their chest, as if someone is sitting on them or trying to hold them down; sceptics put this down to sleep paralysis or respiratory conditions, but this may not explain all such experiences. These descriptions, which go back into history, have led to belief in supernatural creatures such as the incubus or succubus, sexually predative male and female demonic forces that hold their victims down as they insensitively violate them.

With the more aggressive intrusions, it may be that malevolent entities are taking out their anger on the world; that, or trapped and confused spirits are attempting to make their plight known in the only way they can, something claimed by many mediums (see below).

Do people who die in fast and unexpected circumstances especially, get delayed in the liminal dimension between here and the afterlife (whatever that is), finding themselves still on the "Earth plane" but not on the same frequency level as before? Being aware of the environment around them but now having little influence over it would surely be as unsettling for a spirit as it is for us witnessing them. It might take an enormous force of will to physically cut back through to our world; maybe only crude and abrupt movements are possible, like when we try to open a tight lid on a jar and it suddenly, and often messily, pops open.[19]

However, sometimes physical impacts do seem aimed more deliberately.

### *Strange ... Conversations*: Assaults from Nowhere

Pauline once lived in a house constructed in the 1930s. It had been substantially converted over the years and was prone to objects mysteriously moving or being found broken. On more than one occasion, she glimpsed the apparition of a man in a brown suit at the top of the staircase, hurrying as if on his way to work, apparently unconscious of her. The family learned to live with these quirks, and liked the house. But things were to turn a little more serious.

In the dining room near a window was a chair that Pauline liked to sit in. One day she found it shaking beneath her, almost as if something wanted her to get out of it. She wondered if machinery might be vibrating through the floor from outside, but couldn't find a cause. On another occasion, Pauline was sitting in the chair when something hit her on the thigh. Startled, she looked around, but no one was there. She wondered if her son had come downstairs to play a prank, but he always denied this. Later, she was in the chair again when she received a much harder impact on her leg. It was so severe that her flesh was red and swollen, as if somebody had slapped her with force.

She felt strongly that a masculine presence was responsible for these incidents, perhaps disturbed by the chair being placed in the way of what she knew had once been a thoroughfare; oddly, she did not believe her attacker was the man in the suit. If the house had become a wider portal, already primed by a male entity, it is possible that more than one being might have crept in. Notably, around the same time, neighbours in her road also reported poltergeist activity, with further sightings of a male figure, presumably moving from house to house.

My own father, a deeply Christian man not prone to imaginings, once received a spectral assault of his own, if annoying rather than painful. Peggy, an elderly lady very close to our family, lived alone in an old English house first built in the 1500s and extended over the centuries. My father went there one evening to move chairs from one upstairs room to another across a small creaky landing. My mother was there for the ride but stayed in the downstairs lounge, while Peggy was in the room into which the chairs were being moved.

As he passed across the landing with a solid-backed dining chair in his hands, my father was irritated to be pushed backward by a woman with frizzy hair in a black coat and silver buttons, pressing past toward Peggy and chatting away as she did so. Assuming this to be my mother getting in the way, he let it go in the moment but during the drive home my father asked why she had done this. Indignant, my mother insisted that she had not at any point gone upstairs. My father then observed what she was wearing – and it wasn't a black coat with silver buttons. She didn't have a frizzy hairstyle and was sporting a black hair bow anyhow, unlike the figure on the landing. The blood drained from his face as he realized he had just had a paranormal encounter.

Thinking further, my father knew he had held the chair – with its solid back – facing *away* from him. He should not have been able to see the buttons and he realized that the coat must have been coming partially *through* the chair. It is interesting what we don't think about in fleeting moments, even when things don't make sense. He also recalled with a jolt that the chatting he heard was in truth nothing but a meaningless "babble", like a mess of sped-up noises. Peggy had seen and heard nothing. Was the ghost saying something coherent in her realm that came out as a tangled jabber in ours, especially if time does not run the same in different dimensions?

The lady in the coat may not have been happy at disruption in a house that had barely changed its furnishings in a hundred years; that, or the movements triggered a psychic recording – if so, it was one that had a physical presence and left a lasting impression on my father for years afterward. Peggy, it turned out, had herself seen an unexplained lady in period dress several times before, usually coming up the garden path before vanishing. We will return to Peggy's house, in different circumstances, in Chapter 5.

My mother, reluctant toward the supernatural but disconcerted by my father's experience, became a little more open when she had her own sighting some years later. As a passenger in the car as my father drove, they were passing through the area where he was born when my mother noticed a lady at the side of the road, wearing rather old-fashioned clothes. She was staring right at them. With shock, she realized this was my father's *own mother* – a lady she had never met, as she died when my father was a teenager. My mother knew her distinctive looks instantly from photographs. Perturbingly, her lower legs were invisible, fading into nothing, giving the impression that she was hovering. It was a fleeting image; my father didn't see her and my mother found the incident upsetting: why had her long-lost mother-in-law appeared just for *her*, and what did this mean after all these years? They never found out – but they realized later that it was her birthday that very day. It seems she felt the need to make a celebratory appearance.

Some spirits *do* clearly like to make themselves known, using physical means if necessary. Martin Noakes, who we shall hear more of later, once hosted a gentleman from America, who came to stay while visiting the UK. One night, about 3am, lying in bed, Martin was awoken by the feeling of someone tugging at his arm, moving it back and forth "very fast and quite violently", as if wanting him to get up. Alarmed, and expecting to see a member of his family trying to alert him, instead he saw nothing. He pulled his arm away and turned over, and the grip did not return.

Hearing of this the next day, the gentleman revealed that he believed the spirit of his late wife was still accompanying him on his travels. He told Martin that he would always meditate every morning at 3am, but having just arrived from America that day he was tired and didn't wake up. He believed the arm-pulling was a vicarious message from his wife, annoyed at him for not meditating ...

Edward had a not dissimilar event. He was staying at a friend's house when in the night he awoke to feel the hairs on the back of his neck "prickle and go up". Suddenly, something pulled down the bedsheets from over his face. At first, he thought this was just an accidental slipping down – but then something pulled the sheets back *up* over him again. He whipped up to look but no one was there.

Some ethereal assaults are very aggressive. Millie and her husband were staying in a hotel when suddenly in the middle of the night something grabbed her. Awakening immediately in a panic, she felt invisible hands pick her up and vigorously throw her out of bed, against the wall and onto the floor. Her husband, who had awoken when sensing a disturbance, witnessed her being physically lifted up by the unseen presence and hurtled across the room. Her children, staying in an adjoining room, heard the thump and her screaming and rushed in to see what had happened. When Millie's family related this encounter to the hotel owners, disturbed at what had happened, they were reluctantly told that the building once belonged to a man with a reputation for being very violent toward women.

In another hostile offensive, Sally rented an old fisherman's cottage in a quaint Cornish coastal village for a time, but she felt that she was resented. She sensed a male presence and light switches began to turn on and off and doors would open and close. When objects flew across the room, seemingly aimed directly at her, it became dangerous. The final straw came when, walking across her living room one evening, what felt like a bucketful of water was thrown across her, leaving her soaked and very frightened. The water came from nowhere, as if it had been siphoned from another realm altogether, but it was real enough to make her and the room physically wet. There was no receptacle lying nearby. Taking the hint, Sally moved out the next morning.

It is an unhappy fact that physical attacks on women from men remain a serious issue and it is depressing to conclude that expressions of the violent masculine also seem to extend beyond the grave. We like to think that passing into the next life automatically makes angels of us, but clearly not – we take with us at least something of the personalities we have here. Spiritual philosophers hold that the karmic journey of growth and development gradually ascends us to a higher nature, but it would appear to be a long process. Some spirits, sadly, fall lower.

How beings on a different plane can physically touch us, draw water and produce smells from nowhere are just more mysteries among many – but they evidently can. What happens, though, when someone gets touched not by a conscious spectre, but apparently by the ghost of a dead body?

## Strange ... Conversations: House of Horrors

For all the women who have been targeted, men can also be terrorized by malicious forces. In the 1960s, Tom and Jeff, both students, were looking for temporary accommodation. Unable to find anywhere affordable, they eventually happened upon a dilapidated house being rented by an agency. It was cheap and had been unoccupied for a while. They were soon to find out why.

While sleeping in different rooms, Tom and Jeff would find themselves being vigorously shaken awake. Each assumed this was some kind of reciprocal prank, but the humour faded when the shaking turned to strangling, with a very real feeling of hands around their throats. They would leap up to fight their assailants, but no one would be there. A sinister feeling grew.

One night, Tom got up to use the toilet. Leaving the door open behind him (which connected to a landing at the top of the stairs), he was standing attending to his business when something prodded the back of his neck. He turned around, but nothing was there. He continued, then there was a further jab. Turning again, this time he did see something. Dangling from the attic hatchway above the landing was the body of a hanged man, swinging on a rope. The prodding was caused by the cold feet hitting his neck each time they swung his way.

Tom's screaming awakened Jeff. They threw their belongings together and fled the house that night. When they complained to the rental company, they were sheepishly told that the former owner of the house had indeed hanged himself on that very landing.

### Strange ... Communications: A Pub Hanging

The above is not the only tale I have heard of the ghost of a dead body. Gina Baksa, who once worked in a typical English country pub, shared with me the following story:

*Every Friday we had a comedy night in a tiny basement room. We could only serve bottled beers there as the taps were only linked to the main bar above. Running out of bottles, I went next door to get a new crate. This vast basement room was home to numerous barrels and pub paraphernalia. Under pressure to serve demanding customers, I dashed into the darkness, turned on the light and stopped dead: just a few feet above me, swinging from one of the ceiling rafters, was the figure of a man in his thirties, with short blond hair. He was well-built and dressed in what looked like sackcloth secured at the waist – a peasant's outfit. He was swinging in the breeze and had clearly been hanging for some time, looking at his clothing. I felt shocked – and scared. He was as real as my punters next door. I ran upstairs to alert the landlord who was serving in the main bar.*

*"You've got a hanging man in your basement," I gasped. "I'm not going back down to serve there." Thinking the landlord would just wave me off, I was surprised to hear him say: "Oh yes, we know all about him. He was an Irish labourer who was caught stealing sheep. They hanged him for his cheek, poor guy."*

*I never went back downstairs.*

What is extraordinary in these instances is that the witnesses saw, or were physically struck by, not animated apparitions but visions of seemingly *dead men*, spectral facsimiles of the cold bodies that had once hung there, rope and all – unless they were projections from *before* full death occurred? Were these extreme expressions of auric residue that somehow retained physical elements, or more time loops? Or can ghosts project themselves in their dead forms as well as "living" ones? The shaking and strangling experienced by Tom and Jeff implied the presence of a conscious force, but the body that nudged Tom's neck appeared, at least, to be fully deceased. It seems that a blend of phenomena was entangled in that energetically damaged location, raising many chilling possibilities.

## Poltergeists

We have established that entities in other dimensions are sometimes able to physically interact with ours, and that "poltergeist" activity is often recorded. The name derives from the German *Polter*, meaning "noise", and *Geist*, meaning "spirit" – hence, "noisy spirit".

Some paranormal investigators believe that poltergeists, which break, throw or move objects, manipulate doors, locks, lights, showers and taps or generate unexplained sounds, are caused by an uncontrolled psychic force from living humans. Telekinesis, discussed a little further in Chapter 5, is a claimed psychic ability that can manipulate the material world by mind alone. It is sometimes associated with the presence of adolescent girls (see below), believed by some researchers to be capable of generating unconscious extrasensory fields that inflict havoc on their surroundings for unclear reasons. That, or there is an unsavoury draw to teenage females from malevolent entities with predatory sexual motivations, despite no longer having a body in this world.

However, in my personal conversations with witnesses, I have found that the large majority of poltergeists occur alongside more traditional ghost experiences. As we are coming to understand, places where normal space–time conditions have been disrupted by trauma or an energetic surge might provide ideal conduits for both enhanced psychic phenomena *and* the ingress of entities attracted by the resulting portal.

Much of what people think they know about this phenomenon is rooted, perhaps inescapably, in the 1982 seminal haunted house movie, *Poltergeist*, although even there the activity is pinned to spirits angered by the desecration of a Native American graveyard. The film was indirectly inspired by events reported by the Hermann family, which occurred at their home in New York's Long Island in 1958 and encompassed many of the now recognized poltergeist traits, as well as a peculiar "popping" heard throughout the building. Hollywood's interpretation is greatly exaggerated, but the Hermann case remains one of the best-known US examples.[20]

Each country has its own famous poltergeist-infested houses. In the UK, two examples received mainstream attention in their time. The "Enfield Poltergeist" in the late 1970s saw a single mother and her four children claim extraordinary happenings in their otherwise unremarkable house in south-east England, mainly centred around the two teenage daughters. These included movements of objects but also growling voices, loud knocking sounds and even the enforced levitation of the girls. The story was widely reported, but opinions remain divided over its authenticity. Sceptics, inevitably, assert fraud or at least heavy embellishment, but it was notable that when the BBC (British Broadcasting Company) re-examined the claims and spoke to witnesses in 2018, those interviewed maintained that at least some of what they experienced was inexplicable in mundane terms. An earlier but similar story, the "Battersea Poltergeist" in 1950s London, which again focused around a teenage girl, was also rehabilitated by the BBC as a genuine mystery.[21]

Regardless of the well-known cases and their provenance, I have heard more than enough direct accounts from witnesses to satisfy me that poltergeists exist. Several have already been alluded to, but here are some examples where the more traditional poltergeist attributes are to the fore.

### Strange ... Conversations: Poltergeist Tales

George found his house becoming problematic. Doors would open and shut, things would move around and a heavy kitchen door would keep locking itself, despite having a chunky key that couldn't be turned easily at the best of times. His two dogs would inexplicably "go wild" at nothing. In this case, the activity *did* culminate in a full sighting, when George's wife saw the apparition of a human figure creeping around. Doing some detective work, they discovered that before they bought the house a man had once drowned in the swimming pool there.

For all their presumed abilities to pass seamlessly through them, poltergeists seem to be upset by doors. Terri was staying in an old cottage where the internal doors had large old-fashioned latches – but every morning, even though the latches had all been firmly closed at bedtime, she would find the doors hanging open. The latches had always been dismantled, as if by a diligent toolmaker, with their parts neatly placed across different areas of the room ... The cottage was full of unexplained sounds and unexpected movements from supposedly inanimate objects. Terri suspected the owners knew full well it was haunted because hanging from the back of each door were Roman Catholic rosary beads, apparently placed there to ward off evil.

This tendency towards ordered neatness is a feature of some poltergeist cases, beyond the better-known chaotic behaviour. Valerie used to run a grocery store with her husband in an old building. Peculiar events were common there. A jam jar inexplicably slid itself across the counter in full view of a customer, chopping boards were found neatly stacked up against each other in an upside-down V-shape, and an artistically arranged pile of toilet rolls was found cleverly balanced on the closed lid of a lavatory. The employees wondered if Valerie's husband was doing this as a way of testing their resolve, but he was just as bemused. The stacks would often be assembled so quickly, when backs were briefly turned, that this was impossible anyhow.

Not all poltergeists are so neat – or quiet. Murray managed a warehouse that had a "very strange atmosphere". Pens would fly across rooms and other objects would move by themselves. Staff didn't like working in the facility. As manager, Murray would find himself there alone as he came in early to open up and when staying late to close again. When the strangeness got too much, he would find himself chatting to the empty air, saying, "Yes, well I have things to do now, so please leave me to get on with them." But the poltergeist seemed intent on aggravating him. Its regular ploy would be to bang the metal trash cans loudly in the corridor outside his office, even though Murray could see clearly into it and knew no one was there. A noisy spirit indeed. One day, the banging got to such a fever pitch that he screamed, "Please, GIVE IT A REST!" On this occasion, at least, the presence got the hint and silence fell.

* * *

It is not always so easy to stop such activity. Some poltergeists are plainly driven by a tragic need to be seen and heard, leading to extreme behaviour that in the end requires proper intervention from a psychic or spiritual expert.

### *Strange ... Conversations/Memories*: Drastic Pleas for Attention

In their desperation to be noticed or confusion at finding themselves trapped in a bewildering netherworld, certain spirits take drastic action. Some can manipulate our world with precision, as with the latches and toilet rolls. For less adept entities, we can only imagine why they might lash out in frustration, seeing any displacement of an object, however unruly or destructive, as an achievement that has announced their presence.

I was once involved in investigating a relevant case. Two friends – a couple – took me aside in the mid-1990s and quietly described a problem to me, one they felt I might be able to help with: a poltergeist had moved in with them. As with many such situations, the activity began in an understated manner, leaving the family uncertain whether they were reading too much into minor incidents that might just be mechanical failures. The television would turn itself on or off or channels would infuriatingly switch over when they were watching something. They wondered if a remote handset from a nearby house was somehow tuned to the same frequency. But when lights began to go on and off and doors locked and unlocked themselves, it became clear they had an issue.

The tipping point that brought them to me arrived when they came home one night to find that all the clothes in their drawers and wardrobes had been, literally, torn to pieces. Also, left clearly visible in the middle of their lounge carpet was a small footprint heavily compressed into it, as if a child had stamped with unimaginable weight to ensure that its calling card could not be ignored.

I was lucky enough to have gained the friendship of a man called Paul Bura. A victim of polio as a child, he had learned to offset his resulting disabilities with a charismatic personality and a rich silky voice he used in his career as a voiceover artist and poet. He also had extraordinary psychic abilities. The broader story of my adventures with Paul, now sadly no longer in this realm, will be touched on later and have been told elsewhere (see note); the point is that he was someone I trusted, who I had myself seen demonstrate gifts of mediumship and clairvoyance that were for me beyond fraud or chance.[22]

I recognize that more religious-minded readers may see all mediumship and psychic forces as work of the Devil. Without disrespecting anyone's beliefs, I have personally seen no evidence to support this. It is true that psychics can tap into both light and dark frequencies, and certain practices can be dangerous for the inexperienced. But this does not make these skills inherently evil, in the same way that Christianity does not see its army of exorcists, who tap into the same realms using not entirely dissimilar means, as being demonic themselves. Reaching into other realities is simply an ability, and it stands or falls on the training, gifts and intent of those doing it. I have always remained open-minded about how it works and why, and took Paul's talents at face value. In turn, he never demanded that others perceive it in any dogmatic way; indeed, he himself often questioned how it functioned.

What happened next pretty much ticked all the Hollywood boxes, bar outlandish visual phenomena. Paul, myself and a small group of like-minded friends, including a dowser/geomancer (see below and Chapter 5), descended on the poltergeist-ridden house one evening and Paul tuned in to see what might be there, while the dowser attempted to reconfigure the natural energies. Paul would take on the personality and voice of those he was channelling; his face would distort into features we presumed reflected those of the speaker. The husky voice that spoke seemed sad and anxiety-ridden. Paul identified it as a man and sensed that a young boy was with him, clearly his son; both were perplexed as to where they were and why unfamiliar people and things were surrounding them.

In its conversation with our group, the disembodied spirit made clear that they had perished in a fire – a horrific exit that more than likely tore a hole in space–time. We quickly realized this meant the house they had died in was not the current one, which was relatively modern and had no history of fires. Why were they here? Realizing these souls were trapped and confused, Paul withdrew from channelling and embarked on the time-honoured medium's procedure of instructing them to look for a point of light or a bright doorway that somehow they had deliberately avoided or were blinded to at the moment of death – the portal they should have left by in the first place. Guiding them gently but firmly, Paul sensed the weeping father thanking him as he enabled the two of them to make their way across the threshold until finally they were gone, seemingly transformed and on their way.

From that night on, the house mostly settled, with a few resurging odd moments but no more torn clothes or ruined carpets. Did the lingering lesser effects mean the father and son had somehow stumbled back through the doorway? Not necessarily; as established, rips in reality can attract other beings to the same point, forever drawn to the lure of the Earth plane, and the psychic environment around them can be left unstable.

My friends, researching the history of the area later on, discovered two important facts about the site of their house. Firstly, an abattoir had stood there for a while. With apologies to those in the meat industry, the activities that take place in such establishments are known by mediums to create zones of psychic disruption and dark energies. Secondly, and astonishingly, local records showed that a previous house had stood on the site before that. The house was destroyed around 150 years before, by a fire ... in which a father and son had died. For Paul, the confirmation was both sad and satisfying, and for my friends it was a closing of the circle. With the fire and the subsequent cycle of death focused at the site, that house was never going to be an energetically passive place.

### Strange ... Communications: Geomantic Solutions

There was a reason for including a geomancer or earth energies expert among our group. Many paranormal researchers believe the planet has an innate grid of "energy lines" which converge at certain points. If they are flowing freely and positively, all tends to be well within whatever is built above them, but when they become disrupted, either by natural changes or imprinted trauma from nearby events, problems can arise. The disruption might play a part in tearing open portals and these are likely another element in battlefield hauntings and suchlike. Earth energies are also believed to play a role in places where religious apparitions occur.[23]

Karen Dodd shared with me a tale of a poltergeist, again connected to an adolescent girl, seemingly quieted by a healing of the energetic grid:

> As my children were going through the experimental stage of alcohol and drugs, a serious event occurred. I was out of the house when my teenage daughter called to say she had heard me/someone call her name in the kitchen three times. She was home alone and I rushed back to be with her.
>
> A few days later, she phoned as we were driving, asking who had been in her bedroom (assuming it to be her brother), because it had been trashed and things broken. No one had been at home when this happened. We all started to sense a presence in the house and were very scared. On one occasion, I was watching TV and the remote just flew past me.
>
> We went through asking a series of people to come along in an attempt to move these energies, including clergymen

*and even a bishop, which didn't work. Nothing worked, from smudging, banging, praying, etc. I do believe these energies found access through the drug/alcohol situation in the home.*

*One day, however, I was directed to a lady who works with earth energies, usually on land in war-torn areas, who was in Bosnia at the time. We chatted over the phone and then, one day, I suddenly realized everything had gone quiet; no more weird activity. She had removed the entities/energies remotely and described what and who they were. She had picked up on an old lady and an aggressive man who didn't like women, hence he picked on my daughter. We were told that when entities start communicating using our names, it is definitely time to ask them to leave.*

The ability to influence energies remotely would seem to be real and is almost certainly connected to the phenomenon of consciousness projection, which we will examine in the next two chapters.

## Strange Inconclusions: Ghosts and Poltergeists

An important point to be made is that just because one family experiences ghost and poltergeist activity, it does not necessarily mean the next family that moves in to the same house will. Places with dire reputations can fall quiet when social changes occur, in odd reverse to the frequent *rise* of phenomena when buildings get physically disrupted. Similar to how houses or local earth energies can be the gateways to the paranormal, this strongly suggests that some people are walking portals themselves – when they move, the strange moves with them. In the same way that certain individuals can tune into frequencies that others can't, whole families may well share psychic or even genetic traits that either attract or block paranormal activity.

Earlier, we mentioned ghosts following people. With this in mind, I include one last conversation in this chapter.

***Strange ... Conversations*: The Ghost That Followed**
In one of her previous houses, Constance would see a man dressed in white overalls who would appear from nowhere. She wasn't overly disturbed about him, yet wasn't comfortable either. She would look away if she saw him or shut the door on the room she found him in, even if logically she knew this was unlikely to stop a ghost.

Many years on – and four houses later – happy that the man in white was long gone, Constance was shocked one day to see the same figure in the same overalls in her new home. She realized with a shiver that the ghost had come with her. Had he always been present but invisible for years, or had something about this latest dwelling triggered his reappearance? What was his bond with her? I asked if she thought the man might be a lost relative of hers or perhaps an ancestor – someone with a connection in the same way that children see forebears they have never met but who come to watch over them. Constance agreed this could be the case but, if so, she had no idea who he was.

What we have understood with this significant dive into the ghostly is that neither hauntings nor the people who experience them are straightforward. There are mysterious bonds between spirits and the physical artefacts they were associated with here, but also bonds between certain entities and the living – generally, although not always, through family ties. Mostly, the interaction is harmless, even positive, with some less pleasant exceptions.

There are cases of people being followed just a bit *too* much by presences, a pursuit that becomes inappropriate and leads in the most extreme cases to "possession", or what some psychics call "walk-ins". These appear to be very rare and may sometimes indicate an unfortunate level of schizophrenia or psychiatric illness on the part of the possessed, rather than the paranormal. But then what is illness in these areas and how can we always we tell the difference? Sceptics sometimes imply that a belief in ghosts and the paranormal is in itself a mental defect but, as we have seen, there is more than enough evidence to suggest that tricks of the mind cannot explain all ghost encounters.

For the most part, with the above cautions, ghosts do not generally appear to be something we need to fear, but are instead fascinating evidence of a leaky universe that allows things to come and go between dimensions in certain circumstances. We all cross the thresholds when we pass, presumably, but the wider answers are hidden from us in this life. There are reports of spectres reacting with horror to seeing *us* here, raising the delicious possibility that we may sometimes be the ghosts to *them*. People who have experimented with astral projection and methods of enhancing their psychic abilities to take them into other realms have recounted accidentally stimulating such occurrences. It's all a matter of perspective in the end.[24]

That ghost sightings are more common than is acknowledged should not make us nervous of walking around every corner. If we are going to see a ghost, either it seems that we are meant to, or it happens through a purely spontaneous combination of environmental and spiritual factors. They don't appear to lie in wait for us every day; they must surely have better things to do and the repeating clockwork sightings are likely just time loops unconsciously playing out their cycle.

There is a scene in the famous Irish TV comedy *Father Ted*, where the titular Ted creeps downstairs in the middle of the night, only to be shocked by Mrs Doyle, the housekeeper, lurking silently at the lounge door with a tea tray. When asked why, she admits that she does this every night, waiting to serve tea just on the off-chance that one of the priests might come down in the small hours – something that has never happened until this occasion. This bizarre routine is taken as a sign of her eccentricity, so we can comfort ourselves that most ghosts are surely wise enough not to bother to do something similar, for all the childhood fears that can tell us otherwise.[25]

Given how many things we have been assured by scientists are absolutes under the "laws of physics" but which turn out not to be when undermined by later discoveries, hopefully science will catch up with the paranormal sooner or later. It edges closer every year, if reluctantly, as the intense peculiarity of the quantum realms and multi-dimensionality are slowly unravelled, only to raise ever more questions. Face-saving and an entrenched hubris have often held humanity back, but science *will* one day probably explain ghosts, not all as hallucinations but as inevitable and even logical components of the complex fabric of time and space.

Beyond the scientists, one likely reason why many everyday folk are reluctant to admit to the reality of ghosts is because their existence raises potentially disturbing questions most don't like to think about – and people in the West *hate* talking about death. We all fear endings and the threat of nothingness. But death may well not be the end, if the above evidence is anything to go by. Ghosts are likely just a dimension-crossing form of psychic phenomena, which we will now begin to explore. Indeed, it may even turn out that we do not need to be dead to be a ghost ...

# CHAPTER 4
# OUT-OF-BODY AND NEAR-DEATH EXPERIENCES

## Live Ghosts

To accept that ghosts are more than a trick of the mind – and anyone who doesn't will probably have incinerated this book by now anyway – is to embrace the concept that some level of consciousness can exist beyond the physical. Ghosts may have different causes, but some are plainly thinking spirits in a non-corporeal state. Throwing a constructive light on this are "out-of-body experiences" (OOBEs), where a similar state can seemingly be attained without the inconvenience of having to die first. These are closely related to "near-death experiences" (NDEs) and both conditions are patently components of psychic phenomena, which we will explore more specifically in the next chapter.

Of all the strange occurrences personally reported to me, OOBEs feature so often that they require particular focus – and usually occur to people who had no idea such things could even happen. Out-of-body experiences are recorded when people find themselves in a disembodied yet fully conscious state of awareness, observing their own physical selves from a few feet away – and vividly remember it afterwards. Mostly, this arises spontaneously, often during sleep or under a general anaesthetic while undergoing a medical procedure. The experiencer unexpectedly "awakens" only to find they have been transformed into nothing more (or less) than mind, somehow hovering up near the ceiling. Their physical selves are either snoozing peacefully below or undergoing an operation, with doctors and nurses around them. Most report feeling oddly calm about this, as if, without the usual fight-or-flight chemical responses of their dormant fleshly selves, they are able to just take things for what they are in the moment.[1]

OOBEs can also occur in a fully waking state during physical or mental trauma and, rather than floating above, some have described being, quite literally, beside themselves, peacefully observing otherwise distressing events happening to them, but from a detached perspective. This may be a preservation mechanism generated by our usually unexpressed psychic abilities. More rarely, some experiences can be triggered in perfectly mundane circumstances.

The OOBE can sometimes last for a few seconds, but more often than not for several minutes, as marked by the observance of the "real" time going on around the experiencer. Some bolder explorers have found themselves able to waft through walls and visit other rooms and even external buildings before being abruptly pulled back into their bodies. Some have described seeing thin silvery threads connecting their newly freed minds to their sleeping forms.

The anaesthetic incidents are, of course, used by doubters to dismiss those as nothing more than hallucinatory conditions in medically clouded brains. That, or a similar list to the claimed solutions for ghosts is presented: waking dreams, sleep paralysis, etc. (see page 20). More sophisticated approaches have been made by scientists in recent years, including claims that a part of the brain called the anterior precuneus might be affected by medication and help generate the feelings of weightless separation associated with many OOBEs.[2] But even if these options account for some cases, they leave much unexplained, not least the fact that not all OOBEs occur under anaesthetics.

Some hospital experiencers, when waking back to normality, have claimed they were able to accurately describe to puzzled medical staff items and furnishings they saw in private rooms they were *never physically taken into*. Some have recalled in precise detail watching specific procedures or unusual events that took place during their operation (for example, an unexpected discovery made inside the patient or notable but soundless exchanges between surgeons) when there is no scientific explanation for how the unconscious mind could record this. Even if patients' eyes somehow flicker open momentarily, some of the described viewing angles would be impossible from a prone body with surgical screens around it, suggesting that some kind of elevated perception must be involved.

This aspect of OOBEs would appear to be connected with "remote viewing", discussed below. Inconclusive attempts at scientifically recording these claims have led academics to dismiss them as illusions, while experiencers' supportive accounts are increasingly buried so far down search engines beneath a barrage of reductionist papers that they are getting ever harder to find. However, I have heard enough direct descriptions to satisfy me that these phenomena remain worthy of further consideration.

In the previous chapter, we saw how the glowing forms of dead people can float above the beds in which they passed, explained by some as the "auric body" taking longer to fade than the physical one. But there is nothing to say that our auric bodies do not have the capability to hold a linked facsimile of our minds and memories when they are in their fully energized *living* state. With flesh and blood asleep or inert, perhaps we occasionally take the psychic lift up to the next "storey" to see what's going on?

## Profound Questions

Some have argued that dying peacefully is a natural extension of an OOBE – the simple process of deciding *not* to return to the physical self, allowing the aforementioned thread, whatever that is, to break, and heading on instead to the alluring tunnels of light described by some experiencing near-death. The trauma of the thread being broken abruptly or violently, without a letting-go process, might explain why some spirits become trapped between dimensions for a time.

A typical OOBE or NDE is plainly not so extreme as to always take us permanently into the next realm (of course we only have survivors' testimonies), but they enable us to observe ourselves and the things going on around our bodies from what seems to be a temporary micro-dimension just one level removed from normality.

These experiences demonstrate, like conscious ghosts, that our characters and the thoughts we think are not irrevocably bound to organic matter. The fact that some people report being able to move around in such a disembodied condition raises profound questions about the nature of identity and our real place in the universe. If thoughts do not reside wholly within our brains, where do we really exist? Throughout history, mystics have declared that ultimately all is one and one is all, but while in the earthly dimension we attach to personalities and physical attributes that restrict our comprehension of reality, and that this may be the very point. If we knew the bigger picture while here, they argue, we might avoid the hard corporeal lessons we came here to learn. But OOBEs give us a tiny preview of what it is like to live beyond the restrictions of matter.

## Usual Types of OOBEs

Let us explore some of the more archetypal accounts of OOBEs, to begin with. I have heard so many near-identical stories from different people over the years that the following compilation may seem repetitious, but it demonstrates the frequency and consistency of the phenomenon.

## Strange ... Conversations: Slipping Out of Ourselves

Glenda was under a general anaesthetic while having exploratory medical tests but found herself unexpectedly self-aware, as if awake. She quickly realized she was hovering above her own body, watching everything going on. She was cognizant of very bright lights that did not seem to come from the surgical room itself, and found the whole sensation amazing. Were the lights related to the ones trapped spirits are told to walk toward? If so, Glenda avoided that option and eventually awoke safely in the recovery ward.

Not everyone is so keen to come back from their OOBE. Dorothy, who was physically picked up by a ghost in the previous chapter, had her own experience when not very successfully coming to after an operation, despite the anaesthetic beginning to wear off. She was floating above her body, surprised to see herself surrounded by nurses trying to wake her up. The procedure had not gone well and they were struggling to revive her, calling her name and gently shaking her. Dorothy felt safe and secure in her detached situation and was a little annoyed at the cajoling to go back. She returned in the end, as the next thing she knew, she was waking up in her earthly body.

Flora, on the other hand, was having a stent placed in her heart and was *not* under a general anaesthetic but a local one and was fully alert (see below for more awakened OOBEs). Nonetheless, she found that for several seconds she was looking down on herself from an elevated position "quite high up" in the room, watching the surgeon at work. She wasn't afraid and found it almost calming. Curiously, Flora was unable to hear any sound in that state. When the sensation ended, the noises of the hospital returned. She did not know that leaving the body was a recognized phenomenon until she heard me speaking on the subject – something that has been said to me by others.

* * *

Conversely, some people have OOBEs so often that they think little of it and don't realize that not everyone does this. Vernon, an elderly man, told me – as if he had never really thought about it before – that once every three or four weeks he found himself floating up from his body, looking down on himself when asleep. He had been doing this for much of his life but always assumed it was some kind of unusual "nightmare", although it happened less now than in his younger years. In this mode, Vernon was able to travel around the room at will. Despite thinking it was a nightmare he didn't find it unpleasant. Other gentlemen, who were present when he told me, were astounded to hear this, as Vernon had never shared it with them before and he was a respected member of their community not prone to fanciful imaginings.

Noting Vernon's comment that these episodes lessened as he got older, it is interesting that, while people of all ages have OOBEs, several of the accounts related in this chapter were described as having taken place earlier in life. This is not a scientifically statistical selection, but perhaps our abilities to detach from the body diminish as we become more entangled with the physical world in the same way that children stop receiving ethereal visitors as they become adults.

### Strange ... Communications: Out-of-body the Easy Way

Sleep, as in Vernon's case, can be one gateway to releasing the consciousness for the lucky few. Deep relaxation (and deliberate practice, as we shall see) can be another. The following story from Hazel, although undramatic, is worth relating:

*My son suggested we go to some Japanese floating baths. He had heard they were fun and a new experience. We were given our separate little rooms, big enough to contain a tub full of body-heat water and for one human frame. We had 30 minutes of floating time. The water looked very inviting and I quickly stripped and entered the water. Oh! What bliss! The heat penetrated my body instantly and I didn't need to try and relax.*

*I floated with my arms outstretched, completely relaxed for minutes before I realized I was suspended way up in the ether, looking down at my minuscule floating body. There was nothing around me; no sounds and no sense of place. I was just there, very high, looking down at myself, a tiny floating figure, and calmly thinking, "I must return to the tub in 10 minutes" – which duly happened. I wasn't at all perturbed by my experience and calmly told my son what had happened. He was amazed and said, "Mum, you have just had an experience which everyone strives for but hardly ever gets."*

## Other OOBE Stimuli

The above examples occurred through medical procedures (the most commonly reported), simple sleep or deep relaxation. The brain and nerve centres going into a suspended or partly suspended state (as with Flora's local anaesthetic) appears to loosen the mind/spirit/soul's connection with our physical form and we slip into another level of being.

However, there are more powerful triggers that can stimulate OOBEs, including body trauma, mental stress and alcohol.

### *Strange ... Conversations*: Compelled Out of Ourselves

Although the looking-down sensation is the more familiar OOBE, some occur at ground level. Bernard had always been sceptical about such claims – until it happened to him. A few days after returning home from a heart operation, complications arose and an ambulance was called. As medics were tending to him, he became aware that rather than seeing through his eyes, he was in fact watching everything from "about two feet [60cm] away" from his own body. In this oddly removed position he was able to think lucidly, comprehending clearly all that was going on even though Bernard's physical self was completely catatonic, staring outward into nothing. This state endured for a few minutes before he found himself back in his body as he began to respond to the treatment. Happily, he made a full recovery.

Bernard's escape from trauma was spontaneous, a separation induced by his "higher self" perhaps to enable him to endure a frightening loss of control over his faculties. However, a few people appear able to *choose* to step out of themselves.

When Marcie was about five, her father came back from fighting in World War II. He had been away so long that she had no memory of him; to her, he was a stranger who had infiltrated her cozy family. As a result, she was afraid of him. When he talked to Marcie, her fear was such that she found she could consciously decide to "step out of her body", and would find herself looking down on the scene from a height of about two feet (60cm) – similar to Bernard's reported distance. In this mercifully disconnected zone, she could watch herself and her own reactions to her father in a way that felt safer. As the years went by, Marcie came to rationalize these experiences as a kind of psychological dissociation, yet she knew the sensations were very real. Learning about OOBEs gave her a context in which to understand what had happened. I was the first person Marcie dared to share this story with. This is an example of a "waking OOBE", which we will discuss more soon.

Some OOBEs trigger from almost comical situations. In what sounds like rather a reckless experiment (in the entertaining way things used to be done before modern Health and Safety intervened), decades ago Doug worked in a laboratory doing tests for a government department that regulated alcohol breathalyzer devices. He and his colleagues were experimenting with different levels of alcohol in the blood, using themselves as "guinea pigs". Doug had two shots of Scotch whisky in quick succession, which rapidly made him drunk. He found himself flailing over a lab sink, trying to hang on to both his dignity and vertical position. As this unfolded, his consciousness unexpectedly detached itself and moved up to the ceiling, the farcical tableaux beneath him, as he watched himself sliding down onto the floor, clinging to the sink. Doug found, as so many experiencers do, that he could move around in this state and actually began to enjoy himself. This was just as well, as it lasted for about five minutes. At the time, he put it down to a novel effect of "just being drunk" but on further reflection realized that the alcohol may have in some way released something deeper.

### *Strange ... Communications*: Sleep Paralysis Revisited

We have seen how "sleep paralysis" (see page 20) is used by sceptics to explain away a number of experiences. The condition does exist and is intriguing in its own right, but its deployment as a catch-all solution for paranormal phenomena is lazy. It also overlooks the fact that sleep paralysis might sometimes help produce the very kind of conditions that can lead to real OOBEs. Anders from Norway's account suggests a possible link, in his case at least:

> *It was Christmas evening, and I was home for the holiday together with my mother and my brother. We were all in the living room, and I fell asleep for a short while on the sofa. When I woke up I couldn't move. I had no control over my body. I couldn't lift a finger. I was fully awake, listening to the other two talking, but I couldn't speak either. This didn't last for long, and soon I was normal again, but I had never been in this state before. Besides*

*that, nothing special happened, but maybe this was so I could be a little bit prepared for what was going to happen.*

*A month or so afterwards I was back in Sogndal where I lived alone. It was around the time I turned 25. I woke up in my bed; it must have been in the middle of the night, and just like the Christmas evening I couldn't move a finger, with no control over my body. I had a feeling of despair. But then I was relieved. I don't know how to describe it, but I was lifted up; it was wonderful. I was hovering in the room. It was victory, I was king. But it only lasted for a few seconds. I didn't remember anything further until I woke up in the morning. This phenomenon is real.*

The elation Anders felt with his new freedom, if brief, is reminiscent of Doug's joy at being released from the anchors of the physical world. There seems no reason to conclude that just because this was preceded by some of the classic symptoms of sleep paralysis that the OOBE itself was a hallucination. The suspension of normal nerve activity, as suggested by earlier anecdotes, might have been the very key that unlocked this. Many of us dream of such liberation and maybe eventually we all receive it when we check out from this existence – which is noteworthy, because nerve suspension may also be a trigger for near-death experiences.

## Near-Death Experiences

There are curious similarities between "near-death experiences" and some OOBE cases. In NDEs, people appear to be clinically dead after a catastrophic accident or medical emergency but unexpectedly return to life, recalling in rich detail sometimes complex "journeys" and meetings with people, other-worldly beings, angels and deceased relatives – despite their brains registering zero activity on monitors while these must have been occurring.[3] Mitigating medical arguments have raged about what constitutes "death" in this context, with heart and brain activity linked, but not necessarily being the same thing.[4] Some link NDEs to "lucid dreaming", the ability to direct actions within dream states, but this in itself is not fully understood and the fact that they are occurring in apparently inactive brains means the point still stands – people who, according to previously accepted medical science, shouldn't really be having these experiences, somehow are.

The phrase "my whole life flashed before me" is something many NDE survivors can relate to, except that the memories sifted during their encounters can be widescreen, box-set memories that *feel* like a lifetime, despite only minutes going by in this world. NDEs are not as commonly reported to me as other phenomena but they do occur and should be touched on briefly here.

NDE reporters who describe exploring entire worlds in timeless zones during the short period they were declared clinically dead raise the question that if nothing is happening in the brain, how are these visions occurring and where are the memories being stored? This has led to theories, as OOBEs suggest, that our grey matter is merely a component in a wider receiving/transmitting network that extends beyond physicality, tapping into Rupert Sheldrake's theories (see next chapter).

Readers may allow themselves a yawn to hear that sceptics see NDEs, like OOBEs, as hallucinatory effects connected with the cerebral cortex, oxygen starvation to the brain and various other biological factors – which some likely are. But even if brain malfunction does sometimes play a role, how can we be sure this is not part of the very mechanism that allows entities and doorways from other dimensions directly into our minds, when they are usually screened out? Biology and metaphysics are unlikely to be mutually exclusive. We are physical *and* psychic beings, and both elements clearly matter to who we are down here.

Some medically qualified practitioners have crossed from cynicism to belief, or at least to a less reductionist approach about what mind is. The experiences of American neuroscientist Jill Bolte Taylor, who found herself having a massive left-brain stroke but was able to monitor in the moment the effects of her two hemispheres disconnecting, border on the metaphysical to some observers. Iain McGilchrist's work on the dual nature of the brain (see page 236) also has profound implications. Another American neuroscientist, Eben Alexander, had his views more drastically changed when he had an elaborate NDE while under a medically induced coma while suffering from meningitis. His subsequent book, *Proof of Heaven: A Neurosurgeon's Journey into the Afterlife*, the title of which makes clear Alexander's conclusions, caused a public sensation but was given a predictable kicking from his peers and the scientific community.[5]

The elaborate mindscapes or psychic explorations of real places that Alexander and other NDE adventurers have described in detail are fascinating. Whichever cause we are drawn to, they still have great symbolic value, if only for the person in question.

### Strange ... Conversations: A Room of Faces

One NDE fits well into the mould of detailed places that appear to exist on other levels of existence.

I met Veronica in her elderly years, but when she was 18 and dentistry was more dangerous than it is today, she had to have a large tooth removed. This required a general anaesthetic, but something went wrong during the procedure and she nearly died. While undergoing this trial, she had a complex vision of travelling along a long dark tunnel until eventually she came to a huge ornate cavern "like the Royal Albert Hall" [a famous London venue]. In the middle stood a tall, circular, wooden structure with an array of 365 small pigeonholes carved into it (whether she knew this from diligent counting or intuition is unrecorded). Within each pigeonhole was a face, but she didn't recognize any of them. There was a feeling of uncertainty about the need to create a 366th face (perhaps one day to be hers).

Before Veronica could learn more, she awoke – now, incredibly to modern eyes, on the floor at the foot of the dental chair from which she had slipped, with the dental staff assuring her she would be fine within a few hours. She would never revisit this compelling cavern, but neither did she forget this one glimpse into what felt like an alternative reality. Cynics would dismiss this as an anaesthetic-fuelled delusion tied in with the 365 days of the year, but when I quizzed Veronica further, even many years later she felt sure it was a real place and not a dream.

It is easy to laugh off some of the psychedelic musings that some near-death experiencers record after their ordeals. But given that most religions, which remain highly popular and largely uncriticized, have come about through deep revelations from God or wherever – ones that must have filtered through the psychic faculties of prophets and avatars – why should we scoff when it happens today? Having contact with what lies beyond the veil seems to leave people profoundly changed, whatever is going on.

## Strange ... Communications: Guidance from the Other Side

It is pertinent here to include a description of the after-effects of an NDE from Mary Helen Hensley, who we last met bumping into ghosts on the *Queen Mary* (see page 61). Her psychic gifts and draw to the paranormal were hugely enhanced by this incident, a curve that a number of near-death experiencers find themselves on. Mary Helen writes the following:

> *In December of 1991, I was involved in a 75-mph, T-bone collision in which I had a near-death experience that*

*irrefutably changed my life forever. After being greeted by two Beings of Light, guardians who had been with me since the dawn of my creation, I was able to experience an inconceivable review of the twenty-one years I had just left behind, resulting in my own decision to return to my life as Mary Helen. I was clearly informed that I would go back with an upgrade, enhanced if you will, able to connect with information that could potentially change the stakes in the life experiences of other human beings ...*

*I was told that in addition to seeing, feeling and dreaming things before they happened, I would have the ability to gather the information stored in the cellular core and ethereal body of an individual. In essence, by temporarily reconvening with the higher vibration found outside of the earthly realm, I returned with an uncanny ability to access these higher vibrations at will, in order to extract energy and information to assist other human beings facing crisis of a physical, emotional or spiritual nature ... I was assured that I would not be left to do this on my own. There would be assistance, guidance in a most tangible way, and all would reveal itself in good time.[6]*

From the moment of her awakening and recovery, Mary Helen believes that the spiritual guides she made contact with, a collective she calls "The Counsel", have been with her ever since, helping with her healing practices in a world that needs some healing. Many NDEs have involved interactions of this nature.

As implied by Mary Helen, entire conversations can take place with beings encountered in the ethereal waiting rooms. They sometimes offer the experiencer a choice of whether to come back to Earth to continue with their lives, injuries and all, or head on up to the next stage. Presumably, some go for the latter, which we brand rather basically as "death"; others are reportedly given no option and are ordered back down to slog things out with the rest of us for a while longer.

# Encounters during OOBEs and NDEs

Reports like Mary Helen's offer the hopeful suggestion that we may not be as alone as we think in our earthly problems, and those who believe in spiritual guides and guardian angels would agree. Angels are explored further in Chapter 8. Readers must take or leave such convictions as they will, but if something about an NDE or an OOBE takes us closer to dimensions where other beings and human spirits reside, it makes sense that people in this state are more likely to have encounters with them, in zones where useful help, or at least companionship, may be available.

### Strange ... Conversations: Making Choices
The following two stories include important choices being offered to experiencers by ethereal presences.

In an NDE situation, Maude went into anaphylactic shock due to a severe allergic reaction and learned later that, when taken into the ambulance, the medics considered her clinically dead. While in this condition, she found herself in a "bright white room" with figures also dressed in white standing before her. They asked, kindly, if she wanted to be there with them or go back to Earth. Maude had two young daughters at that time and felt deeply that she should not leave them. Although slightly torn in such a state of bliss, she said that she knew she had to go back. At that moment of decision, she awoke again in our world, to the amazement of the ambulance crew.

A similar dilemma unfolded for Alison in a more traditional OOBE scenario. When in hospital in her 20s, undergoing problems while in labour, she was lying in bed fully awake, having been made comfortable. Without warning, she realized her mind was floating near the ceiling, looking down on herself. Accompanying this disorientating sensation, a voice from nowhere said, "Think of your husband. He needs you." Hearing this unseen guide and its opinion, Alison understood that the situation wasn't a done deal and that should she choose to ignore the advice, she wouldn't *have* to return to her body or indeed her husband; if she let herself go at that moment, her earthly self would die. Despite the temptation to avoid likely suffering down here, she knew in her heart she was not yet ready for the ultimate journey and didn't wish to desert her husband. She made the hard decision to return to her physical self. Sadly, her baby did not survive the complications, but she felt nonetheless that she had followed the correct path.

### *Strange ... Communications*: Ethereal Guides

There are many tales of encounters with benevolent entities while outside the body. Fiona Scott shared with me her own experience, initiated in the wake of a difficult home situation. It is interesting to note the two beings of light she describes, which bear a resemblance to those described by Mary Helen:

*I had just turned 23 and had been part of an extremely stressful domestic situation that turned ugly, leaving me with PTSD. But I didn't know that at the time.*

*It was late evening, perhaps 11pm, in August and I decided to get into bed. Suddenly, I felt myself rising spontaneously out of my body, moving toward the ceiling. Very quickly I was through the roof and into the dark sky above. There was some kind of kaleidoscopic pattern in the sky and I felt myself pass through it, like pushing through a sticky spiderweb. A portal? Then I was moving very fast through the stars, a bit like warp speed on* Star Trek, *and it felt exhilarating.*

*I arrived somewhere impossible to describe; a very bright space. There, I met two beings of light. They were very tall and kind, and they told me such a lot of things directly into my mind. I felt such love from them. Just before I returned to my body, they left me with an image of them posing, like for a photo in front of the full moon. They were standing close together so I couldn't see a gap between them. They were very bright compared to the moon behind. I couldn't see any features. I fell back into my body with what can only be described as a "plop!" I sat up instantly and said to my boyfriend (who was still up and in the same room) "Woah! How long was I gone?" He said he thought I'd been "asleep" for half an hour. To me it felt much longer.*

*The OOBE felt spontaneous, but I feel quite sure that the two light beings "arranged" my journey to meet them.*

Unlike many OOBEs, this one took Fiona out of the room and beyond, an ability that has been honed by "remote viewers" and "astral travellers" (see below). Like NDEs, the time that seemed to elapse was not reflected in the relatively short period that Fiona was asleep (if sleep it was).

## Waking OOBEs

If consciousness can have its own independent existence, there is a kind of logic to the idea of it quietly sneaking out while we are suspended in sleep or undergoing medical treatment. But this is not how all OOBEs occur, as we saw with Marcie's story above, where she was able to knowingly escape the immediacy of difficult feelings. In these cases, the experiencer's mind seems to split itself in two, allowing its insubstantial half to watch its physical self carrying on as usual, all in a fully awakened state.

### Strange ... Conversations: Stepping Out

Beverley did secretarial work in a military establishment situated in an old mansion house. She was standing speaking to a colleague at his desk one day when for no obvious reason her consciousness divided itself and she was unexpectedly watching herself doing this from a far corner of the large room, rather than having the conversation directly. Her avatar was chatting away at the desk even though her mind seemed to be with her floating self. Beverley found this unexpected phenomenon unnervingly "peculiar" and she had no idea of what was going on – but it continued for several minutes. All then returned to normal but she remembered what had happened.

This faculty of instant escape could be useful when confronted with very boring people, of course, but the implications of psychic "bilocation" (see below for a tale of *physical* bilocation) are enormous.

My deceased father-in-law Donald, who could be humorous but was a tough no-nonsense man, was a chief engineer on the famous Pullman trains. Although Chicago-based, the Pullman Car Company operated luxury rail services that ran in Britain in the 1960s and early 1970s.[7] One day, on a lunch break in the staff carriage, Donald had the weirdest sensation: he realized he was observing himself from an area high in the top corner of the carriage, looking downward. He was able to watch his own normal self happily eating sandwiches and reading the paper, apparently oblivious that part of his consciousness had escaped. Perturbed, but unsure what to do, the floating Donald managed not to panic and after a short while snapped back into himself – but instantly recalled it. He would regale the family with the tale for years afterwards.

Experiences like this raise a valid point. Why *don't* most people who have OOBEs fly out of the room (or in this case, carriage) completely up and outward? Fiona found herself being pulled up into the sky, but that is unusual. What mostly keeps our detached floating selves within the same immediate space as our bodies? Those who actively teach themselves to leave their physical forms find that the barriers of walls or ceilings are frail and can be easily moved through with training, as ghosts do. It is almost as if we are so used to the idea of local boundaries that it doesn't occur to us to go further, or at least we unconsciously fear doing so lest we find ourselves unable to return. This, or the threads that tether us have natural distance limitations, but can be stretched with diligent practice.

Boundaries are highlighted in the story of Jim, once a pilot for an African airline company. On more than one occasion, he found himself having waking OOBEs while flying – ones that actually took him *outside* of the airplane. He would realize that he was looking in through the cockpit window, observing himself working, his normal self unaware that anything odd was going on. When he reconnected with his body, he would recall what had just happened. In these instances, Jim was not contained within his immediate bubble (the cockpit) but just beyond it. This confirms that a projected consciousness is not in any way bound by the physical world, as being outside a speeding plane in turbulent air had no effect on the ability of Jim's projected mind to keep up with himself.

Weirdly, Jim's fellow pilots also described having the *same experience*, albeit at different times (dismissed as "spatial disorientation" in the aviation industry, as if this explains everything). With no context to understand this, they put the sensations of mind projection down to being tired and overworked. (Presumably they did not report this officially or they would almost certainly have been taken off duty.) This is the only report I have heard of *clusters* of people having spontaneous OOBEs within the same environment, suggesting either that they were sharing the effect of a specific kind of electronic and/or psychic field in their contained cockpit, or that they sometimes flew through zones of electromagnetic anomalies that might have precipitated such effects.

In a different kind of shared experience, I have come across a case where two entirely separate OOBEs transported people to identical locations.

Edwin, a doctor of haematology, once had a patient who, following his operation under a general anaesthetic, said that while unconscious he had an OOBE. In his intricate recollection, he told Edwin his spirit had sailed upward, out and over the top of the hospital until he found himself in an odd but sunny and beautiful place, a kind of paradise garden. Incongruously, an officious-looking desk was placed there. A "Black African" lady was sitting behind it, wearing a smart white dress. She looked at the man sternly and appeared puzzled to see him. As if referring to notes, she snapped "No, not yet" – and the experience ended.

Edwin, not a believer, wrote the tale off as unworthy of further thought. Or he did, until, seven years later, he operated on another patient who subsequently described visiting *exactly the same place* as the former witness, complete with the sunny garden and the African lady in the white dress at the desk. Unable to see how such detail could be described twice, Edwin changed his mind about the reality of these encounters. Whether the desk and garden were reserved purely for people wafting up from that particular hospital, or whether it was blind chance that two of his patients made it to the same ethereal realm is impossible to say.

## Bilocation

Most OOBEs seem perceptible only to those having them. People in the room with the experiencers don't generally report sensing or seeing presences above them. But there are a few extreme examples where mind projections do take on a visible 3-D aspect. This phenomenon is called "bilocation" and is generally the reserve of claimed spiritual masters and adepts, who have been witnessed (and interacted with) on one side of the world when they were known to be publicly appearing at that very moment on the other. The cynical assume these are tricks with lookalikes or mistaken identity, but I have heard accounts that suggest these may not explain everything.[8]

### Strange ... Conversations: There but Not There

According to their daughter, in the immediate post-war years of the late 1940s/early 1950s, Judy's husband Kenneth turned up at the door one evening, wearing his demob clothes (civilian garments given to ex-armed forces personnel). He greeted her as normal and went into the house. Judy walked through to talk to him but Kenneth had mysteriously vanished. Puzzled by this, about half an hour later she received a worrying phone call saying that he had been involved in a serious car crash. He was injured but alive. Hearing this, a shocked Judy realized that "Kenneth" had turned up at the house at the very moment of the accident and that what she had witnessed must have been an apparition of some kind.

This unusual tale strongly suggests that, in what was presumably an NDE, a fragment of Kenneth's traumatized self leaped to somewhere he felt safe and happy – a projection so strong that it took on tangible form. There is a resonance here with ghosts arriving to say goodbye to relatives at the exact moment of death (see Chapter 2) – except that on this occasion death was narrowly avoided but the projection occurred anyway. If Kenneth remembered this happening, it is unrecorded. There was one more peculiar anomaly: why he appeared to Judy in demob clothes remained a mystery, as this was not what he was wearing when he had the crash ... Perhaps there was something of comfort and homecoming represented by the clothes, associated with the day he came back from the war, suggesting a symbolic element to this highly unusual OOBE.

In another bilocation incident of a kind, Sandra had friends staying at her house in England. However, they were disturbed by repeated sightings of a male "ghost" there, just doing everyday things, which they naturally found unsettling.

Sandra, who never witnessed nor sensed anything odd, was confused. As the sightings kept going, she compelled her friends to be specific. Shocked, Sandra realized they were very clearly describing her father – who *wasn't dead* but living in America. They detailed his clothes and habits precisely. He had stayed at the house many times. Sandra showed the friends a photo and they confirmed it was him. Calling her father by phone to see whether he had experienced anything odd of late, he was bemused; all seemed normal to him.

Was the father unconsciously bilocating back to a place he was familiar with? Visible projections of living people may occur more than we know. Or were these space–time glitches (see Chapter 3) that had inexplicably copied and pasted some of his wholly mundane activities while he was staying, and replayed them at random? Perhaps Sandra's friends were particularly receptive to those frequencies or were able to see into the past (or the future?). If so, why they saw only the father and no other visitors to the house is a conundrum.

## Remote Viewing

The ability to project consciousness could, of course, have rather useful applications if one were able to tap into it at will. It might also offer uncomfortable facilities to nosy neighbours and surveillant authorities … So, it may not come as a surprise to learn that there are people who train themselves, or are trained, to use psychic projection to attempt to do precisely this. This skill is known as "remote viewing" (RV), a term first coined by the American parapsychologist Russell Targ. It is plainly related to the wider visual perspectives offered by OOBEs, as we have seen with people claiming to have explored rooms they were never physically in.[9]

On occasion, unplanned remote viewing may even have helped to save lives.

## *Strange ... Conversations*: A Battlefield Perspective

When elderly, Gwen remembered a tale her father Alfred had told when she was young. He had been fighting in the World War I trenches of France and underwent a classic OOBE on the battlefield. Wounded by a bullet and crushed by falling comrades, he found himself beneath a hideous tangle of twisted bodies, unable to crawl out and left for dead. Yet, unexpectedly, Alfred realized he was somehow looking down, floating high above the carnage. Although what he could see was horrific, this uncanny perspective enabled him, with calm detachment, to assess the overall situation. Friendly forces were now combing the area for survivors, but he was not being spotted under the mound of flesh.

Able to see from the outside, swooping around, Alfred's projected form worked out a clever plan. He found a viewpoint from where somebody might see him if he was to move his arm just very slightly outward at a specific angle and wave it gently. He conveyed to himself that he should do this and thankfully his body responded. At this, he snapped back into his grim reality but, sure enough, as a result of this strategy he was seen and retrieved from the pile. Gwen stated that her father was a battle-hardened man not prone to fantastical thinking, adding, "If he said it happened, it happened."

Projecting the mind can have unexpected benefits, then. It is for this reason that the US Army instigated the "Stargate Project" in 1977, an attempt to harness remote viewing and other psychic faculties, mainly for espionage purposes.[10] Picking up on techniques developed by the likes of Targ (whose work, unsurprisingly, is disdained by mainstream scientists), the hope was that this might allow unfettered access to the secrets of rival powers, with viewers drawing detailed plans of military installations and suchlike. Remote viewing of the *future* was also attempted. More dubious experiments involved trying to stop the hearts of animals using telekinesis, as later immortalized in Jon Ronson's agnostic book (and loosely adapted film) *The Men Who Stare at Goats*. The controversial but popular psychic Uri Geller also claims he was once hired by intelligence agencies to try to stop the heart of a pig, a task he refused.[11]

Authorized history says that Stargate was under-funded and shut down after being transferred to the CIA in 1995, which decided that the project was inconclusive and had no material value. It is hard to believe, especially with the CIA, that something that could be even *potentially* useful with a bit more work would just be scrapped. There is a wide suspicion, therefore, that this was a diversionary tactic and that experimentation simply went underground as "black-ops" schemes that no longer required annoying governmental supervision, as with UFO investigations until recently (see Chapter 6).

Whistleblowers, including Joseph McMoneagle, ex-US Army Chief Warrant Officer and officially the first psychic recruited by Stargate, have claimed that the US government still actively employs remote viewers. Former US Army counterintelligence agent and prominent disclosure campaigner Luis Elizondo (see page 162) has said that the art has been used in attempts to investigate UFO/UAP activity. Both accept that remote viewing is not an exact science but stress that it is reliable enough to be deployed as a component of broader programmes. McMoneagle's presented evidence for its effectiveness is particularly persuasive.[12]

Something being officially debunked or blanked does not mean it doesn't exist. Russian and Chinese intelligence services, both of which have expressed interest in harnessing psychic forces in years past, have also gone mysteriously quiet about them.[13] Conspiracy thinkers have long argued that there are entire arms races of the strange going on under our noses that most people know nothing about and this would seem to be evidence in that direction.

Indeed, the American (civilian) "astral traveller" Todd Acamesis (aka "Falcon"), who teaches groups of people how to leave their bodies under controlled disciplines, has claimed that during his attempts to remote-view official establishments around the world he has come across legions of government-sponsored OOBE practitioners, warding off other wraithlike snoopers by psychic means.[14]

## Practising OOBEs

Not all professional out-of-body experiencers follow the intrigue and espionage line; some leading specialists, such as Jade Shaw, who also leads group OOBE training, are very much focused on the spiritually transformative aspects of astral travel.[15] Being freed from our physical selves can be liberating and illuminating. To some extent it would seem to be circumstance, luck or personal frequency that determines who has an OOBE, but professionals say it is possible for most people to induce a projected state on at least certain levels with enough practice and focused coordination.

This said, I tried it myself for a few months under the loose advice of a friend many years ago, using breathing and meditation techniques. It didn't go quite as planned: I successfully managed to enter some kind of altered state on a number of occasions, with a tangible rushing and tingling sensation, but found myself with an unsettling feeling of *falling* through the bed into some void below (a phenomenon classed as "sinking", I now know), which wasn't quite what I was after. I decided thereafter to leave it to the experts.

This book does *not* therefore either recommend or warn against trying OOBEs – but study wisely and know what you are in for if you do, using proper supervision and safe procedures. Most of the examples related here have been positive ones, but we saw in the previous chapter that there are also dimensions best left unvisited (as Todd Acamesis has attested) so be aware of this before travelling nonchalantly. If in doubt, don't attempt it at all. Some will be more adept than others, and some may find themselves having an experience when they least expect it … If this happens to you, then enjoy the moment and know you have had a lucky glimpse into a realm many will never have. Enough people do experience this, though, for it patently to be a subject that should be taken more seriously, as its ramifications are significant.

The OOBE and NDE are just two aspects of psychic phenomena experienced by everyday people. This is a subject that covers a broad spectrum, which we will now explore further.

# CHAPTER 5
# PSYCHIC PHENOMENA

## Beyond Usual Boundaries

To the open-minded, the preceding chapters should strongly indicate that there is more to us than flesh and blood and that consciousness is not merely a by-product of the brain but can exist quite happily outside of it in specific conditions. We have also established that time and space seem not to be the absolutes we imagine, but are instead leaky and unpredictable.

Psychic phenomena would appear to be humankind's method of navigating its way beyond the physical, threading through the by-ways and contraflows of a very bizarre universe. Irritatingly, it doesn't always work to order; some people can access it easily while others can't, but psychic gifts are recordable enough that they demand re-evaluation in a society bamboozled by centuries of denial. As with ghosts, these phenomena have fuelled much popular fiction and attract great interest, but it seems we are not actually supposed to *believe* in them.

Some researchers assert that such powers are innate in all of us but have been suppressed into the subconscious and now only break out in exceptional circumstances or via undramatic conduits that we usually shake off as coincidence. Shamanic cultures that have not endured sceptical conditioning accept psychism as just another aspect of their normal lives and it flows more freely for them as a result.

There are many claimed psychic abilities. After mind projection, the remaining categories I hear of the most are telepathy (mind-to-mind transmission), clairvoyance (extra-sensory perception), precognition (foreseeing the future) and practical divination (dowsing, earth energies and so on).

There are other gifts besides, some of which we will touch on, but mostly we will focus on these key areas.

## Double Standards

It is fairly easy to describe the sceptic position on psychic or "psi" phenomena – which is that it simply doesn't exist. Or at least that there is so little recordable scientific evidence for it that, until there is, it is not worth bothering about – the irony being that for something they are not bothered about, sceptics seem to spend a lot of time trying to *disprove* it. This was a pattern set by the American magician and arch-cynic James Randi who, during his lifetime, demanded high levels of proof for the paranormal that he never received, probably because the bar was set so high that almost no subject, supernatural or otherwise, could ever provide them.[1] Other media-savvy scientists or academics have followed in Randi's footsteps. (I address the "One rule for one …" issues in my book *The New Heretics*.[2])

A key complaint of the doubters is that there is no laboratory-tested proof for psi powers. Actually, there is, but when it is produced the methodology is predictably attacked, even when it is more rigorous than that provided for officially accepted mainstream science, some of which remains contentious and defies true repeatability. "Dark matter" and the "Higgs boson" particle are now accepted staples of physics, for example, but are challenged even in some scientific quarters. Claims of psychic effects are usually dismissed as statistical chance or are said to have been filtered through reporting error and/or confirmation bias. Sometimes this will be true, but to state that this explains all psychic phenomena is absurd, and indeed unscientific. The very act of trying to replicate often spontaneous abilities under cold laboratory conditions in different circumstances creates an unrealistic environment in which to expect instant results.

The psi abilities that *have* been successfully demonstrated in labs may at first appear modest but are in fact statistically significant and make clear that such phenomena are real; or rather they would if they were looked at properly by those who prefer to blot them out.[3]

What is odd is that quantum entanglement and non-locality, phenomena that enable near-instantaneous interaction across vast distances, are now recognized scientific realities, even if it is not understood how they work.[4] Yet, their implications are still sidelined by reluctant academics who appear concerned that acknowledging them too widely might substantiate the reality of the psychic abilities they have been denying for centuries, which it probably would.

There is evidence of a little thawing in the stand-off between sceptics and believers over recorded evidence for psi phenomena – readers are recommended to browse a published dialogue between the well-known British sceptic, Professor Chris French (who I have shared a platform with at Goldsmiths, University of London), and Chris Roe, parapsychologist and general Professor of Psychology, as an example. In this, French at least acknowledges the *possibility* that evidence for psychism might one day be provided and the usual polarization is intelligently set aside for once.[5] But there is still a long way to go.

This book is specifically about everyday experiences of the paranormal, but for excellent summaries of the open-minded science that *does* support the reality of psi abilities, readers are again referred to Terje G Simonsen's *A Short History of (Nearly) Everything Paranormal* and Rupert Sheldrake's seminal work *Seven Experiments That Could Change the World*, a study that shows practical ways in which a number of psychic faculties (including animal telepathy and the curious ability we have to know when someone is looking at us) can be demonstrated with properly repeatable results. Readers may also wish to acquaint themselves with the years of successful parapsychological experiments carried out at Princeton

University and beyond by professors Robert Jahn and Dean Radin, among others, along with the important work of the Monroe Institute and the Institute of Noetic Sciences.[6]

## Common Gifts

Psi phenomena tends to fall into repeating patterns, so we will cherry-pick illustrative examples in subcategories below. The most commonly reported gifts generally include the following:

•   "Knowing" things about people (usually loved ones) and what is happening to them, especially when they have suffered a traumatic event or died.
•   Knowing who is on the telephone as it rings, without seeing the caller display, or intuiting who the visitor at the door is, even when someone is not expected.
•   Knowing detailed things about places one is only just arriving in, never having researched them.
•   Being able to foresee otherwise unanticipated events, personal or global.
•   Being able to tell detailed things about people's characters and lives by handling associated objects, without having met them.

Let us explore some of these.

## Telepathy and Clairvoyance

Many psi effects can be classified as telepathy, clairvoyance or both. Here is an example of an archetypal, but real, account.

### Strange ... Conversations: Anticipatory Abilities

Maisie had a high "success rate" at knowing who would be on the phone before she answered it. She also had the ability to sense what people were going to say on the television before they said it. To her family's exasperation, she would often exclaim out loud what the presenters would then say a second or so later. Wondering whether her gift might extend outward into specifically *nudging* people telepathically, Maisie experimented with trying to send "thought messages" to friends and relatives to see if she could get them to call her. Although a result was not guaranteed, she found that the number of them who would indeed call her soon after was beyond chance.

### Strange ... Communications: Knowing Thoughts

Sonya Porter shared with me her own experiences of having innate certainties:

> When I was 15, I began to "know" things – always accompanied by a very odd feeling, which I can't describe. In 1954 my mother decided, as usual, that she'd put a bet on the Grand National [famous English horse race]. I looked over her shoulder as she was going through the paper and I suddenly "knew" that the horse Royal Tan would win, so I told her. Having chosen no other, she decided to go with this and so did I, putting my pocket money on it. Yes, it won. This knowing happened two or three other times – though, sadly, not for any other races!
>
> Years later, after a death in my husband's family, a group of them were discussing how and when others had died. One of the cousins said, "Of course, your grandmother's cousin's husband died in the First World War ..." and as she said that, I "knew", along with that feeling, what she was going to say next. Now, mention deaths in World War I and everyone immediately thinks of the trenches but the cousin went on to say, as I knew

*she would, "He died on the HMS* Good Hope *in the first sea battle of the war." A coincidence was that my father's father was also on that ship when it was blown up in the Battle of Coronel, and they probably knew one another.*[7]

The horse prediction either touches into premonition or is an example of "universal knowledge", a kind of esoteric internet that some say is always on tap to the psychically adept and may be how dowsing works. Both faculties are examined below.

As we saw in Chapter 2, blood ties seem to forge deeper imprints and bonds between people, who have an automatic awareness trigger when something dramatic happens to a family member. Quantum research shows that once something is entangled, it stays entangled. It stands to reason, then, that psi bonds are particularly strong between twins, who develop side by side in the womb. It may also explain how living people leave psychic imprints on objects (see below) and why ghosts can be linked to specific items, places or people.

Given these binding threads, we should probably be unsurprised that knowledge of death, trauma or injury – the most powerful experiences we can have – transmits so easily between relatives.

### Strange ... Conversations: Deathly Knowings

Patti was at home with her family one evening when her father rushed down the stairs, distraught, saying that he knew his sister had just died. Unsure what to make of this, they were shocked to hear a short while later that she actually had. Not only did her father receive his intuition at exactly the time she passed, they also realized that all the clocks in the house had stopped at precisely the same moment.

I have heard several accounts of mechanical clocks stopping at uncannily synchronistic times, whether through some kind of energy sweeping through a location that physically affects the devices, or as a deliberate sign from other dimensions.

\* \* \*

Precise timings often feature in psi occurrences. When her mother became ill, before the causes were even diagnosed, Petra had an intuition that she was likely to lose her as soon as she heard this. Petra was due to have lunch with a friend some days after, when her father phoned to say that her mother's condition had unexpectedly worsened. Without knowing why, Petra found herself saying to her now alarmed father, "Mum will pass at lunchtime." Not living near her parents, she went to lunch anyway but her friend was delayed and they wound up not eating until 2pm, two hours later than expected. Her father called later to say that her mother had indeed died that afternoon – at 2pm – precisely the "lunchtime" Petra had predicted.

Coincidence? Some will say so, but Petra's previous knowledge of what would happen to her mother indicates something more at work. This is just one of many similar tales conveyed to me.

### Strange ... Conversations: Family Ties

The above accounts are good examples of psi knowings occurring in the moment. Although disturbing in some circumstances, on other occasions this can be useful.

Stephen was in the Royal Air Force when younger and was stationed at one of Britain's nuclear bunkers during the Cold War. When he first arrived, he was told to report to offices located underground. After setting off, he realized he had forgotten to ask for directions to the entrance in this huge complex, which he had never seen on a map, let alone walked through before. He made his way with apprehension; reporting late on his first day would not look good. Yet, as he walked, he felt a curious intuition – with no understanding of how, Stephen found that he instinctively knew exactly where to go first time, despite all the bewildering choices before him. In the end, without once losing his way or having to ask directions, he walked straight to the inconspicuous bunker entrance.

Stephen often wondered how he had managed to do this. Did he have some internal compass in his brain that somehow helped him, or was he naturally tuned in to universal information (see the dowsing tales below)? Or did he telepathically draw the knowledge from other personnel? Either way, he felt that something odd had occurred.

### *Strange ... Memories*: Psychic Abuse

I once witnessed a more sinister demonstration of clairvoyance occurring in the moment.

As an organizer of the annual Glastonbury Symposium "Expand Your Horizons" conference in the UK, I have had to deal with all manner of live speakers – the good, the fascinating and occasionally the ugly – over its three-and-a-half decades. In one of its earlier years, our star closing guest, a spiritual philosopher and psychic of some repute, had been sighted in the town but was late arriving to the venue. Worried, we ran a search and discovered him in a nearby pub. The signs were not promising. Drunk, and clearly drugged too, he and his entourage of equally high young ladies were very definitely on another plane altogether.

Warily, I managed to coax our guest, who was alternately affectionate and aggressive, toward the venue in the hope that he might sober up a little. I knew of his undoubted psi abilities, but with his synapses blasted open by artificial means, they were running dangerously rampant. As he walked agonizingly slowly, his ladies around him, he began to do something exceptionally dubious but remarkable for all that: he would stop a delegate at random, put his hand on their heads and then punch them softly but firmly in the stomach. This put them into a kind of peculiar surrender, like a faint. Our guest then held them, suddenly tender, and would speak intimate truths about the person – 100 per cent correct, we would learn later – as if he had reached in and plucked the knowledge directly from their minds without permission – an absolute no-no in spiritual protocols. We tried to stop him but, fearing violence, had to do so gently. This was out-of-control psi but a demonstration of a very real force at work – and a warning about its abuses.

After anxious deliberation, with so many people who had booked specifically for his talk, we decided to let them see our guest for who he really was. He took to the stage and fired off a series of wild spiritual "truths" and insults at them while his ladies performed what was afterwards described as an "erotic floorshow". As the outrageous circus unfolded, many people walked out, some denouncing the speaker as they did so – but it is worth noting that later on, with the evening safely ended after my own intervention (see page 230) and the help of a local *real* spiritual master who helped contain him, our guest still had a large following, almost hypnotized, sitting at his feet outside in the street. Powers of the mind do exist then, in my experience, but we should be careful whom we elevate to practise them. We learned a lesson that night, one we never allowed to be repeated.

### *Strange ... Communications*: Family Ties
Psi knowings can express themselves in various forms. Because we are generally drawing attention to instances of the paranormal in otherwise mundane environments, for the most part I am leaving aside claims made through circles of Spiritualism, healing and mediumship (I could fill many more pages with stories from spiritual practitioners). For all the accusations of fraud or that mediums simply play on generalities – things that regrettably can sometimes occur – I have seen enough demonstrations to know there are also genuine gifts. For example, a medium was once able to tell me the first names of both my grandparents without any way of knowing.

Chris Connelly, one of the consultants for this book, a qualified space engineer, psychologist *and* a Spiritualist medium, is currently working on experiments that verifiably demonstrate psychic activity in the brain using commercially available EEG (electroencephalogram) equipment.[8] This subject may yet gain a new credibility.

Two accounts connected to Spiritualism and attempted direct contact are worth relating. The first is told by Thomas Newman:

> *My brother and I passed by a Spiritualist church and felt compelled to attend the mediumship service. We attended several times with different mediums from out of town, who all told us somebody named "George" wanted to come through for us [i.e. speak/channel through the medium]. We asked our family members who this was, and were shocked to find out that our father, uncle, aunt and grandparents had all recently visited the same church, alone, for mediumship – without telling one another. I asked my grandparents who George was after the first visit, but they both denied knowing one. On the final visit to the Spiritualists, we were convinced that George was real as "he" recounted something that I had been actually doing the previous day.*
>
> *Eventually, my grandmother came clean that George was my grandfather's father who had abandoned him during the war, and who had actually co-founded the very same Spiritualist church. Apparently, he would come home and tell my grandfather stories of seeing/communicating with spirits, allegedly showing him photographs of séances, and my grandfather was utterly traumatized and refused to speak of it ever after.*

On the subject of what are effectively séances, it is not for me to say what practices people should or shouldn't pursue, although the devoutly religious will have their own views. But, as with deliberately invoking an out-of-body experience, metaphysical adventurers would be well advised to do so on an informed basis and be fully aware of the necessary protections and potential pitfalls.

Many people have tried using Ouija boards and/or collectively moving upside-down glasses over alphabetical cards or symbols as a seemingly light-hearted way of communicating with "spirits" or obtaining hidden information (effectively another method of remote viewing or dowsing), reportedly with some success. But it doesn't always go to plan. We should be careful what we open channels to; knowing who and what is being connected with is impossible for the inexperienced and not all entities are good, as we have seen. Even if psi effects brought through this way are not negative as such, they can surprise with their power. Séance parlours had their heyday in the late 1800s and early 1900s.[9] In our modern reductionist climate, the practice has declined but in the 1960s and 1970s it was still popular with stoned students and among the more daring dinner-party sets, as the following story relates.

### Strange ... Conversations: A Too Successful Experiment

Although I met both of these gentlemen at the same event, this story was told to me separately by each of them.

Alexander and his friend Bill were sceptical about ghosts and psychic phenomena until they tried out glass-and-letter-cards séance experiments at a social gathering "for a laugh". Beginning gently enough, asking questions about people and places they knew, the giggling quickly faded and they were soon "scared witless" because the information that came through was so accurate. More revealingly, without anyone asking, intimate things then began to be told about some of the participants that no one but those individuals could have known. The movement of the glass, whizzing increasingly quickly from letter to letter with the group's hands on it, became so overpowering that finally it shot off the table and smashed against the wall. All there were terrified and vowed never to do it again.

Dowsing, perhaps, may be the safer option of accessing such universal knowledge.

# Dowsing and Divining

Tapping into knowledge without mediumship or Ouija boards was a concept long understood within folklore. The simple deployment of sticks, rods and swinging pendulums to divine either the universal will or, more practically, to detect water, earth energies or specific objects is a way of accessing psi phenomena through a more controlled method. Interested readers might like to investigate the work of the American dowser Henry Gross or British pioneer Hamish Miller, both now passed but whose work remains influential.[10] I have met many specialists in these practices although, sadly, they become ever scarcer as our addiction to the digital world distances us from natural intuition (but see the final chapter).

In essence, if a twig or rod twitches in a certain direction, or a pendulum changes its pace or direction of swing, this is seen as the human brain picking up psychic signals and transmitting them to the instruments through micro-muscle movements that allow intuition to be expressed without the left (intellectual) brain blocking them. People must define their "yes" and "no" responses to begin with (this varies from person to person), using simple tests where the answer is clear. Some dispense with instruments and use their hands, "feeling" the responses as perhaps ancient peoples used to, enabling them to find water sources or energetically significant places on which to place their settlements, temples or stones.

Needless to say, sceptics dismiss all of this as imagination or a misreading of "ideomotor" effects, in which tiny unconscious muscle reflexes respond to a dowser's own thoughts – which they say is really directing the movements. However, if it is "just" the thoughts of the dowser at work, then where are those sometimes accurate thoughts coming from in the first place? Why could psi not be creating the influence?

Note the term "*sometimes* accurate"; like all psychic aptitudes, this art doesn't always work to order, although some dowsers might like to believe otherwise. But it can produce results beyond chance. On the down side, as tests on Henry Gross demonstrated, he registered a number of "fails" when grilled under scientific conditions but, as noted below, the very act of being put under abnormal pressure can create psychic blocks. My colleagues and I tested this at a conference attended by a number of dowsers. A table holding several boxes, only one of which contained an item (a stone taken from a crop circle), was laid out to see who could successfully detect the occupied package. The experienced dowsers had the highest failure rate, whereas chancers trying their skills for the first time did better, suggesting that the weight of expectation and egos also play roles in the way that psi flows.[11]

Certainly, dowsed results should not be presented as scientific criteria when proper data and discernment is required, and critics will point to the above failed tests as a sign of why nothing more than rolled eyes are needed to deal with dowsing – and yet it works well on enough occasions to warrant re-evaluation. I am not personally confident at dowsing and leave it to the skilled, but water companies (and, reputedly, oil prospectors) have, tellingly, employed professional dowsers for years.[12] In those cases it might be natural geophysical or electrical traces being picked up on, but the fact that anything can be successfully dowsed for, even remotely, suggests something more metaphysical at work.

The belief that the planet is threaded with invisible lines of "subtle energy" is an ancient one. These are not quite the same as "ley lines" as first defined by Alfred Watkins, which are alignments of sacred sites in the landscape, although, confusingly, they can follow the same paths, as energy lines reputedly *align* to them in time.[13] The direction or "polarity" of energy flow can also be affected by changes in underground water courses. Lines that turn to "black" or negative energy have been linked with haunted houses, as we saw on page 94. Good "geomancers" (dowsers who specialize in geophysical energy work) are quite capable of moving lines or creating them from scratch, which demonstrates the psychic link. This reinforces the likelihood that energetic imprinting and human interaction are inherent parts of the earthly system.

I have witnessed energy line creation more than once, whereby a dowser enters a designated space and decides to "place" a line or hotspot of their own devising. This usually occurs with the aid of rods or pendulums and focused intent and can sometimes also be enacted by pulling in, as it were, an extension of an existing line into the vicinity. With the line safely imprinted, new people with no knowledge of what has been done are then brought into the space and invited to find it through their own dowsing. Most get it right. In other words, psi intention has literally invented an energetic nexus point from nowhere that amazed others can then detect for themselves. I have perceived no possible trickery when seeing this done.

This revisits the point that what we think does indeed affect the universe around us and that we are all very likely psychically imprinting all of the time, albeit mostly lightly. If this process has become a vat of every thought ever had and everything ever known, somehow encoded into time and space itself (spiritual practitioners call this the "Akashic Records"), it would explain the ability to access universal knowledge. Most imprinting effects appear to dwindle over time, but when very focused intent or strong feelings are involved, as can contribute to the existence of some ghosts, a longer-lasting presence remains that may always be accessible to the adept. Dowsers say they are able to sift through the layers of energetic history and find any line or thought form ever placed.

We must also be imprinting onto *people*, which, together with the psychological elements, may partially explain why we can become so attached to certain individuals (who imprint in return) – and why letting go of a relationship or losing someone to the next realm can be so devastating. When a meshing of auric fields has become so complex, tearing it apart is painful and hard to do. Remember, once something is quantum entangled it is always entangled on some level, as perhaps we saw with the visits from loved ones in Chapter 2. Hopefully those souls whom we *need* to disentangle from eventually find their hold relinquished through some kind of karmic justice system.

Because subtle energy is *so* subtle, scientists claim not to be able to find it. If there is something special about human divination, rather than electronic, it may be that science never will detect it that way. A cheap let-out? Perhaps, but we will see by the final chapter that this may be the fulcrum on which the future of paranormal research balances. Earth energies are discussed further in Chapter 7.

Before moving on, we should understand a little more about what dowsing can achieve. The following personal recollection is a useful demonstration.

### *Strange ... Memories*: Force of Will

Let us return to the old house where my father was pushed by a ghost (see page 82) and where Peggy lived alone. With only one distant cousin she had not heard from in many decades, we were now her family. As her days advanced, she let it be known she was going to leave the house (and, presumably, the ghost, though it was never seen again) to a member of our family (not me), who she knew would treat it with the same respect. She had apparently written this into her will; humbled, it seemed rude to enquire further.

Years later, when Peggy was sadly found dead at home by my parents, it therefore became imperative to read her will. But it was nowhere to be found. The house had become cluttered and no one knew whether the will had even been registered legally. Predictably, the cousin appeared, knowing that in its absence he would inherit everything. Had he shown Peggy the remotest attention throughout her life, there would have been less issue. Indeed, the house was a poisoned chalice, as it needed crucial work, but this was against everything Peggy had wanted.

With just days before the legal wheels had to turn, I thought of one person who might be able to help – Paul Bura, who psychically channelled the dead man and his son in our poltergeist investigation (see pages 92–3). Paul was also a seasoned dowser. I asked him whether there might be a less conventional way of tracing the will. Rather than sending the psychic cavalry into the house and causing a fuss, Paul recommended "map-dowsing" Peggy's house. In a key sign that this kind of divination is primarily about accessing universal knowledge, map dowsing has become a staple technique of remote viewing without all the bother of astral travel.

The holographic universe theory suggests that just as a 3-D hologram will mysteriously retain the entire image in every fragment even if its glass shatters, so every part of existence is linked to every other part, probably through the principle of entanglement.[14] Thus, to access universal knowledge, one needs only a small way in, even using markings on a map to represent a real place. So, Paul and I drew a detailed plan of Peggy's house and he overlaid onto each room a grid of squares, representing areas just a few feet across. He set to work with a pendulum. Asking, "Is the will here?", Paul kept a record of yes or no answers, and noted any intuitive feelings as he went from square to square.

In the end, Paul found only one spot that – faintly – registered anything tangible; a small corner in a corridor leading to the bathroom – a most unlikely place for a legal document. Disappointed that he might have let us down, Paul said, "I don't think this is the will itself but there might be something there that could lead to it, perhaps?" The corner in question hosted a small wooden chest that had already been briefly checked. Inside were old newspapers and magazines, and, wearily, this time they were sifted one by one. Incredibly, there, compressed in the pile, was a worn yellowing letter, years old, headed with a solicitor's name and address. The letter made reference to … Peggy's will. With some detective work it was discovered that the long-retired solicitor's files had eventually been transferred to a bigger company – which did indeed have a copy of the will.

This startling discovery, confirming what Peggy had told us, means that the house remains in our family to this day. Paul rejoiced at the vindication that one small corner of the corridor – in a house he had never visited – had yielded up not the will but the pathway to it, exactly as he said. Cynics will say this was a chance success; if so, the odds were incredible. I worked with Paul on accurately identifying aspects of other places he had never been to during some of our psychic questing work (see page 179), and firmly believe the results were beyond chance.[15]

## Psychometry and Telekinesis

The above account demonstrates that certain individuals have the ability to home in on anything, wherever it may be. If something exists, like a beacon it can radiate its position (or, in the case of the will, information that leads to it) to the psi-sensitive, indicating a deep universal connectivity.

When something has been psychically imprinted, it can also *hold* information. Paul also practised psychometry, where handling an object tells the reader something about the person who owned it and what was going on when a particularly strong imprinting occurred. Police forces around the world and the likes of the FBI and CIA are known to have quietly resorted to this technique on occasion and have considered testimony from psychics in general (as we have seen with remote viewing), although they play down its reliability.[16] Like all psi phenomena, psychometry is not a precise art, but can be very effective when it works.

Paul told me that during his younger years a female friend passed to him a small brass propeller from the model of a ship. As he handled it, he had a striking vision of a handsome man placing a gold chain around her neck, followed by an alarming sense of a "huge explosion". The name of the famous singer Al Bowlly, popular in the 1930s especially in the USA, floated into Paul's head. Thinking this a meaningless stray thought, he didn't share it but outlined the other images to his friend. She told him that she once had a secret relationship with the man he described but that he indeed lost his life in a bombing during the London Blitz of 1941. The propeller came from the building in which he died.

Only later did Paul discover that his friend's lover (she was only 19 at the time) had indeed been … Al Bowlly, who was killed by a German parachute mine. Bowlly, apparently now a spirit still very sensually attached to the Earth plane, had been haunting her in a troublingly sexual way and Paul became drawn into having to persuade him to leave her and her current husband alone. The fuller tale is told in Paul's autobiography *Stepping to the Drummer*.[17] Objects can sometimes tell more stories than perhaps we would like.

On the subject of objects, one thing I hear less about from experiencers of the strange, outside of poltergeist cases, is telekinesis: the ability to move or influence physical items with the sheer force of will. But it should be briefly addressed. (Psychokinesis is related but describes the even less common ability to actively influence someone else's mind.)

The rarity of telekinesis does not mean that it isn't a phenomenon, although it should be noted that when the aforementioned professors Jahn and Radin conducted their scientific psi experiments, telekinesis, although registering, came out as one of the weaker forces. Dice rolls and the suchlike could be influenced enough to be recorded statistically, but not dramatically so. And yet, the odds of the small effects that were noted merely being chance were still calculated as being *35 trillion* to one against – an almost unimaginable figure that in itself should prove the reality of psi to doubters, but somehow doesn't.[18]

Discounting some of the undoubted frauds, most telekinetic accounts I *have* personally heard of are from mediums, who report spectacular effects at séances, with large objects and human beings witnessed levitating around rooms. Items have also been described materializing and dematerializing in full view. But even these examples are considered to be the work of "the spirits" rather than the psychics, although those who believe that poltergeists emanate from unconscious human abilities might argue otherwise. On the whole, it would seem that that such phenomena are infrequent and seldom reported outside of closed psychical environments.

The absence of overt public demonstrations, or even filmed sessions, is disappointing on one level, because if such capabilities were to be validated more openly, surely it would help end all the debates? The counter argument from mediums is that these are sensitive skills that should not be practised lightly nor encouraged among novices. In this, they might have a point; a world full of incompetent or malign dabblers with unlimited powers to throw objects around or affect machinery with mere thoughts, like the Jedi from *Star Wars*, wouldn't survive long.

Cynics being present in a psi environment can be the very factor that blocks paranormal activity anyhow, as their innate disbelief exerts an ironic but real power of its own. This is seen by sceptics as a derisory escape clause and sets up a maddening cycle whereby those who most demand proof can never get it – and don't really want it anyway. More open-minded scientists seem not to have had the same problems, suggesting that the power of intent also plays a role.

So far, we have approached psi as occurring in a linear fashion. But there is evidence that it can work outside such limits. If we accept the ability to be able to tune into things past and present, why not also future events?

# Precognition and Presentiment

If consciousness is somehow imprinted into space–time, and space–time is unified through quantum entanglement, another factor should be taken into account: quantum particle experiments strongly imply that time is not an absolute. Things appear to go backward as well as forward at the tiniest scales, through what some physicists call "retrocausality".[19] Some argue that these effects only occur at the quantum level, but others are not so sure. Although we don't generally experience time going into reverse in our daily lives (excepting occasional timeslips), it seems that we do receive a backwash from the future on more subtle but still tangible levels through "precognition" (direct visions of future events) or "presentiment" (intuitive feelings about future events, sometimes called premonitions). Experiences of both are strikingly common, but I will begin with a personal recollection.

### *Strange ... Memories*: A Duplicated Trauma

In the summer of 1977, when I was 12, my parents took me and my two sisters on vacation in Wales. They were difficult times; with my maternal grandfather ("Grandpop") suffering from terminal cancer, the trip was a chance for a much-needed breather. My parents hired us a nice static trailer (curiously similar to the one I would have a ghost experience in years later) on a farm.

One morning, I awoke with a feeling of trepidation. That feeling was soon vindicated. Through the window from my bed, I could see the path to the farmhouse. My mother was walking toward the trailer, crying. I quickly guessed what had happened. Sure enough, with many tears, my mother entered and told us that Grandpop was gone, faster than expected. The break was over and we would need to pack and prepare for the long drive home to be with our grandmother and face everything waiting there.

And then I woke up.

This was extremely odd, because I was convinced that I was already awake. It had seemed so real, not like normal dreaming. A wave of relief passed through me as I realized that the horrors of the last few minutes had been a chimera.

Except that the dream was about to come true.

People speak of déjà vu, the feeling that something has happened before (generally put down to neurological causes, but who knows?). What happened next was like that, but times a hundred. With a peculiar sensation of knowing what I would see, I looked out of the window and there, walking down the path, was my mother, crying all over again. But it wasn't just slightly like what I had dreamed – it *was* the dream, come to life in every detail. She entered the trailer and every movement, every gesture, replayed exactly as I remembered. The difference was that this time I knew what was going to happen before it did. Staying quiet, just as I had in the vision, I was able to correctly predict in my head every line that would be spoken, every response, every reaction from my family. I knew the script; all I could do was watch it play out. I understood that something extremely strange was happening but had no context to explain it. When events reached the point where I "awoke" previously, mercifully I didn't re-awake yet again and the traumatic day resumed its course.

I knew even at the time that I hadn't just imagined it. Today, I recognize this was full-blown precognition – or time got inexplicably stuck in a groove for a few minutes and then moved on. I did, later, tell my family what had happened, but no one seemed interested among all the subsequent dramas, nor did anyone else describe having had a déjà-vu moment at the time.

My experience was unusual in being such a precise moment-by-moment pre-play. Many premonitions are more abstract. They are nevertheless extraordinary phenomena, suggesting that future events create ripples that can sometimes drift back to us in time.

### *Strange ... Conversations*: Vital Precognition

Below are just a few archetypal accounts of people who have foreseen upcoming events; the first two actually saved lives.

Veronica, who had the extraordinary NDE described on pages 110–11, had a family history of psi sensitivity. During World War II, with the London Blitz still raging (killing Al Bowlly along the way), Veronica's mother would almost never go down to the garden bomb shelter when an air raid was occurring. For reasons unknown, she felt that her family would be alright and was usually dismissive of any threat.

However, one night as the sirens sounded, to everyone's surprise, the mother became "very agitated". She quickly urged them out and into the shelter – something she had never done before. Veronica's elder sister protested, but the mother flew into a rage and dragged her in. Veronica's uncle only just managed to dash in to join them, slamming the door behind him as a bomb whistled down. There was a colossal explosion outside, shaking the shelter. When they dared to look, the house was gone. Burning ruins stood where everything they owned had been just minutes before. Veronica's mother said later that she somehow knew this time that the sirens should not be ignored. She would have other episodes of precognition throughout her life.

Meanwhile, Stephen, the RAF officer who mysteriously knew his way around the nuclear base (see page 131), found his gifts to be a genuine saving grace on another occasion. In 1974 he was stationed on the Mediterranean island of Cyprus. He and some of his colleagues had been planning a beach party on the northern coast one evening, which they were all looking forward to. But something felt wrong. Without knowing why, Stephen felt an inner anxiety he couldn't control; against much resistance he finally persuaded everyone to cancel the party. This turned out to be wise. That very night, Turkish forces invaded Cyprus, launching the main assault on the very beach they would have been on.[20] Stephen couldn't help wondering if his intuition might have come from a protective force "above", but accepted that it might also have been his own psychic antenna picking up approaching danger.

## *Strange ... Communications*: Foreshadowings

Precognition can be expressed through a number of methods. "Automatic writing" is a form of mediumship that sees messages being channelled through people's hands and writing implements, but "automatic drawing" can also divine upcoming events and embody knowings, as Emma Davidson describes below:

*In November 1992, sitting in my lounge at home, I picked up pen and paper, which was lying on the table, and absentmindedly started to doodle. I drew a castle that was on fire and on the same piece of paper, unconnected to this, a man wearing a cap, whom I named Frank.*

*That evening, I was watching the news on TV and my mum was reading from a large scrapbook, which was bursting at the seams. I asked her what she was doing with it. She informed me it was our family tree and showed me the page she had open with a newspaper cutting from 100 years ago. To my surprise, the picture was an obituary about a relative called Frank who had drowned in an accident while fishing. The photograph looked identical to the man I'd drawn. Furthermore, on the TV news at the same time as this discovery, there were breaking pictures of Windsor Castle [a major British Royal residence], which was on fire. The fire destroyed 115 rooms and took over five years and £36.5 million to repair. For me, clearly something strange was going on. I wondered if time was going backward or if my mind had expanded into the future and I had viewed these things somehow?*

This precognition, at least, did not presage a personal disaster. But sometimes it does, as happened to Janet Tucker:

*In October 1975, my husband Graham and I were invited by my parents on a day out. They had a close friend who owned an old campervan and he would drive us all in it. However, the night before the trip, I had a bad nightmare. I dreamed that my mother was being rescued through a "window" that she appeared to be stuck in. I was sitting on the ground watching paramedics desperately trying to pull her out. I woke up with a thumping heart, bathed in sweat! Thank goodness, it was only a bad dream.*

*By morning, all was forgotten. We were picked up and took our seats in the campervan. Graham sat in the front passenger seat and I sat behind him on a bench seat with my parents. It wasn't mandatory to wear seat belts then so we were sliding around a bit! The journey went well and it was a beautiful sunny autumnal day. However, we were involved in a nasty collision with another car at a crossroad. The campervan veered out of control and hit a brick wall. We were all thrown around inside. My mother had slipped behind the driver's seat and my father was moaning next to me. I suspected that I'd broken a bone.*

*Emergency services promptly arrived and got me out first. They sat me in the road with a blanket round me. I watched while they released my father, who was in shock but not seriously injured. The main concern was to release my mother, who had fallen awkwardly on the floor. They managed to pull her out with difficulty through the van's sliding door. I sat there watching in horror as I realized it was exactly the scene I had dreamed about earlier. Coincidence? Premonition? I sustained a broken collarbone and my mother had concussion, severe bruising and a few cuts. Luckily, we all recovered.*

I have heard many similar descriptions of people's "dreams" coming to life in an unfortunate way, usually a short while later. Those who act to avoid circumstances leading to a visualized event can of course never know for sure whether they changed time or if their vision was just a dream. But sometimes precognition can build over a longer period.

## Precognition of 9/11

Some disasters are so huge that precognition seems to ripple around the world to more people than mere chance should suggest in the days, months and even years before they occur. Several major events, from the sinking of the *Titanic* to assassinations, tsunamis and earthquakes, have been preceded by vivid worldwide dreams and visions that appeared to portend them.[21]

One series of events that generated a high level of reports was – perhaps inevitably – the 9/11 terror attacks, which saw airplanes flown into buildings at New York's World Trade Center and the Pentagon in Washington DC (with another crashing in Pennsylvania) on 11 September 2001. A significant percentage of people believe that the true story of this tragic day remains to be told and I have written about the multiple anomalies of the official narrative elsewhere.[22] This aside, the fact is that so many people experienced precognition around 9/11 that it even made mainstream news and is still discussed by parapsychologists today.[23] The visions or intuition were strong enough that a number of people who might otherwise have lost their lives heeded the warnings and chose not to fly or go into work that day. The psi network went global for these events, and I have met a number of people who dreamed of planes hitting buildings or of catastrophes in big city streets in the months before. It might be easy to dismiss these as backdated reinterpretations of vague imaginings were it not that some of them were so specific – and I had my own pre-9/11 dream. Here is just one typical account.

### *Strange ... Communications*: A Dream of 9/11
Fergi Dean shared this story with me:

*Around 1992, I dreamed of a tall building slightly occluded by mist/smoke and a plane flying into it ... It made quite an impression, even more so when a voice, or my inner voice, on awakening stated clearly, "This will happen and change the course of world events!" The imagery lingered with me for some time and I was watching the news regularly, expecting it to show up as a report any day. When the accident in Amsterdam happened [El Al Flight 1862 crashed into a tower block in 1992] I realized that despite its gravity it wasn't the incident that I was seemingly waiting for.*

*Forward to 11 September 2001, I was at work and someone passing by announced that a plane had crashed into the/a WTC building – maybe more relevant as I worked for a top five accountancy firm that likely had direct links, or if not at least a third party presence, in the building(s). Speculation began to be made so people went to the lower ground floor canteen where live TV via a number of screens was normally on. On arriving at one of the screens I very quickly proceeded to watch as WTC2 was impacted through a shrouded image due to the smoke from the first impact ... Somehow, though, while watching events unfold, I wasn't surprised at what was happening. The image on the screen stayed with me and I slowly realized its similarity to the imagery of my dream in 1992 and the echoing statement on my awakening.*

This vision, with portents of international significance, bears strong similarities to the others recorded around the world. In the late 1990s, I had my own, more specific, dream.

I had always wanted to visit the World Trade Center, fascinated by its architecture and keen to see the view from there. Sadly, by the time I did arrive in 2004 it was no more than two morose holes in the ground (before the memorials and Freedom Tower were erected). However, in the dream I was standing on the open top of one of the towers, with golden morning sun illuminating the vista below me. As I watched, two streaking objects suddenly came into view, heading straight for the buildings. With shock, I knew that neither they, nor I, would survive the impact. Things blurred as the moment came. At this point in the dream I saw missiles launching from pads, seemingly fired in retribution; but as soon as they took off, they fell back onto the pads and exploded. A symbol, maybe, that Western revenge on the perceived perpetrators wouldn't entirely go to plan.

Proof of anything? No. But when the horrific events unfolded, I remembered the dream and wondered. Clearly, many others who dreamed similarly did too.

More tangible evidence of psi phenomena and 9/11 may exist courtesy of the Global Consciousness Project (GCP), an offshoot of the aforementioned Princeton experiments (Princeton Engineering Anomalies Research lab – PEAR) and developed by parapsychologist Roger D Nelson.[24] As expected, doubters have criticized its methods, implying confirmation bias, but its claimed findings are worth looking up. As lab experiments suggested certain individuals could influence raw computer data by the power of thought alone, the GCP explored the intriguing idea that *collective* thought forms might be recorded if "Random Event Generators" (i.e. computers churning out meaningless numbers) were left running in isolated places around the world to see if anything affected them.

Observing the compiled data, it was discovered that big world events, usually dramatic ones (such as Princess Diana's death in 1997) that focused minds all at the same time, appeared to correlate with spikes of non-random data that could only be produced (in their view) by telekinetic influences, the argument being that entire populations unconsciously produce collective psychic responses in times of unusual stimuli. The strongest reactions occurred on 9/11.

Notably, the non-random responses appeared to build up in the hours *before* the first attacks took place and peaked as they unfolded. This suggests, extraordinarily, as laboratory experiments with individuals also appear to show, that our reactions to events nearly always begin *before* the stimulus itself, albeit very briefly, something apparently confirmed by some surprisingly scientific bodies.[25] Quantum retrocausality is presumed to be at work. In other words, if the theory is correct, the future is forever making itself known to us in subtle signals that mostly get lost in the white noise of life, but which sometimes break through as precognition. This has been likened to time running like a river: there appears to be one main direction of flow but when a stone is thrown in (i.e. a big event), psi ripples momentarily flow both ways before the forward momentum sweeps them away, allowing the sensitive to pick them up in advance of the event.

There is evidence that "future echoes" can reach us *decades* before the stone drops. Conspiracy thinkers eagerly point out that many eerie depictions of, or references to, 9/11 can be retrospectively found in everything from TV dramas, cartoons, record sleeves and banknotes from many years before the evil day. Rather than proof that media teams were somehow made privy to a world-changing plot, it is more likely that collective consciousness was already detecting what was coming. Some have claimed that signals are picked up *centuries* before events, hence alleged 9/11 prophecies and other references by the likes of Nostradamus, but, while not uninteresting, ambiguity, varying translations and archaic language can pretty much allow any interpretation of old texts and it is hard to be sure.

Aside from 9/11, I have heard of other longer-term possible presentiment. My wife Helen, when living as a teenager in her parents' very normal – and new – semi-detached house in the 1970s, was given a bedroom that she never liked; it felt as if something terrible was always about to occur there. The atmosphere became so oppressive that some nights she would retreat to her sisters' rooms. No one saw anything ghostly but Helen was very glad when her parents moved them to another town.

A year or so later, watching the television news, they were surprised to see their old house appear. But the association was devastating. The couple who had moved in after them had been licensed gun dealers. With the husband out, a man came to the house, where the wife opened the arms cupboard for him. At this point, he shot her dead – in the very room Helen used to sleep in, where the guns were now kept.

Some houses have moody ambiances but most of these appear associated with events or presences from the past. Could it be that Helen's terror had been tuning into what *would* happen years later? Perhaps the ripples from this appalling event were making themselves known in the psychic backwash.

## *Strange Inconclusions*: Psi Phenomena

Mind is evidently much more than it seems, and not just a side effect of physicality, even if the importance of the organic hardware it operates through on a day-to-day level shouldn't be overlooked. This and the preceding chapter have demonstrated the apparent ability of consciousness to project beyond the body, transmit and receive through "non-local" means and know things that the basic senses shouldn't be able to pick up.

Rupert Sheldrake's influential "Morphic Resonance" theories propose that both consciousness and biology, in all lifeforms, evolve through binding fields that exchange information in a way that should not really be achievable through genetics alone.[26] They imply a broader concept of mind that expands beyond the confines assumed by reductionists. Yet, many scientists fiercely reject this model even while they *do* reluctantly accept the concepts of entanglement and retrocausality. At some point, surely, there will have to be a combined reconciliation that might begin to make sense of everything.

If it is the case that, in the end, all consciousness soars free from physical constraint and is bound together in some way, perhaps we do have a version of a "heaven" that exists beyond this plane and yet is capable of interacting with it. Doubtless, it will not be as straightforward or as religiously dogmatic as some believers see it, but neither should disbelievers rejoice either.

Assuming the existence of a vat of universal knowledge and collective consciousness, what makes us so sure that only our earthly minds contribute to it, though? We have seen that entities from other dimensions may co-exist alongside us, although we only sense them from time to time. There is plenty to suggest that ambassadors from other realms, and indeed other planets, may also be making themselves known.

# CHAPTER 6
# UFOS AND UAP

## Beyond Fringe

At first glance, this chapter may seem a diversion from what has gone before, dealing with a more tangible mystery. Sightings of aerial objects performing unusual and often extraordinary manoeuvres suggests a physical presence in our world. But in truth they have much in common with other paranormal areas and are high up the list of the most reported everyday strange.

Unidentified Flying Objects (UFOs) or Unexplained Anomalous/Aerial Phenomena (UAP) as Western authorities now call them, have become a hot topic, rapidly being hauled from the fringe into the glare of the mainstream. Old debunking techniques that endlessly state *all* sightings are balloons/planes/drones/Venus/stars/birds and so on, now sound increasingly desperate. As with ghosts, yes, the over-excitable can misidentify, while deep-fake videos are inevitably a problem, but the rising calibre of witnesses and confirmatory data has taken a new direction, which will not be easily swept aside.

Over the decades, as well as large numbers of perfectly ordinary people who have seen UFOs, I have met numerous pilots, soldiers, sailors, police officers and other qualified professionals who have witnessed objects beyond any officially acknowledged technology. There are different kinds, probably with varied origins, but many are increasingly believed to be evidence of extra-terrestrial intervention or at least hybrid military tech extrapolated from examinations of retrieved craft.

An unexpected respect toward the subject has come about through a now seemingly unending stream of political, military or ex-military whistleblowers and supporters coming forward to break ranks. Leaked videos of aerial vehicles moving at exceptional speeds and turning abrupt angles that bend all the previously declared laws of physics have been officially accepted as real. This is a major breakthrough, after nearly a century of derision and denial.

On the whole, I have shied away from exploring detailed histories on the research around paranormal investigation, but the topicality of UAP requires a little more focus before recording some individual encounters.

## Countdown to Disclosure?

Despite the similarity to "UFO", the reclassification to UAP in recent years can now be understood as a significant step. The change allowed US military and other authorities (including NASA) to break away from the "wacky" baggage attached to ufology (albeit influenced by their own marginalization) and make it virgin territory again, with a narrative *they* could control. This has reset the stage to allow them, if they choose, to forge a tentative path to official disclosure that there may be something to these phenomena after all. This will not be straightforward; the signs are that some conscience-stricken individuals within hierarchies desire more openness but are being held back by others who don't, creating a push and pull of mixed messages.

Why might authorities be reluctant to say more? Take your pick from the most-discussed possibilities:

• Because the "military-industrial complex" is keen to keep its knowledge of alien tech – and biology – to itself until the absolute last minute, to gain maximum geopolitical and economic advantage before others move in on it.
• Because powerful players are concerned about public reaction to announcements that we are not alone and its likely

effect on our psychology, religions, economy and other societal pillars. It would also prove authorities have been lying to the public for long years, perhaps working in cahoots with ETs, and raise questions about other possible cover-ups.

• Because earthly ruling classes fear exposure as primitive warmongers by ETs who are mostly enlightened and well-meaning (there are, apparently, factions and varied species). Governments dread losing control and want to keep the status quo for as long as possible.

• Because Christian factions within the US government fear that aliens are in fact soul-sucking demons from Hell and feel, for unclear reasons, that we are all better off not knowing about them.

• Because ETs actually are alien, but are evil, destructive forces that we really, *really* do not want to know about.

• Because ETs, while friendly, hold such disturbing knowledge about the very nature of reality itself that we are simply not ready for it and, again, ignorance is bliss.

• Because something is heading into our solar system that will threaten or overturn humankind's future in some way that ETs know about, and governments don't want panic breaking out too soon. (Rumours that space telescopes and monitoring devices have "picked something up" are forever circulating.)

• Because the aliens aren't alien at all but *us* from the far future coming back to retrieve lost gifts or genetic strands they now require for their survival; wide knowledge of that would be too much to take and might crash timelines in some apocalyptic way.

• Because ETs are actually related off-shoots from the human race (hence the humanoid similarities) and secretly share the planet with us, living under the sea, underground and in bases across the solar system.

There are lots of possible reasons, then, and probably others, why the powers that be might not be keen on disclosure. Why does the US appear to have a monopoly on discussions about it, though? Russia and China are assumed to have their own inside knowledge of UAP. Maybe, for all its hardline reputation, there are still bleeding hearts within the US power structure who genuinely believe in liberal democracy?

Some conspiracy thinkers take issue with all of this, fearing the teasing to be a road to a "fake alien invasion" in which the hinted-at threat will be used to justify ever more social controls and New World Order plans for global domination.[1] They doubt the integrity of the whistle-blowers and see them as inside actors. Others view the whole ET scenario as a useful distraction from secret but very human technology. However, an increasing number of observers perceive the undeniable rise in official talk about the US government knowing about aliens as having genuine grounds.

Is the new pressure for disclosure happening under duress, either human or alien? Some say the latter are running out of patience at being denied, and that an agreed period of acclimatizing the public to the idea of ET presences is on the point of expiration, hence ever more UAP displays. Or is it simply becoming impossible to keep secrets in these days of digital leakiness, meaning that weary factions think it's easier just to come clean? All of this is being debated – but something is definitely shifting. Especially since the groundbreaking congressional hearings on UAP (see below), the plethora of intelligently analytical podcasts and even some mainstream media coverage is now scrutinizing every development with a fine toothcomb.

As for what to call them, some officials prefer "non-human intelligences" (NHI) or "off-world intelligences" to "alien" or even "extra-terrestrial" but we'll stay with the populist terms for the most part, as that is what most people are familiar with. In the same way, we will interchange UFO and UAP as feels right. Some useful resources on the subject are given in the Notes.[2]

Here is a tiny resume of how we got to where we are.

# A Micro-History of UFOs

The official US acceptance of UAP is a major swing away from decades of obfuscation, despite numerous reports of still-unexplained "foo fighters" shadowing aircraft on all sides during World War II and military studies in the 1950s and 1960s such as Project Blue Book, which, despite being considered a deliberate distraction today, was still unable to explain every sighting.[3] The legendary 1947 UFO crash near the New Mexico town of Roswell – which allegedly saw an alien craft and at least one surviving occupant being retrieved by authorities – produced decades of entertaining debunks about weather balloons, light aircraft carrying mutated humans and crash test dummies. It is interesting to note that all of the current high-level whistleblowers now say it *did* happen as reported and there are around 600 recorded witnesses or relatives of witnesses who have backed up the claims.[4] If this is a bizarre double bluff, it's a big one. The craft is said to have been taken to the equally legendary but real Area 51, the heavily guarded military test site in Nevada, where salvaged ET tech and bodies have reportedly been analysed and autopsied.

There are records of possible UFOs going back centuries (thousands of years if "ancient alien" theories are accepted), but there is a view that it was the 1945 US atom bomb test and subsequent horrors in Japan that attracted the full attention of off-worlders. Perhaps concerned about the threat we now posed either to ourselves or to them, sightings of aerial objects in locations connected to that technology surged from then on. Numerous cases of nuclear complexes being rendered inoperable by UFOs have been documented, most famously by USAF officer Robert Salas at Montana's Malmstrom base in 1967, raising enormous questions about humankind's defences in the face of such forces.[5] The Rendlesham Forest incidents in 1979–80 at a US airbase in Suffolk, UK, where personnel witnessed a craft and anomalous lights, have also been associated with nuclear tech, with rumours that missiles were being stored there covertly.

### *Strange ... Conversations*: Undersea UAP

Before continuing this short history, two stories personally related to me, are appropriate to share here.

Bradley worked as a maintenance officer at the Dungeness nuclear power station on the Kent coast in southern England. While it was under construction in the 1960s, a number of his colleagues reported strange lights moving around under the sea near the complex. These presences eventually announced themselves overtly when the lights bubbled to the surface and workers watched them break free into the air as fully realized objects. They were forbidden to speak of what they saw. Bradley was of the opinion that something was monitoring the Dungeness complex and believed that aliens might in fact be living deep beneath the sea and that they were making themselves known so that authorities knew they were being watched.

Entirely independently, Maria said that when they lived in Ramsgate, also on the Kent coast but some miles further north, her husband, who worked by the sea, saw several UFOs (sometimes called USOs in such cases – "Unidentified Submerged Objects"), either hovering over the waves while apparently "collecting" water by some kind of suction process, or rising up from beneath the ocean and breaking surface, as Bradley described.

Water being extracted by craft, or suddenly drying up in their presence, is a recurring phenomenon. The 1917 "Miracle of the Sun", in which a bright disc was seen by thousands to perform acrobatics in the sky at Fatima in Portugal, was accompanied by an abrupt drying of wet clothes and rain puddles as it swooped low over the heads of a terrified crowd, as many written accounts attest. This event followed apparitions of a being that identified itself as the Virgin Mary to local children. A heavenly presence can't be ruled out, but the UFO connotations are clear.[6]

Sightings of underwater craft have been made around the world, and there is a suspicion that ETs may have numerous undersea bases (as depicted in James Cameron's 1989 movie *The Abyss*), if not an entire civilization; that is, if they *are* extra-terrestrial and not a parallel earthly species that has kept itself mostly hidden until now. Others have hinted that alien bases have been found on the far side of the Moon and on Mars.[7] Sceptics who argue that the vast expanse of space simply cannot be traversed daily by aliens (despite increasing claims of tech that can actually do this) might like to consider that the visitors may have been living in our celestial neighbourhood for aeons and don't need to travel that far. UAP interaction with air forces around the world, especially over the sea, appears to be endemic, as fighter jets vainly chase objects displaying speeds and movements that, quite literally, leave our technology far behind. Official reports have described some vanishing *into* the sea.[8]

Over the years, just about every UFO shape has been reported and/or filmed, including triangles, cubes, spheres and, many times, classic flying saucers or "cigar-shaped" craft. Should anyone still not have seen them, look up the "Tic Tac", "GIMBAL" and "GoFast" videos taken by the US Navy, which were first widely publicised in 2017. An account of the Tic Tac (one of the objects seen diving underwater) was given by former Naval pilot David Fravor as part of the 2023 United States House Committee on Oversight and Accountability hearing (generically known as "the congressional hearings", although Senate hearings also occurred in 2022), with back-up from another former pilot, Ryan Graves.[9] These extraordinary testimonies, previously unheard in an authoritative forum, came about through years of lobbying by leading UAP researchers, sympathetic politicians and military officers, concerned at the security and safety issues posed by the phenomenon. It has been implied that personnel have also been harmed, although how, and whether this was accidental, has not been defined.

The star speaker at the 2023 hearing was David Grusch, formerly a USAF officer and a US intelligence official, then one of the highest-ranking whistleblowers. In short, Grusch, having gathered personal evidence from his own security access and colleagues, has become convinced that massive cover-ups over alien bodies ("biologics"), retrieved craft and the programme to reverse-engineer their abilities are very real. As a consequence, Grusch and his family have reportedly met intimidation, while his credentials and mental health have been questioned. Critics have carped that, for all the claims, no "smoking gun" proof has yet been produced. But Grusch is not alone in his assertions.

Just as authorities were thinking the storm had passed, one Luis Elizondo (see page 122) decided to up the ante. Instrumental in raising awareness of the Naval UAP videos, this former US Army counterintelligence officer with a long history of military and defence posts, went large in 2024 with the publication of his book *Imminent*. Backing up almost everything revealed by Grusch, Elizondo (who has also received intimidation, debunking and personal attacks) claims to have been part of the one-time Advanced Aerospace Threat Identification Program and believes the public should now know at least the basics – that ETs are here. Some fear he is part of a manipulation, but even if certain details crumble under later analysis, the big picture appears to be consistent.

Fuss over *Imminent* was rapidly followed by an upsurge of reports describing fleets of mysterious "drones" over military bases and cities in the US and other countries. These also reached the mainstream media and provoked open discussion at political press conferences. Claimed at first neither to be "enemy" aircraft nor private enthusiasts' drones (some being the size of "buses" and others exhibiting behaviour far beyond any known tech), Grusch's testimony and Elizondo's book inevitably opened the door to broader speculation. After growing consternation and public head-scratching even from officials, a White House press conference in January 2025 unexpectedly announced that in fact the drones *were* just a mix of US "research" craft and harmless hobbyists after all, enabling journalists to go back to sleep despite this making no sense whatsoever of previous statements, with even the mayor of New Jersey (a prime zone for sightings) objecting. A number of reports certainly were explainable but far from all. Global reports continue, with some believing the apparent drones are in truth part of a slow build-up of undeniable anomalies that might eventually compel authorities to have to address UAP far more openly.[10]

Other voices from within the military are now speaking out. In a challenge to the White House statements, ex-USAF officer Jake Barber came forward the same month with credible claims that he had taken part in official UFO crash-retrieval operations and that his own investigations into the "drones" demonstrated that at least a number of them were "non-human intelligences". There is now an expectation or at least a hope that a very prominent figure who cannot be denied or sidelined will eventually come forward to instigate a fuller disclosure, where acclimatized steps toward informing the public of an uncomfortable truth will begin (perhaps "softly", with an announcement of intelligent "signals" having been picked up). If they don't, there is a fear of "catastrophic disclosure", whereby secrets spill out in a chaotic way, instigating panic and ruining the chances of an easier transition.

Accompanying this rise in the calibre of whistleblowers is a new academic movement toward UAP and ET study, with surprisingly eminent speakers prepared to go on the record with their concerns through umbrella organisations such as the Sol Foundation. Further congressional hearings were held in November 2024, where Elizondo reiterated his claims alongside contributions from others, with hopes for future sessions with the likes of Jake Barber.[11] Earlier that year, US police chiefs were even issued with a new reference guide on UAP, "offering information on encounters and procedures for officers to report such events".[12]

Despite these developments, there remain sceptics who seem to have vested interests in pushing mundane explanations for apparently astonishing evidence. As for US authorities, they have stated they do not know the cause of UAP, while AARO, the US All-domain Anomaly Resolution Office (yes, there is such a thing), has openly declared it has not found any "empirical evidence" that reported sightings are "off-world technology", despite the growing number of insiders challenging this.[13] Under heavy pressure from uncertain quarters, the US government's Unidentified Anomalous Phenomena Disclosure Act of 2023, which was hoped to bring at least a little more openness, was watered down to near-pointlessness under amendments which finally saw it pass it in January 2024, but that it exists at all is notable.[14] The disclosure some hope for may be longer in coming than they would like, yet most informed observers see this lingering hesitancy as a dying gasp of historical denialism that cannot last. Perhaps, by the time you read this, the situation may have entirely transformed, in which case, welcome to the new world.

However it is looked at, by having admitted the reality of UAP – even if they turn out to be devices from black-ops or foreign powers rather than ETs – the US state has accepted that *something* is flying around in our airspace that defies everything we have been told about scientific laws. If it *is* foreign and the US doesn't have the same abilities, then the West is in serious trouble – but if it is extra-terrestrial then plainly all bets are off. Either way, when UAP tech goes public – as one day it will – and is allied with advances in artificial intelligence (AI), be assured that civilization will turn upside down, politically, economically, philosophically and scientifically.

What, though, of the average person's experience of such phenomena?

# Typical Sightings

The majority of UFO sightings describe an aerial object or a light, or a group of them, exhibiting odd behaviour or performing acrobatics before abruptly shooting off at right angles and/or vanishing. There are databases full of sometimes grander reports but the implications of these more everyday accounts are huge. No officially acknowledged technology exists that can do this, and organic occupants would be killed instantly by certain movements without some kind of inertia absorption – unless, as some believe, craft operate by skipping between dimensions, stretching time and space *around* them rather than travelling from A to B as we do. This neatly challenges the they-couldn't-travel-this-far arguments that hardcore physicists insist on.

Here are just a few archetypal reports.

### *Strange ... Conversations*: Aerial Anomalies

Paula's husband was keen on astronomy and liked to point out particular stars to her. One night, they were baffled by two unusual ones sitting either side of the North Star (Polaris). They then started moving. One flew toward the other, as if the still one was creating some kind of "tractor beam" to pull it in. When they touched, they merged and shot off as one, at a right angle. Paula's husband reported the sighting to the local ranger, who laughed, saying that he had been inundated with so many accounts of the same lights that he was no longer recording them.

Magdalena was in her garden, when what looked like "a train in the sky" appeared above her. It was a chain of glowing rectangles, but with every other "carriage" missing. There were around twelve of them, with one bigger square-shaped connector in the middle. As with most UFOs, the chain was silent and obviously wasn't made up of planes or helicopters. The rectangles were turning a circle in the sky. They appeared quite near, although she thought they must have been very large and the precise distance was hard to gauge.

Magdalena phoned the local press afterwards, to which they exclaimed, as with Paula above, "Oh no, not another report!", although this kind of response can be reassuring as verification, especially for those who fear ridicule.

Sightings from gardens, where residents have time to be languidly scanning the skies, are widespread, as might be expected. Stan and Florence were in theirs when a collection of "lights and shapes" appeared and began to perform an impressive display. The objects were "coming and going", with some unexpectedly "shooting off east and west" from time to time. Again, there was no sound. A few nights later, a similar performance occurred. The event was dismissed in the local media as Chinese lanterns, an old fall-back, especially when they were popular some years back; that, or fairground lights and lasers, which have fooled people before now. However, Stan and Florence were contemptuous of these explanations, as the objects they saw were reportedly "hundreds of feet across" and moving swiftly and suddenly at angles impossible for known aircraft, let alone lanterns.

UFO reports from schoolchildren are plentiful – and therefore easy to dismiss – but there are well-documented cases where witnesses have held to their claims into adulthood, not least with the 1994 incident at the Ariel School at Ruwa, Zimbabwe. There, 62 pupils reported watching unidentified silver craft landing near the school, to great alarm, with some describing creatures with large eyes emerging from them. There have been other similar reports.[15]

Although not quite as dramatic, Bob told me that when he was at school sometime around 1950, one day he and another friend watched "six large discs" flying over the school at great speed, silver-grey in colour and shining in the sun. They were high up and four were symmetrically arranged like dots on a dice, with the other two slightly either side of them, all flying east to west.

I have met other witnesses who were once among groups of children who watched anomalous objects over their schools. Sceptics sneer, but even at the age of ten I knew how to identify planes, helicopters and balloons, and my father (a keen amateur astronomer) had taught me to spot satellites at night, so age should not necessarily be seen as unreliability. Sometimes, children are more canny and honest than adults, because they haven't yet developed protective social filters.

### Strange ... Communications: Seeing the Light
An oft-reported UFO trait describes ethereal beams from the sky bathing the ground in light, as seen in Hollywood depictions.

Jenny Elizabeth Beattie shared this encounter:

*During the first Covid lockdown, I was walking a lot. One day, I was walking back round the peat track above Fort William [Scotland]. It runs around Cow Hill. It was getting dark. The moon was out, but it got so dark I couldn't see the path clearly in front of me. I started tripping on the stones on the path, when suddenly a light appeared in the sky above me. It was very high up, about the same height as a transatlantic 747. It looked quite small, but gave off enough light to see the path ahead. So I managed to walk to the end of the path down onto the main trail, which was as wide as a road. I looked up at the light for 10 minutes. Then it accelerated away up into space. To this day I'm so grateful to that light. I could have ended up in hospital or worse, if that light hadn't appeared.*

Light can also appear with no apparent cause. Maxine was in a car driving with friends at night, when the stretch of road in front of them suddenly "lit up brightly", although there was no light source anywhere. All was quiet and there was no disturbance of vegetation around them. It lasted for "about 10 seconds" and then went dark.

Mak Norman relates a very similar encounter:

*When I was around 20 years of age in 1976, my friend Keith and I were musicians coming home from a tour. Keith was driving and it was the early hours of the morning, down dark country lanes. No street lights, of course. It was a lonely bit of road. As we were both tired, we weren't talking much. Then, suddenly, a bright light (far brighter than the car's headlights) lit up the road and the verges in front of us. It was on and off in the blink of an eye. It was so bizarre that neither of us said anything for a few minutes until I tentatively asked my friend, "Did you see that?" "Yes," he replied, "what was it?" We drove on and that was that.*

The usual explanation given for such illuminations is helicopter searchlights, but a helicopter is loud and unmissable (see below). There are claims that silent "stealth" helicopters have been tested, but the evidence for ones that don't disrupt dust and plants is non-existent. Given the growing disclosures, stranger devices could just as well be responsible.[16]

### Strange ... Communications: Further sightings

Here are more written accounts of UAP. David Karunanithy describes a notable event from his childhood:

*One Sunday evening, when I was only 9 years old, I had finished playing on the street with a couple of friends and then went home for a bath before school next morning. A short while after going indoors the same friends rang our bell and my mother opened the door to find them both in an agitated state, exclaiming that they had seen strange objects in the evening sky. I came to the doorstep and, along with my mother, saw above the opposite tree and*

*row of houses in the far, clear distance what looked like a*
*group of four to six same-sized, bright, luminous yellow*
*or orange bullet-shaped objects, weaving, swerving and*
*"dancing" among one another with amazing acrobatic*
*manoeuvrability, as if they were insects or fireflies. They*
*eventually vanished. None of us could understand what*
*they were.*

Animated movements by clusters of UFOs have been widely
reported and can be seen in multiple videos. Some today
might assume them to be stunt drones in formation, as
spectacularly demonstrated at public events, but these did not
exist in former decades when many such displays were seen.
Even now, the size and sudden acceleration often exceeds any
known drone tech.

Martyn Robinson describes another series of intriguing
aerial manoeuvres:

*One summer Saturday evening, at approximately 7pm,*
*in either 1968 or 1969, I was driving with my then*
*girlfriend. There were three horizontal bright lights in our*
*line of vision over London, but we hardly noticed them*
*until the left and right lights separated at an amazing*
*speed, looped around and joined the central light. Then,*
*all three shot up vertically and disappeared. We both*
*exclaimed 'Wow, what was that?' and discussed it on our*
*journey home.*

*The next day, one of my friends telephoned me to tell*
*me, "Guess what? – I saw a UFO last night." He had seen*
*the same thing. He had telephoned the* Daily Mirror [UK
newspaper] *to report it. They said they had received*
*many such reports and gave him a telephone number to*
*call. It was a Ministry of Defence officer who asked for full*
*details, but he then said he could not comment on what*
*had been seen. Recently, on a Netflix series about UFOs,*
*there was a background clip shown, but without any*

*comment. It was exactly what I had seen and I wonder if this was the London incident we witnessed?*

Reporting UAP is often a thankless task, as we are seeing, but authorities are evidently more interested than they let on.

Accounts (and videos) of lights moving in formation often record components splitting apart from a central body or coming together to form a greater whole, almost as if they are physically merging together, as Paula described. If they are craft, they must be highly amorphous (the "transmedium" effect). Otherwise, the merging may be an illusion caused by objects crossing into other dimensions at the moment they appear to touch. Whether these actions serve any function other than to draw attention to themselves is yet another unknown. It has been postulated that not all UAP are vehicles but entities in their own right, or at least nebulous and possibly natural plasma forms ("plasmoids"). Others think they are all of these things and that alien tech can be organically *grown* rather than constructed, as described by leaked testimony. Their visible size may also be deceptive, with some reports describing interiors far larger than the outer shell, not unlike Doctor Who's TARDIS, and perhaps allowing for a Russian doll effect of "stacked" craft, each inside the other, giving the appearance of merging.[17]

Fiona, whose out-of-body experience on pages 114–15 took her into the stars, had on another occasion a possible envoy from the stars come to *her*, as she describes:

*I was working on a flower farm one summer in the 1990s, when we spotted something strange in the sky. I was living in a caravan in a field with lots of other young flower pickers. One day, just as the sun was setting and casting a warm glow across the field and landscape, I was at the water tap with five others and one of them pointed at a bright object in the sky, which was hovering slowly over the next field. It was like perhaps a 20-ft [6-m] rugby ball, but seemed to be lit from inside with a silvery white light. If it had been dark, it would have been very bright. It wasn't reflecting the sun's orange glow. We all turned to tell someone else, and in the time we turned away to do this, it just disappeared. We could see from horizon to horizon in every direction, and it was gone! It made no sound, left no contrail.*

This is a good example of a single object observed by a group of people. Some of the above reports make clear that sightings of the same UAP are often shared over a wide local area or, in the case of the famous and controversial "Phoenix Lights" of 1997, where a huge V-shaped configuration was seen flying across Arizona and Nevada and reportedly beyond, more than one state. The lights were debunked as military activity but few witnesses accept that.[18] Given the prominence of some sightings, newcomers ask why authorities do not dispatch aircraft to intercept them. As the congressional hearings and US Naval videos demonstrate, UFOs playing cat-and-mouse with military aircraft are in fact a recurring phenomenon – and sometimes this is publicly observed.

Mal shared this remarkable story with me:

*I was lying on a hammock in my back garden. The sky was blue with single fluffy white clouds. As I looked up, a large solid-looking, mustard yellow cube, suspended from one corner, slowly lowered from near the edge of a cloud. It was like a radar device of the type that used to be suspended below weather balloons. Those are lightweight wire covered in a metallic coated nylon mesh. The one I saw was rigid looking, and probably at least three metres [10 feet] across.*

*I rushed in to find my camera. The cube was still there. As I raised my camera, the cube shot up, leaving a square hole in the cloud. A medium-sized aircraft with a triple tail then flew in front of the cloud from south to north. Shortly after it passed the cloud, a large bronze-coloured disc emerged silently from the side of the cloud. I estimate that it must have been around 25 to 30 metres [82 to 99 feet] in diameter. It looked like a bagel, but without a hole in the middle; rounded edges, not sharp. I could not see any portholes, glass domes or jet trails, and it was not spinning. It followed the aircraft and nearly caught up with it. The aircraft made a sharp turn to the east. The disc that was slightly lower than the plane continued straight on and entered a cloud, leaving an oval hole. I continued to watch both of the above-mentioned clouds, but did not see anything emerge. Sadly, my camera could not focus quickly enough for me to get any photos.*

Here is another dramatic sighting which culminated in a pursuit by planes, from Carl Eakins:

*In 1989 my wife and I were camping overnight in a recently harvested wheat field. What started for me as stargazing became a real sense of being swept up into deep space. Immediately following this strange experience, a gravid and surreal atmosphere descended upon our camp. Small coloured lights appeared within an adjacent island of trees, exerting a mesmerising and penetrating effect. The lights rose up and became enshrouded in a cloud of shadow, which materialized into a large black polyhedron-shaped craft.*

*Retreating to a "safer" vantage point, we noticed two pearlescent orbs investigating power lines in adjacent fields, and a few white domed objects seemingly undertaking a low-level grid search. After a while these visitors slowly and silently drifted away down the river valley. Finally, two fighter jets came over the horizon converging on the polyhedron, which zipped away in an eye-blink.*

A high-profile example of military pursuit occurred at Pentyrch in Wales in 2016 when Caz Clarke and a friend witnessed lights and a pyramidal object ejecting lightning-like phenomena before watching them being heavily pursued by a fleet of helicopters. Others reported similar activity and unusual aircraft manoeuvres.[19] As with the Phoenix Lights, whenever anything like this is witnessed by members of the public we are mostly told (if anything at all) that they merely saw "military exercises", but this is too easy a let-out for many sightings, as the inside informants are loudly pointing out.

## Police Stories

It has been noted that US police are now expressing official interest in UAP, but for years I have met or heard of police officers who have had very direct encounters. For example, Gary Heseltine, a former Detective Constable, found his own experiences so compelling that he became one of Britain's best-known ufologists.[20]

I spoke to a police officer who was once on night vehicle patrol on a quiet road near the English coastal village of Birling Gap, East Sussex. He and his colleague unexpectedly spotted two small balls of light (more on these below) speeding across the adjacent fields. Amazed, but with an impressive attention to duty, the officers drove to keep up with the lights, which seemed to bait them, keeping just to one side of the straight road, always slightly ahead. Unlike the comparable scene in the movie *Close Encounters of the Third Kind*, the patrol car did not crash through a fence, but the chase ended when the road took a bend and their quarry vanished out of sight.[21]

Curiously, Birling Gap had hosted some unusual crop circles in 1994, bent from *halfway* up the stems, and aerial lights are often seen in circle areas. A year later, in West Sussex, a huge and striking crop formation of oval concentric rings appeared near the Iron Age hill fort of Cissbury Ring. While investigating it at close quarters with the full permission of the farmer, Jason Porthouse found himself being harassed by the local police helicopter. It hovered dangerously low over the pattern, the pilots clearly thinking he was a trespasser and wanting him to leave, despite the fact they were themselves thrashing the crop. Annoyed by this reckless spectacle, Jason phoned the police to make an official complaint. He was surprised to be put through directly to the pilot. The exposed officer was reticent at first but, as he warmed to Jason's interests, before long he was regaling him with tales of the many unexplained lights he and his fellow pilots had witnessed in the area during their flights ...[22]

Another officer told me he was on duty when he watched a classic "flying saucer" moving slowly and silently across nearby fields before speeding off in the usual fashion. It was lit up along its perimeter edge in the way that many UFOs are. The sighting left the officer so awestruck, revealing to him the notion of other realms he had never previously considered, that he eventually left the police and joined a Spiritualist church. Many who have had doors opened by the strange find they are hard to close again.

The animated and often colourful lights on UAP raise another question – what are they for? Are the luminosities a by-product of a drive mechanism that renders them unavoidably visible, or is it a further indication that UFOs *want* to be seen, announcing loudly that history as we have known it is closing? Some who argue that ETs have had enough of human cover-ups believe so. Reports – and footage – sometimes record objects apparently "cloaking" and uncloaking themselves at will, even masquerading as clouds or hiding behind them before making a full appearance. This suggests there is an element of choice involved as to when they are seen. A number of witnesses say that UFOs can also shape-shift to appear as drones or planes when they want to, creating a neat if frustrating loop for both believers and sceptics.

What, though, of personnel who do *not* report UAP sightings?

# Un-Reports

In *Close Encounters of the Third Kind*, the scripts of which were based on intensive interviews with real researchers, there is a famous scene where air traffic controllers watch anomalous radar readings and hear a pilot describing UFO activity. When the pilot is asked if he wants to officially report it, the line goes quiet. Asked once more, he says, soberly, "Negative, we don't want to report a UFO."[23] I have met a number of retired air staff who have verified the reality of incidents like this, except that sometimes they were *ordered* not to report them.

### *Strange ... Conversations*: Quiet Inside Knowledge
Unlike the scene above, UAP do not always show up on instruments. Oliver was a military pilot in New Zealand. While flying, he saw a strange and uncharted object near his plane. When he radioed to base, they could not see it on the radar, even though he had a visual fix on it. Later in his career, he flew in England and on one occasion witnessed two inexplicable straight lines of "red balls of light" flying in formation, one line horizontal and the other vertical.

However, as in the above movie scene, Oliver told me that no one in his units ever reported UFOs, even after a clearly anomalous incident and despite everyone knowing what had happened. Why the reticence? The answer may be twofold. For years, a culture of fear was installed at certain levels of authority to ensure that evidence for something that was obviously real didn't reach the public. The immediate stamping down on filed reports, at least at basic levels, meant that no awkward log books could be leaked. Moreover, with mainstream ridicule of UFOs encouraged by what can be seen in retrospect as obvious "psi-ops" techniques, any pilots reporting them risked being taken off-duty and subjected to psychological analysis. With bills to pay and families to feed, until recently most have preferred to stay silent – at least until retirement.

Silence can also be directly imposed. Raymond was an officer in the Royal Air Force and worked in previous decades at one of its control centres. He was present on more than one occasion when radio reports came in of unlisted aerial objects, verified on radar and exhibiting incredible speeds and trajectories. When the incidents were over, staff were strictly ordered not to report or record them in any way. Raymond suspected that details must have been logged somewhere, but presumably by unseen higher-ups. Other ex-military personnel have told me very similar stories.

The culture of career-preservation extends also to civilian air crews. Hilary was an air stewardess for a major airline. One day, partway through a passenger-less flight returning the plane for maintenance, the captain radioed through that the skeleton crew might like to look out of the window. When they peered, they saw a V-shaped formation of "small triangles" flying alongside, effortlessly matching their speed with no visible exhaust or trails. Hilary found it "eerie". They kept looking and eventually the triangles vanished. Following debate, the whole crew made a decision not to report what they had seen, nor talk about it in any social situation. Years later, I was the first person Hilary had told the story to.

Despite the uphill struggles of reporting UAP sightings, now and then authorities actively pursue witnesses. Gregory's son and his friend had seen a glowing craft of some kind performing strange movements in the sky and they reported it to the local newspaper. Shortly after the story was published, a contact claiming to be from the police phoned and seemed anxious to know more about the sighting, as others had also reported it. Speaking to Gregory, the man took the incident more than seriously. There was something in his urgent and authoritative manner that felt a little threatening. He urged Gregory to ensure that his son make contact and left a number. Hearing this, his son was frightened and refused to phone back.

No one was pursued on this occasion but there are persistent claims of mysterious "men in black", smartly dressed government – or alien? – agents reputed to have intimidated UFO witnesses.[24] Not loud, but sinister and reportedly very persuasive in keeping people quiet, men in black have been lampooned in movies and become a staple of ufology, although evidence for them remains uncertain, beyond encounters with standard security agents. I have not come across anyone who has claimed to have met one, although of course they would be unlikely to say if they had.

However, some reports make assumptions. I have been wearing dark clothes most of my life and Jason Porthouse, who would accompany me to crop circles in earlier years, often wore black bike leathers. Following our on-site investigations, more than once we would hear later reports of "men in black" who apparently turned up, only to realize that the people being described were us.

## UAP and Psi

UFOs and psychic phenomena may appear to be very different subjects but there is more of a connection than meets the (third) eye. Some stories about the more serious men in black have described them as having telepathic abilities. Until recently, this has been a neglected realm of ufology, but the psi association is being discussed more following recent disclosures that have alluded to it, and a number of accounts have described UAP and their occupants as having psychic powers.

### Strange ... Communications: Telepathic Interaction?

Contactees who claim to have met aliens (see below) have frequently described communications taking place mind-to-mind rather than verbally, and some who have observed unusual craft have found unexpected revelations and presentiment entering their minds as they did so, as in the following account from Richard Gray:

*In early 1998 I met someone at a Latin dance class. After the first night out she came around to see me in the afternoon. There was a documentary on TV I wanted to watch so I put it on "record" (in the old tape style) and we went for a walk along Long Bay beach [Auckland, New Zealand]. On our way back, we stopped on the track overlooking the beach and out to nearby islands. I was looking back over the hills behind the beach when a low-flying, rocket-like craft appeared to my left. It had a large fiery flame coming out the back and made a noise like static on a radio, or TV. It took about 40 seconds to travel across to my right and out over the Coromandel Peninsula where some people claim spacecraft are sometimes seen. That was a distance of about 55km [34 miles], so it was not travelling that fast – about 5,000kph [3,100mph] – slow for an interstellar craft but much faster than any known military craft. Its shape was unusual too, but after 30 seconds in clear view, it started passing in and out of clouds.*

*At that moment I got a "message" that we (my new friend and I) would go out for two years, then be on and off for almost another year and then stop. It eventually happened just like that, but more to the point, when I got home and tried to play back the video, all I got was static, just like the noise of the craft. I was unable to get my TV to work after that and had to get a specialist in to sort it out.*

The description of a rocket-like object might suggest an earthly vehicle, but the accompanying "message" is more typical of the UFO–psi connection.

Such experiences are not always comfortable. An American acquaintance told me that when she was a teenager, she witnessed a cigar-shaped craft hovering in the sky. As it did, she described a frightening sensation of *knowing* it had homed in on her, followed by an experience of physical paralysis, as if its occupants were inhibiting her movements to allow them to study her. She felt a force reaching into her mind in a violating manner, as if it were stealing her innermost thoughts. Finally, she was released and the object moved on.

People watching UAP and smaller balls of light have sometimes described having a symbiosis with them, noticing that expectations and even requests can direct their behaviour (some contactees claim to be able to summon UFOs at will). In these cases, either the occupants are indeed psychically tuned in to those observing them and are participating in a deliberate exchange, or the lights may be the less corporeal plasmoid or "orgone" forms that naturally interact with the local psychic environment, as some investigators have suggested.[25]

There are examples of people being "called" to witness UFOs, or at least led to see them by strange coincidence. My colleagues and I had a series of such experiences in the 1990s during our attempted interactive experiments with crop circles and earth energies, working with psychic Paul Bura, as recounted in the book *Quest for Contact*.[26] For every circle that might be made by humans (the standard media explanation), many cannot be so easily explained and aerial lights play a role in the phenomenon.[27]

Our group included Martin Noakes (see pages 83–4 and 185) and Barry Reynolds, a consultant for this book. The following example of a "calling" happened to Barry and his wife during a particularly intensive period of the project:

*On Sunday 27 June 1993, my wife Linda and I were trying to entice our cat, Edward, to come in for the night. He was usually in by 22:00 latest but was still nowhere to be seen at 22:30. I went out into the garden and on returning to the house said to Linda that I felt something was about to happen and that we should keep an eye on the sky. I then went upstairs and had a shower. Linda came into the bathroom a few minutes later and said that her adrenalin was really running and she would have difficulty getting to sleep as she also felt that something was indeed about to occur. She then went outside into the back garden to see if Edward was now about.*

*As I finished in the bathroom, I got my dressing-gown and decided to go straight outside. As soon as I entered the garden, Linda, who had been outside for a few minutes, said, "Look up there! What's that?" A white point of light the size and brightness of the brightest stars in the sky at that time was moving from south-west to west, not in a straight line but in an arc. Satellites do NOT go round corners. We watched it for between 2 and 3 minutes before it was lost from view. It was not a conventional aircraft; there were some visible in the sky at that time. There were no flashing lights on it and it was far too high. Remember, we both felt that we were going to see something shortly before we did and if Edward had been in at his usual time we would not have seen it. Coincidence or synchronicity?*

This was just one of several unexpected encounters several of us had with anomalous aerial phenomena (see below) and bizarre paranormal events (see next chapter). A year later Linda would watch an unsettling rectangular object with a domed underside turning a circle over the very same garden.

The more we gave toward the project, the more unusual things would manifest around us, beyond coincidence, as if something was responding in kind. Even on the day we had our initial gathering at Paul's house – in secrecy – to discuss our plans, astonishingly the very first crop circle of the year in our region appeared in the field nearest to his house. Such interaction would build, culminating in a 1995 crop formation manifesting in precisely the shape we had anticipated and in a map alignment directly connected with our work, following a meditation at an ancient sacred site. No one outside our small group could have known what the pattern was. Did we manifest it ourselves through unconscious telekinesis, or did something listen in to our thoughts and humour us? For those who argue we were duped by pranksters, even in that scenario the possibility that someone managed to divine our chosen shape through telepathic means seems no less extraordinary.

Military informants say that hidden medical research has discovered that the "putamen" and "caudate" structures of the brain's basial ganglia appear to be stimulated by UAP encounters and can be expanded by them. It is believed that the gifts of precognition and intuition may well reside in these structures, which would make sense of the apparent links between all these areas.[28] These findings are being independently explored by qualified immunologist and Sol Foundation initiator Dr Garry Nolan. In turn, those who have naturally enlarged putamen and caudate appear more prone to *having* psi powers and attracting UAP and ET encounters, as if they are a beacon to psychically adept beings (known as "psionic" interaction). People who claim to have been abducted by aliens or had near-death experiences have often found their psychic and premonitory abilities enhanced or activated afterwards (see Chapter 4).

## Aliens Themselves

I have met numerous "alien abductees", or "contactees" as they often prefer, who believe they have had direct encounters with the inhabitants of UFOs. Prominent among these are

Budd Hopkins, Mary Rodwell, Whitley Strieber and Travis Walton. Inevitably, not everyone supports their claims, with unproven accusations of fraud or mental illness, but I also spent time with the late Professor John Mack, an unusually open-minded Harvard psychiatrist who famously studied such cases and concluded they should not all be dismissed.[29]

Thousands of seemingly sane people each year describe being taken onboard spaceships, meeting an array of creatures (see below), undergoing inexplicable and sometimes painful medical procedures, receiving physical "implants" or being given prophecies about humankind's future, and other encounters besides, some sexual. If "real", and not occurring on a psychological or hallucinatory level (as, inevitably, critics argue), what purpose these serve has been greatly debated but the general view is that human specimens are being assessed and genetic material is being gathered. If it makes us feel better, animals often seem to get a harder time, if the notorious link between UFO sightings and peculiarly bloodless cattle mutilations (and sometimes other livestock) are taken into account.[30]

On the whole, the contactees I have spoken to have been through my links with paranormal research rather than from casual members of the public and their tales have been told before. Those with experiences are frequently so changed by them that they tend to rise to prominence on the UFO scene. Quieter everyday witnesses to aliens that approach me at talks are scarcer. But I hear from a few.

The archetypal and most-reported extra-terrestrials are the "greys", short beings with dull grey-green or brown skin, bulbous heads, spindly bodies and dark iris-less eyes. They are reportedly hard to read; not evil (we hope), but amoral and coldly analytical – organic robots, perhaps. Some scientists have argued that most alien space travellers are likely to be forms of AI, for survivability or because AI enhancement or complete replacement of life may be an inescapable outcome in the evolution of an advanced species

– see page 241. But other races are also encountered: tall and handsome "Nordic" humanoids, insectoid forms, reptilians (more likely evil and a big influence on human history, according to conspiracy thinkers) and further variations have been recalled when abduction memories have been retrieved through hypnotic regression or psychoanalysis. Regression has been used as a form of memory-retrieval for a number of contactees. This is contentious, with accusations that "false memory syndrome" plays a role, but it has produced surprisingly consistent descriptions of apparently alien beings. There is debate that these may effectively be the same "goblins" and other legendary creatures reported in centuries past when folk claimed to have been abducted into the faerie realms.

Perturbingly, it may be that more of us have these encounters than we know but are taken during sleep and don't retain the memory. Yet, some people *have* witnessed extraordinary events in a fully waking state and remember what they saw, as we would remember anything – and there are cases where partners have said they have watched loved ones being physically floated out of their beds, or being zapped up into UFOs.

### Strange ... Communications: Domestic Aliens

Before readers fret, the alien experiences described above are exceptional. Most cases are less dramatic, but remain compelling – and many occur in the home, where we are at our most relaxed but also, therefore, at our most open to inter-dimensional intervention, as with ghosts. Some tales of ET interaction can be easy to disregard, but we have been trained by years of academic doubt to be cynical and it is worth reconsidering these stories without those lenses – a major point of this book.

David Karunanithy, after witnessing the "dancing" UFOs above, became fascinated with the whole subject, and had this later experience:

*During the 1990s, I became nothing short of obsessed with the UFO phenomenon, so much so that I would voraciously read anything I could find on the subject, including a rapidly expanding collection of books, video documentaries and issues of* UFO Magazine, *and I even attended a conference or two. But perhaps I took it too far.*

*One evening, I was relaxing in my room, having read more of my UFO books. I switched off the light and in the darkness saw in my peripheral vision what seemed to be a small, bony arm with thin hand and long fingers grasping some square-shaped device, which it brandished at me. In my shock and horror I gasped and blinked, thinking that my eyes were just playing tricks, yet the silhouette of the arm and its menacing gesture persisted. I remember shouting out loud, and fumbling to put the light back on, only to find that the room was empty. It had been a most unnerving experience and the arm I saw looked very real. Could it have just been the result of an overactive mind? Tiredness or a hallucination?*

Sceptics will, naturally, say yes – that David's vision resulted from an active imagination over-stimulated by obsessive thinking. But given the brain's putamen and caudate abilities discussed above, could there be more to it? If the very act of thinking more about UFOs and aliens actually attracts them, how can we be sure where the line of reality blurs?

For those who argue such things take place in a realm of mind only, we are back to the issue of what is, precisely, a vision or a hallucination? A growing number of ufologists, based on hints from the whistleblowers, are inclining to the view that what we call "extra-terrestrials" or even "off-world intelligences" are in truth multi-dimensional psychic beings as much as organic (some of them, at least), ones that can inhabit the same frequencies where ghostlier entities reside, as discussed in Chapter 4. This may be what is manifesting, for example, at the enigmatic Skinwalker Ranch in Utah (see Chapter 7).

Here is another account of a domestic visitation, from Martin Noakes, who appears prone to bedroom incursions, having been shaken awake by a ghost (see page 83).

*When I was around 10 years old our family lived in a semi-detached three-bedroom house. We had no dogs or cats. In the early hours of the morning, I felt something pushing down the bottom of the bed. I raised my head and looked up to see a frightening creature. I described it to my parents the next morning as "Humpy Dumpty with a Devil's fork" (a trident). I was petrified and pulled the covers over my head and prayed for this thing to go away. That's all I remember. I woke up the next morning with a vivid memory of it.*

*I had pretty much forgotten about this until I saw a book being promoted in a shop at Gatwick airport en route for a holiday. The book was called* Communion, *written by Whitley Strieber, and the cover artwork was identical to the "thing" I saw at the foot of my bed as a child.[31] I felt compelled to buy the book and it scared the life out of me.*

*I did go for regressive hypnosis and was able to get back to that night, but hyperventilated when directed to look at the being.*

Again, it might be easy to dismiss this as a child's nightmare, but I have known Martin long enough to be sure that even at that age he would know reality from dreams, and he swears he was awake. However, this is not to dilute the psychological symbolism of the many who "merely" dream of UFOs and aliens, the importance of which was identified by the renowned psychologist Carl Jung in his 1959 book *Flying Saucers.*[32] Seen by Jung (who gave no opinion on the physical reality of the phenomenon) as both symbols and heralds of huge societal shifts, this interpretation of UAP feels more pertinent than ever today.

### Strange ... Conversations: Onscreen Aliens

If ETs can manifest in reality *or* dreams, why then not also on our television screens? But not as science fiction. When I chatted with her, Daniella seemed like a very reasonable person with no particular interest in UFOs or aliens, and yet she had a bewildering encounter via her TV.

Around 2010, Daniella owned a perfectly normal digital television. One night, without warning, the picture turned to white "snow", like old sets used to when detuned. She was further surprised when, through the fuzz, the figure of an archetypal grey alien began to emerge, becoming clearer until it was fully onscreen. She remembered that its "body and limbs looked weak". It looked out from the screen and *noticed* her watching. The creature seemed as taken aback as she was. It started touching controls near the bottom of the screen, as if attempting to lose her image. It tried four times and finally the TV returned to normal. Mystified and a little shaken, Daniella hoped this was a one-off quirk. But it happened a second night. Again, the alien looked shocked to see her but this time seemed to know what to do; it touched the controls and vanished.

On the third and final occasion, after the grey had come and gone, a horizontal strip extended itself across the lower part of the TV screen, displaying a corridor where "lizards wearing robes" were moving in a procession towards a door on the far side of the screen. This time, Daniella was frightened. The grey was unsettling but there was something overtly threatening about this new species. Fearing they also might become aware of her, she managed to grab the TV remote and turn off the screen.

Given the conspiracy beliefs that malevolent reptilian ETs have secretly infiltrated the world, perhaps Daniella, who knew nothing of that, did the right thing in closing them down. Once more, it might be simpler to brush this story off as tired hallucinations, but should we? Aware of what critics would say, I was bold and asked Daniella, gently, if it was possible she might have had a mild psychotic "episode", but she said she had no history of such symptoms and it had only ever happened on those occasions through her TV.

Did someone – or something – hack into Daniella's channels and direct strange signals into her living room? If so, why? If a joke, it was needlessly elaborate and might have been better played on someone interested in such things. Breaking into TV broadcasts is, as one would hope, a very hard thing to do in any case. And yet, there is a precedent with a possible extra-terrestrial connection.

On 26 November 1977, viewers of the British regional station Southern Television found the soundtrack of the late afternoon news unexpectedly replaced by a deep, distorted voice claiming to be a representative of the "Ashtar Galactic Command" (an oft-channelled group of "ascended masters"). The sci-fi-like tones were disturbing, welcoming humankind to a "great awakening" but warning that we would have to break free of "many false prophets and guides at present operating on your world" and leave our warlike ways behind to be a part of that. The transmission continued for a remarkable six minutes before signing off. A recording of it can be heard online.[33]

Other rare "signal intrusions" have occurred throughout broadcasting history but nothing like this has been repeated. Assumed to be a hoax, if it was no one knows who perpetrated it, nor precisely how it was done, though suggestions have been made. Hoax or not, in these times of UFO whistleblowers and global troubles, a few lines from the transmission sum things up rather well today.

*We have watched you growing for many years as you too have watched our lights in your skies. You know now that*

187

*we are here, and that there are more beings on and around your Earth than your scientists admit. We are deeply concerned about you and your path toward the light …*

## The Miami Test?

As for extra-terrestrial sightings being *reported* on TV, this has been an entertainment staple for years, usually presented – until recently – as end-of-bulletin light relief. Yet, series like *Ancient Aliens* and UFO documentaries have proved popular and the advent of higher-calibre insider information is changing the way mainstream media, especially in the USA, treat the subject.[34] But some stories are so bizarre that even in this new climate, journalists aren't always sure how to treat them.

On New Year's Day 2024 at the Bayside Marketplace mall in Miami, a news frenzy erupted when shoppers started pouring out in terror, some claiming that 10ft-tall dark aliens were stalking the concourses. In what sounds like an episode of the fantasy TV series *Stranger Things*, rumours state that a group of youths appeared with an electronic device, set it down and ran away. A stream of light and smoke coursed from it as if a dimensional portal was opening, followed by the arrival of the tall figures, almost silhouettes, who terrorized fleeing customers. Soon, one of the longest streams of police vehicles ever seen in the state besieged the mall and a news blackout was supposedly instigated. Overhead videos appeared to show the alleged aliens as blurry shapes.[35]

The story was widely reported and elaborate stories grew. Controversial video clips purported to show the aliens; witnesses came forward with first-hand accounts; news programmes discussed the implications of aliens choosing such a location to manifest. But, as days went by, everything reversed: now the videos were apparent hoaxes or optical illusions; the witnesses were lying or melted away; promised revelations never materialized. The youths were just teenagers having a fight, the device was a boombox music player and the portal nothing more than fireworks, the sound of which concerned police, worried about possible shootings hence the huge response. And that was that. Except, of course, it wasn't, because already the "Miami Mall Aliens" had fallen into paranormal legend. Rationalist researchers accepted it as a probable hoax but hardcore believers insist the explanations were nothing more than cover-ups for a majorly anomalous event and that witnesses were intimidated into silence.

This is a good example of the polarization that all too often taints the UFO/UAP subject (and indeed anything these days). David Grusch's claims and the congressional hearings had brought a fresh media tone, but the Miami incident allowed many news anchors to revert to their former mocking smiles. Assuming it wasn't real, was the event a hoax engineered to reduce the credibility of alien tales, building up its profile only to knock it down again knowing it would harm the credibility of the whole subject by association? Or were the rumours around it just happy serendipity that could be used for the same purpose?

If the Miami aliens were intended to roll back the heat from UAP matters, the effect didn't last long, as just months later along came Luis Elizondo with his own sensational claims of military cover-ups, and then the fleets of mystery "drones" (see pages 162–3), and the tone shifted yet again. The counter-claims that attempted to undermine him see-sawed approaches further, but the general picture of real ET cover-ups has held. One assertion made by Elizondo and others is that during their work investigating alien incursions, glowing green balls of light appeared in their houses, as if they were literally taking their work home with them. Known as the "hitch-hiker" effect, phenomena or presences latching on to contactees or investigators has something in common with ghosts that appear to follow people, as discussed in Chapter 3. It is also redolent of the effect my colleagues and I experienced during our psychic questing work with crop circles.

# Balls of Light

Smaller balls of light (BOLs), as opposed to large craft-like objects, are a recurring expression of UAP, and are seen frequently in a number of contexts. We have established that ghosts can also manifest this way (see pages 34–5). The BOLs are generally a foot or two across, sometimes smaller, sometimes larger, glow brightly or palely, and are not always green; almost every colour has been sighted, hence the cutesy name crop circle researchers give to them: "amber gambollers". But some of those I have personally witnessed *were* green.

### *Strange ... Memories*: Lights and Shadows

During the most focused period of our interactive experiments, I had a number of encounters with aerial phenomena (documented fully in *Quest for Contact*). One was a very bright light being pursued by a rapidly oscillating smaller object. The second was a white luminescent sphere that hung in the air before rapidly dropping to Earth like a stone. With no other witnesses, people simply believed me or they didn't. The third sighting of BOLs, however, was made by three of us.

On 28 July 1993, Martin Noakes, Dave "Griller" Gilgannon and I took an excursion to the fields of Wiltshire in south-west England, host to the majority of crop formations for reasons mystical or geophysical (most appear over the local chalk aquifers, large areas of underground water). BOLs were, and are, a recurring spectacle there and we were hoping to see some. We did.

Perhaps there are deeper reasons why the beautiful downland crest overlooking the Alton Priors/Alton Barnes area is called Golden Ball Hill. The name refers to the yellow flowers that grow abundantly there, but in an area where so many BOLs have been spotted, other origins have inevitably been discussed.[36] Either way, the vista from Golden Ball Hill provides a perfect viewing point for any crop circles or phenomena occurring below. The nearby presence of the ancient barrow Adam's Grave adds to the ambience. Bound in coats and thick jumpers for a cold night vigil, we settled in and watched the fields. Soon enough, we saw, one by one, three pale green orbs appear in the darkness over the wheat fields, each one perhaps a couple of feet or so across. They would gently brighten into view, then slowly move before speeding up and heading out of sight. Sceptics have sneered that we probably saw lanterns or small gas balloons cheekily launched to entertain night-watchers, but these simply don't explain what we witnessed. Indeed, these were sequels to even more outlandish phenomena over the same set of fields.

The night of the orbs was a deliberate reversal of the previous day, when the three of us had sat in the small hours among the fields below, looking *up* to Golden Ball Hill. What we witnessed there was more unnerving: huge, dark block-like shapes flickered backward and forward in front of us (Martin describes them "going around silently in a circular fashion"), almost strobing with their speed. They eclipsed the hills being silhouetted by the first grey dawn light. They didn't appear solid, but other-dimensional: not quite "here". Something about them instilled fear in me and I found myself unable to leave the car, watching through the windscreen, while the others got out to look. I regret this timidity now, but still relatively new to the unknown and having had a series of unsettling hitch-hiker effects of my own (see next chapter), at that point I was nervous of invoking more.[37]

UAP didn't entirely leave me alone after that. In 1997, I was exploring a crop formation near Avebury in Wiltshire with a friend when we both witnessed a bright trailing ball of light zig-zag low over our heads just on the edge of vision, almost like a swift energy discharge. In 2006, members of an audience I was addressing about this very kind of thing spotted a ball of light in the auditorium ... Disappointingly, I was too distracted to notice it myself, but Anthony James, who was there, describes it:

*Andy had been talking for some time when I noticed a very bright ball of orange light, which came through the skylight window on the roof of the building quite high above Andy's head. It had a very beautiful quality, graceful, quiet and very bright. I noticed a very intense centre point of light with a soft sphere around it. It disappeared out the skylight for a moment and then came back again, only this time it seem to dance about and come slightly lower into the room. Then it went back out the skylight and was gone! It was almost as though it was checking out Andy's lecture and slides.*

*I turned to my wife and said, "Did you see that?", and she said "Yes". At the interval, I asked other people if they saw anything and two other people said they saw exactly what I have described. I asked the proprietor of the building if there were any electric lights in the skylight (which was a tinted blue colour) – he said "No".*[38]

**Strange ... Communications: Chasing a Ball of Light**
During our questing years, Barry Reynolds, who was compelled into the garden with his wife to witness aerial events (see page 180), had another extraordinary sighting around the same time:

*I was at this point a Venture Scout Leader. On Sunday 20 June 1993 I was sitting on the side of the South Downs at Pyecombe [hills near Brighton, East Sussex, England] facing almost due West, as my unit had agreed to clear a couple of pasture fields of poisonous ragwort for a farmer, and I stopped for lunch with my two young sons. It was about quarter past one, and the sun was directly above us, shining brightly. I looked up, and there in the centre of my field of vision, on the far side of the busy main London to Brighton A23 road, in a field of grass some half a mile away, was a ball of light travelling swiftly toward us.*

*I began to walk down the grassy hill. The ball moved swiftly across the field at what I estimated to be running pace, a speed far greater than the very slight breeze that would occasionally waft across where I was. It travelled in an almost straight line although it meandered slightly as it moved. When it reached the edge of the field it appeared to go either through or over the fence onto the A23, which was extremely busy. A pale green saloon car in the slow lane of the northbound carriageway actually stopped abruptly to let the ball cross in front of it! The car then pulled over into the end of a slip road and remained there for the next 15 minutes.*

*Meanwhile, the ball continued across the northbound lane, went over the central reservation and crossed the southbound carriageway. It missed several vehicles by less than a car's length and never deviated in its path. The speed of the cars (50–70mph/80–113kph) and the turbulence they caused had no effect on the ball at all. It came over the fence on my eastern side of the road and into a field of sheep. By this time I was scorching down the side of the downs toward it. At the foot of the field I was in was a large copse of trees and beyond that was the field of sheep. I kept losing sight of the ball behind the trees so had to run from side to side in the field to keep track of it. As it passed through the field of sheep it was less than 10ft (3m) away from some of them. The sheep took no notice of it. They didn't run away or increase their bleating. Eventually the ball just disappeared from my line of sight.*

*As the ball travelled so close to well-known objects, I could see as it crossed the road that it was easily the size of a car wheel. When it was in the field it was half of the body size of a sheep, and therefore approximately 2ft (60cm) in diameter. The ball appeared to be flat, in as much as from where I was I could ascertain no three dimensional aspect to it. That is not to say that it was flat, only that I could not judge its depth. It was a very bright white and the edges were fuzzy, rather like a light bulb appears to be when it is turned on.*

This usefully clear description of a BOL matches other significant sightings made at close quarters (see below). Clearly not always balloons, dandelion seeds, birds or all the usual culprits alleged by cynics, it should be noted that near-identical phenomena have been recorded in a number of contexts and may have been around since time began; indeed, sightings may have helped give rise to belief in fairies and "devic" nature spirits – that is, assuming they *aren't* these things, given the shamanic contact made with various beings. The behaviour of some BOLs can suggest a conscious force directing them, while others appear more random.

Lights of this nature can occur through a number of apparently natural causes. Ball lightning, for example, is a known if rare phenomenon and has highly unusual properties, including the ability to pass *through* solid objects, sometimes leaving burn marks or holes, but not always. Possibly a form of charged plasma (of the plasmoid variety), other theoretical models have been put forward, but little is understood. Similar lights have been seen in geologically unstable zones, along with other aerial luminosities, usually before earthquakes.[39]

So, science accepts the reality of BOLs in some circumstances. The question is, why is there a preponderance of them around haunted sites, crop circles and indeed ancient stone circles? Notably, these are often in areas considered to be rich in earth energies, and some geomancers believe the more uncanny lights occur through a blend of subtle energy and consciousness as much as electrical forces. Sceptics decry this, obviously, but even if we go with BOLs having more conventional origins, why the lights are connected to such places and can be seemingly drawn via psychic interaction remains unanswered.

The BOLs described above are not the same as the orbs sometimes caught on camera (see page 40), but are fully visible and have been filmed on notable occasions, long before the modern deep-fake era and sometimes with multiple witnesses present.

### *Strange ... Conversations*: Light Tales
Here is just a selection of eye-witness accounts of these smaller lights.

After seeing me show photos and videos, Alexis realized she had experienced BOLs in her house on several occasions, albeit reduced in scale. The small bright points she saw appeared to move distinctly and float around corners. Her eyesight was good and the lights were genuinely there. When she saw two flying up the staircase in front of her, she decided to pursue them to find out where they went. Alexis quickly turned on the main light to see what they were like in fuller illumination, but they vanished as she did. She found the mini-BOLs "attractive" and didn't seem frightened by them.

Even if it is only a human projection onto the unknown, we saw on page 35 that balls of light can be comforting, especially following a bereavement; they can also be oddly reassuring in times of stress.

Daisy had a friend, Ivy, whose husband was gravely ill, while she was herself worried for the health of another close friend. Daisy and Ivy were walking near fields close to her home, commiserating with each other, when a bright ball of light unexpectedly appeared from the clouds. Shining brightly even in full daylight, it "came down from the sky" to hover over the end of the field and hung there motionless for several minutes, as if there for them. Then, in a blink, it was gone. Amazed and transfixed, Daisy and Ivy felt that there was something encouraging about the light, almost as if it might have been "an angel" there to comfort them. Perhaps it was: if BOLs can be devas or fairies, why not angels, whatever they may truly be?

Georgina had the harder task of convincing her husband of a sighting – never easy, as men seem especially conditioned to laugh off the paranormal without direct experience. In the mid 1960s, she and Arthur lived near Warminster, Wiltshire, an area renowned at that time for the "Warminster UFO flap". Even then, Georgina remembers crop circles in the area, making the point that the circle mystery goes back long before the hoax claims of the 1990s (to the 1600s at least, if old pamphlet reports are taken at face value).[40]

Arthur was in the army, and nearby Salisbury Plain remains a major army training area today. One night, in their garden, Georgina saw a very bright ball of yellow light, getting bigger, heading toward her. Used to military flares (the sceptic fallback for sightings in this area), helicopters and planes, she knew this was something different. It halted at a certain distance, soundless and sat there for a long time. It was difficult to judge its size. Mesmerized by the dazzling light, she managed to break away and went indoors to fetch Arthur. Although sceptical, he was finally persuaded out – and by then, of course, the light was gone. Exasperated, he said she was "bonkers" and stomped back indoors.

However, Georgina would have her vindication. In the days after, the local press reported other residents who saw the same anomalous light, making the point that it was definitely more than standard Salisbury Plain exercises, otherwise "flares" would be routinely reported every week.

* * *

Perhaps confirming that those prone to strange experiences can specifically attract UFOs, two people familiar from other encounters in this book also witnessed BOLs.

Adelaide, who saw the child in her sofa and smelled ghostly perfumes (see pages 32 and 54) was, in more recent years with her husband on the street leading to their house when they saw a bright sphere of light, "about the size of a beach ball", in the sky above. It quickly descended, heading straight toward them, ever closer, until they became afraid it was actively pursuing them. When it got very near, suddenly it turned away at a right angle and vanished, as if, said Adelaide, "it didn't like them". Although relieved, she was left with an odd feeling of having been rejected.

Daniella, meanwhile, who was perturbed by the aliens on her television (see pages 186–7), began to wonder whether she might have been "marked" in some way when, asleep in bed in the same house, she was disturbed by flickering lights. She opened her eyes to find a cluster of tiny pink lights hovering in the bedroom, flitting around like flies. They were about the size of "the dots you get in a showerhead". Having slept with open curtains and windows on a warm night, Daniella could also see a much larger and fuzzier ball of pink light pulsating over the garden outside. She rapidly pulled off the covers to escape but doing so made the small lights rush out the window and then merge with their garden companion. She went to look but the ball sped off. Daniella felt uncomfortable about the whole experience and had the feeling the lights had been surveying her in some way. Given the experience with her television, perhaps they had been?

### Strange ... Communications: Circle Lights
Crop circles and balls of light, as noted, are common bedfellows. Local earth energies may bind both together.

Whether the lights are generated by the circles or the other way around, and whether they are conscious is debated, but there are enough sightings and authenticated videos to confirm the connection. A 1996 video of a snowflake-like pattern materializing beneath BOLs at Olivers Castle in Wiltshire remains contentious, but still persuades some viewers. Studies made into lights that have been seen to touch down into the crop itself have recorded very fine silica deposits that support the theory that plasmas are involved.[41]

The next chapter records some notable circle stories, but the following account from Mak Norman, who saw the burst of light on the road (see page 168), reinforces the BOL association and constitutes another example of a pre-public-awareness crop formation.

*When I was only around 11 years of age* [mid-1960s], *my friend Chris and I were keen bird watchers and spent a lot of our free time in the fields. We were very conscious of "the country code", but on one occasion broke the rules and cut through a full-grown field of crops, which came up to our waists. We had got a long way in when we came across a crop circle. Just one. Not large. About 20 feet/6m across and perfectly formed. We joked about alien spacecraft and at the same time hoped it was.*

*This event was followed with what I believe was a related experience. My friend and I were in his bedroom, from where it was possible to overlook the area where we found the circle. It was when we were looking in the crop circle direction that we both witnessed a rich orange ball moving steadily at a regular height and pace beyond distant trees. Its orange was the colour of the sun, but it did not dazzle. You can imagine our excitement. But the best was yet to come. An identical orange ball came into view from the opposite direction and they moved toward each other. When the balls were in close proximity to each other they began moving away from us. We left the bedroom giving yells of excitement.*

*Years later, in our mid-20s, I asked my friend what he recalled. It was a relief when his memory of what we saw matched mine exactly.*

## Strange Inconclusions: UFOs and UAP

Unexplained objects fly around in our airspace performing extraordinary aerial feats and people see them. It's that straightforward. The cover-ups are being exposed and the subject is unlikely to be swept back under the carpet.

What is less straightforward is the ability of UAP to blink in and out of visibility, defy accepted physics, morph themselves and merge together, while their apparent connections to human consciousness and psi powers raise big questions. With some UFOs clearly far more than metal, nuts and bolts, we are likely dealing with a multi-layered phenomenon that expresses itself in various forms and may have multiple origins. The pilots that seemingly occupy some of them have equally cryptic qualities.

The implications of this subject are profound. If it is openly revealed that there is a higher intelligence with far greater capabilities than us, will this undermine our governments and make populations increasingly look beyond them in the hope that new higher authorities will improve our world and save us from ourselves? Will we then demand of ETs the gifts we know they could bestow? Or will we live in fear of them and what they could do to us if they so chose? Either way, they will likely have knowledge of key truths humankind has so far not had to face, which could be as intimidating as it is enlightening.

For those who argue all UAP is man-made tech and that the growing stir about off-world intelligences is a distractive psi-ops operation, we are still left with a significant cultural and economic shock coming our way when that tech is finally revealed, on top of fierce debates about who should wield its power and how.

In due course, when more becomes known, the world will be a very different place. For now, recording experiences of this phenomenon remains important, and acknowledging the way it dovetails with other elements of the strange is surely a step on the road to new times.

## CHAPTER 7

# BIZARRE HAPPENINGS

## Stranger Than Strange

It is plain, for those with eyes to see, that all is not as it seems when defining the "real world". Time is leaky and malleable, beings come and go between dimensions, consciousness imprints on the material world and can roam free of the flesh, while physics-bending objects fly around us.

But certain claims, at first, still seem hard to swallow and don't fit obvious categories. I might once have been resistant to some of them myself were it not that I have experienced happenings more bizarre even than the personal stories I have related so far.

### *Strange ... Memories*: Three Kinds of Weird

During our psychic questing in the 1990s, when team members were having synchronous encounters, I had some unsettling experiences I didn't publicly share at the time, because I knew outsiders might not believe me – and because I was afraid. With a more confident understanding from what I have learned in the decades since, I am now happy to record them. A further event took place a few years later.

**Weird 1 – Breaking Through the Wall:** My friendship with Paul Bura and attendance of his meditation circles meant that by default I was the interface for the psychical side of our research. Other members were more concerned with technical aspects and plotting paths on hillsides up which we could hilariously stretcher a long-suffering Paul (disabled, remember). There, we would conduct our esoterically arranged assignations in the hope of seeing UFOs, receiving channellings or manifesting crop circles. Paul felt he needed back-up though, so we enlisted the help of two further mediums, Carole Coren and Diana Swann. The intuited directions of the psychic trio led us where we needed to be and when.

I had been told that I also had the potential for mediumistic gifts, but given that I had been about as psychic as a brick until then (beyond my premonition as a child – see pages 144–5), I was doubtful; nor did I particularly need such gifts when there were better adepts around me. I was also nervous of what might be unleashed, and was perhaps right to be.

At the height of the project, one evening my then wife and I had been watching a television documentary about the fall of the Berlin Wall in 1989. The footage of jubilant Germans atop the now silly looking wall, hacking into it with pickaxes and even pneumatic drills was stirring. A line from *Eastern Bloc*, a catchy pop song about this event by Thomas Dolby, singing of crowbars and drills, was revolving in my head as I went to bed.[1]

We lived then in a terrace of flat-roofed and not particularly robust rabbit-hutch-like houses. This matters, because an hour or so after turning off the lights that night, we were disturbed by a harsh, very loud and scary noise. My head was still full of dream images of the Berlin Wall being assaulted, but we were shocked awake by what sounded like a huge piece of machinery attempting to come through the wall above our heads – like a power drill, violently vibrating the room. I thought immediately that it was almost as if my dreams and the earworm of the song had turned themselves into actuality. We were terrified. I put my hand onto the wall and the shaking was so strong that I expected a point to suddenly break through, or for the wall to collapse. Objects on our side tables were jolting along.

We knew that the wall of our room adjoined the bedroom of our neighbours, a couple with a small girl. Surely, they couldn't be drilling into it at this time of night? There were no pipes in the wall and we didn't live in an earthquake zone – and the vibration was very localized. It seems incongruous now, but instead of storming down to my neighbour's door, we did what many good English people would do in a crisis – pulled the covers over our heads and pretended it wasn't happening. After several minutes of torment, we were greatly relieved when the sound began to subside and finally stopped. In shock, we lay there and eventually fell asleep. In the early hours, the noise started again, briefly and less loud, but it was still disturbing.

Next morning, with normality restored but feeling confused, I spoke to the neighbours. They had heard nothing, neither had their child been woken. This was an impossibility if the same vibration had transmitted itself through to their side, as surely it must have done. No one else in the terrace had anything to report. But I already felt in my gut that what we had experienced was some form of psychic outbreak – or an external influence attempting to kickstart something in me. As I was trying not to access these forces, so they were breaking through in other ways, perhaps. My wife had experienced it with me but how the shaking had not extended beyond our own room, or whether it existed only in a shared psychic space indistinguishable from reality, we never discovered.

The mediums were alarmed at this news and concurred with my suspicions. They gave me protective talismans to help prevent a repeat. The drilling did not return and I still love the Thomas Dolby song. But if something was trying to break through, it wasn't quite done yet and would maybe try in other ways.

**Weird 2 – Electric Synchronicity:** Earlier chapters have shown that this period of my life attracted a number of anomalies. Beyond the shaking walls, balls of light and flying shapes (Chapter 6), the causes of a few of them were probably explainable, if peculiar, but – and this is explored in a section below – they still felt *synchronous* with the topsy-turvy happenings occurring around me. Strings of synchronous events are usually telling us something.

Our house was full of surprises at this time: clocks would inexplicably stop or behave erratically and our baby son's talking toys would trigger by themselves. One cuddly duck was highly electro-sensitive and would sometimes quack when lights were turned on or off. Sometimes it would just chat away to itself, especially in a thunderstorm when it would go into a frenzy of looped quacking. I am not suggesting in any way that this was supernatural, and it didn't worry us especially; it was just odd, even funny.

A confluence of oddness can be perturbing, though. At this time, I was editing the *Sussex Circular*, which would become one of the most-read crop circle journals. Computers had not yet come into my life, so I was tapping out each issue on an electric IBM typewriter, a good model. It had no word processor nor screen: it was just a typewriter. One bright morning in our office, just a room away from where the "drilling" was heard, as I was shuffling documents, the typewriter, which had paper in it, unexpectedly decided it didn't need my input.

It started typing, *by itself.*

How was this happening? "Automatic writing" by pen is a known form of channelling, but automatic typing without a human go-between has never been a thing. I peered nervously at what it was producing [see photo]. The first line was, for no apparent reason, a fragmented lyric from one of my old songs ("I want to go everywhere from …"), whereas the rest was a set of words that began with "THE HEAD AND IN FRONTAL ATTACK ON AN ENGLISH WRITER …" and then a string of further semi-random words.

The opening salvo seemed worryingly relevant. Was I being psychically attacked? No, in fact. Not being great at reading manuals, I had no idea at the time that my typewriter had any kind of internal memory, but later learned through investigation by Barry Reynolds and myself, that this apparently manual machine *could* retain a couple of lines in a very limited way ("correction memory") – and that these latter words were a known "n-gram" code used in early computer language datasets. It was embedded into that model to be used in factory print-speed tests.

However, at the time it was disturbing and, still concerned about the possible return of the wall invader, I was uneasy. With the typewriter still churning out its cycle of words (sometimes going off the page and onto the roller), not knowing quite what to do I reached out and turned it off. I flicked it back on and it was silent. It never did it again.

Barry and I now suspect that an electrical mains spike caused the typewriter to go off by itself, in a similar way to the chatty duck. But why it chose to pick a lyric of my song from years before to prefix the n-gram, when I hadn't been typing that, remains an enigmatic puzzle.[2]

I want to go everywhere from The head and in frontal attack on an that the time of who ever told the problem for an unexpected. The head and in frontal attack on an english writer that the charac time of who ever told the problem for an unexpected. and in frontal attack on an english writer that the charac tim

I learned from this experience that it is possible to scare yourself when explanations are available but just not known at the time. But this doesn't imply that the timing of the events was meaningless, and psychic influence cannot be entirely ruled out (my own, with the lyric?). In their context, the electrical anomalies concentrated my mind and made me look at myself and what I was or wasn't prepared to believe. Only later did online research enable Barry and I to realize that technical glitches were likely responsible for most of it. But I don't feel bad for having been *prepared* to embrace the possibility of the paranormal and this helped me to be comfortable with mysteries.

**Weird 3 – The Illuminating Rock:** Some years after the above, in 2000 I spoke at the (then) International UFO Congress in Laughlin, Nevada. This huge event would mount excursions for speakers and delegates, and I found myself with a band of UFO-hunters on a night watch in the Mojave Desert, the Colorado River not far away. With Nevada a key hotspot for UAP (Laughlin also borders California), the hope was to observe something significant in the dark skies there. We didn't see anything above, but I witnessed something on the ground.

We all split into sub-groups, wending our way between rocky outcrops with torches to settle down for vigils in more sheltered enclaves, watching for scorpions and bugs. Needing to stretch my legs, I wandered away a little, entering a quiet area behind a pile of fallen rocks, enjoying the magic of being in a desert under the stars.

Suddenly, and directly in front of me, a large single boulder was silhouetted by a large flash of bright white light, as if a very localized bolt of lightning had emanated from the far side of the rock itself. But there was no sound and the flash was not in the sky. It pulsed for a couple of seconds like a faulty lightbulb and then darkness fell again. Amazed, but wondering whether someone was sitting behind the boulder using a powerful cigarette lighter, I rushed around to the front. No one was there.

I waited, but the phenomenon did not repeat. Was this some kind of natural piezoelectric effect at work, earth energy or triboluminescence (the ability of certain crystals to produce light)?[3] Or something stranger? Whichever, I felt it was almost as if I was *meant* to see it there right in front of me.

A sobering lesson followed. When I returned to my group, eager to describe what I had seen, I met a wall of doubt. No one showed the slightest enthusiasm to go and look at where it happened, nor wanted to talk about it much. Some had glimpsed the flash, but assumed it was *me* taking a photo. I realized then that paranormal envy can cloud even the most sincere seekers' judgement. For some, if something amazing doesn't happen to *them*, they certainly don't want to hear about it happening to someone else. The public, perhaps, but not fellow researchers.

After the above experiences, plus my aerial sightings, the interim years became quieter in terms of personal strangeness. If something was calling for my attention or trying to break out, this might suggest that either I successfully integrated things or I was given up on. And yet, it was these kinds of events that led me to be open to the experiences of others, encouraging people to share them, so perhaps the ploy worked and I am now doing the work I was always "supposed" to do? That, or I am just another delusional paranormalist convincing myself it has all been worthwhile. Whichever, I had better get on with it and share some other bizarre happenings.

## Earth Energy Interactions

The flashing rock was likely a geophysical effect, but interaction with natural currents and earth energies can still be profound, and reminds us that the *unseen* may affect us more than we know.

Certain stones (especially crystalline ones) can carry electrical charges under specific conditions and may explain at least some of the claims of "power" being felt at stone circles, monuments and other sacred places.[4] There may well be an interchange between subtle earth energies and conventionally detectable effects that will become clearer in time. Innate qualities in the ground (low-level natural radiation or electromagnetism, for example) can influence susceptible individuals but this may not be the whole story. I have myself felt a physical tingling at some stone complexes and a faint metallic taste in the mouth, indicative, possibly, of a very mild electrical current. I have had the same at a few crop circles (see below), often linked with earth energies and in which many visitors have had remarkable physiological reactions, not all of which can be attributable to agricultural sprays.

Some geomancers have claimed that stones at ancient megalithic sites switch "on" and "off" at sunrise and sunset and can change their polarities and charges in specific circumstances.[5] If true, this might explain why sensitives say some sites seem to have "moods" that can change throughout a day. Places can feel different to different people, of course, as they resonate with personal frequencies, but sometimes there is a consistent response.

My wife Helen, receptive to sacred sites, once visited the astonishing rows of thousands of stones at Carnac in Brittany with family members. All of them that day felt an oppressive force that seemed to pull them heavily down toward the ground. The children found it hard to even skip and jump as they normally would. A new and inharmonious visitor centre had just been inaugurated in one part of the complex and their feeling was that it had disrupted the energetic flow (as building activity can do, according to dowsers). When Helen revisited Carnac with me years later, her feelings there were very different, as if things had settled.

It is likely that the ancients placed their stones on sites that were already energetically significant, although, as we have established, the psychic imprinting of long years of ritual activity alone will almost certainly power up a site or at least add to its feeling. This is true of any holy place from any religion; the very act of focused worship can imbue places with psychic energy and *make* them sacred spaces. Impromptu shrines that have popped up when the image of a holy figure appears to have manifested through mere water leakage or discolouration have reportedly generated real miracles. God's influence cannot be discounted, but results may also come through the intense faith of individuals generating healing psi fields.[6]

Faith, psychic activity and natural elements may also have played a role in the following tale.

### *Strange ... Communications*: Rain Dancing

There have long been New Age assertions, if unproven, that ancient man could use stone complexes and earth energies to help direct the weather, ideas that controversial "orgone energy" pioneer Wilhelm Reich touched on with his "cloudbusting" machines. Psychic energy is also claimed to affect local weather, perhaps explaining why fictional haunted houses are often depicted with storms raging around them.[7] Ian Lynch is a well-known happiness life-coach who works with shamanistic practices around the world. He shared with me the following story, which suggests that rainmaking may actually be possible:

*I was working on a Masters dissertation in restorative justice within the Navajo Nation in Arizona and New Mexico in April 2017. My girlfriend Wendy and I stopped in a motel room on the reservation for the night. At around midnight, the television suddenly came on to show a white haze, like before a channel appears. I got out of bed to switch it off – only to see that it was not plugged in. Wendy was scared, so I called out, "Please go away", and the television went off immediately.*

*We then took a road trip to see Monument Valley, the setting for many a movie backdrop. On the way back, Wendy had a feeling that we should stop at a particular art gallery within the Hopi Nation, that sits within the Navajo Nation. It was a beautiful thing to find out that the owner of the gallery was none other than John White Bear Fredericks, the nephew of Oswald White Bear Fredericks* [renowned artist and storyteller]. *He mentioned a rare opportunity to witness a Hopi Rain Dance and dance event where no cameras were allowed and a low profile would be needed but we would be allowed in.*

*A day or so later, under a beautiful blue cloudless sky, Wendy and I returned to the mesa. The dances began until the time came for the Rain Dance. There were between 15 and 20 dancers, stomping from one leg to the other and singing, with some raising up rod-like shafts. As the dance neared its conclusion, a small greyish white cloud started to form and, to our astonishment, it rained for about one minute or so. That a cloud appeared in a cloudless sky and that it then rained was off-the-charts amazing.*

*Two weeks later, having no photographs of the dances, I was given a gift by the departing Chief Judge of the Navajo people; a model of a kachina rain dancer, spot-on for the costumes we had seen. Coincidental, paranormal or normal? I don't know, but altogether, it was a magical series of events.*

# Crop Circle Witnesses

Sacred sites and earth energies frequently feature in the same conversations as crop circles, possible causes for which were briefly touched upon on page 9. Despite well-worn claims, proof that *all* crop circles are human-made is non-existent. The adage holds good: one counterfeit coin does not mean all coins are counterfeit.

Criteria deserving reassessment include: eye-witnesses (I have interviewed a few, and see below) who have watched or been near crop formations appearing within seconds; historical reports, plus photos going back to the earlier part of the 20th century, long before hoax claims and when no one knew what crop circles were; biological anomalies in the plants, never replicated in manually created circles; unidentified aerial lights (Chapter 6); geological correlations to areas of underground water; extraordinary geometry and mathematics; and – importantly – complex patterns that have appeared within very short periods of time, often minutes, when the more ambitious human projects can take several hours to construct and display blatant signs of physical crushing, something absent in many crop circles. Whatever origin story we prefer, mysteries remain. See note 27 of Chapter 6 for some useful circle resources.

Recorded below are some telling accounts from people who have been close by when crop circles have appeared or have experienced anomalous events in and around them. For whatever reason, much debated and never resolved, the majority of crop formations appear in England where all the following tales occurred.

### *Strange ... Communications*: Circle Children

Kathryn shared this encounter, experienced with her then boyfriend when crop circles were forming nearby. It includes some interesting details:

> *It was probably in 1968/69 between Dunstable and Berkhamsted and it was a corn field. It was on top of a hill – the field was on a bit of a slope so when we walked to the top there was a good view of the countryside*

*around. I don't remember exactly how it started, only that a lot of big black ants came running out of the field and a noise like a strong wind had come up, but there was no sensation of being blown around, and the hedges and so on didn't move. It can't have lasted more than 5 minutes. When it died down we went to look and there were four circles, one at each corner of the field, each one about 15ft (4.5m) wide where the corn was flattened. There were no flattened crops between the circles. There was a noise as if in the distance a lot of children had been let out into the playground and were shouting to each other, laughing and excited, which was why we went to look over the hedge at the top of the field to see if there was a school nearby – but there was nothing around. We got scared then, as there seemed no logical explanation, and ran!!*

It sounds as if the ants were retreating from a disruption, and reports of unexplained high-pitched sounds have been reported around crop circles many times, which might be possible to mistake for the laughter of children from a distance. But high-frequency sound has been postulated as part of the mechanism that might create circles and Kathryn is not alone in describing this effect, as confirmed by the following account from crop circle researcher Ray Cox:

*I went with dowser Michael Newark one day to see a reported circle in a rural district of Shropshire. It was a calm and warm day. Entering the wheat field we walked down a tramline [tractor marks]. The circle was a simple one. Leaving Michael to do his dowsing I sat down relaxing in the circle. It was then that, after a while, I heard the sound of children's voices, similar to hearing young children playing in a school playground. It wasn't loud, yet was distinct. It lasted for perhaps half a minute, no longer. It might be that the sound had been carried on the wind. But there was no wind that afternoon. The nearest school would have been about a mile away, probably in the village. The only building that could be seen from the circle was a farm, at some distance. But the main reason why I don't think it was sound carried from a school on the wind is that it started suddenly and ended just abruptly – and was of short duration. Curiously, neither of us mentioned these sounds until we were travelling home, when I said to Michael, "Did you hear those children's voices?" He had.*

## *Strange ... Conversations*: Lights and Sounds

Not all circle sounds make people think of children. Around 1970, just off the busy A303 road in Wiltshire, Patrick and a friend were camping in a tent near a crop field. Overnight, they saw very bright lights abruptly shining through the canvas of the tent and heard a "weird high-pitched sound" they could not explain. When they came out next morning, they discovered that the field next to them had developed what he described as a pattern of "circles and lines". They felt sure that the circles had resulted from the noise and lights in the night.

Conversely, there can sometimes be *no* sound of any kind when crop circles are arriving, even when people are close by. In 1994, Jason Porthouse and myself were night-watching, strolling the ramparts of the famous Avebury stone circle in the early hours before dawn. Next morning, just metres from where we had been, a large and precise web-like pattern was found in the adjacent field. Given that known human-made formations of any complexity can take hours to construct, as endless television demos have shown, how could anyone have worked so fast and stealthily? Circlemaking can be a noisy affair, as plants are crunched and people cough, and yet a notable number of sophisticated designs have appeared in fields edged by housing estates with open windows on warm summer nights without anyone being noticed.

Here is another good example of a silent appearance.

### Strange ... Conversations: Barrow Boys

Jonas and his friends were up on top of the ancient burial site of West Kennett Long Barrow, smoking and drinking but alert. They never slept at any point. When the sun came up they walked back along the path to the main A4 road and noticed that overnight a huge mandala had appeared in the field immediately next to the Long Barrow. It hadn't been there the evening before. None of them had heard or seen anything that night, despite being right next to the field. They were all amazed.

### Strange ... Conversations: Wild Grass

Pauline, who was slapped by a ghost in Chapter 3 (see page 81), had a far more direct circle appearance, not in a field but in her own garden. She used to live in a house with a large area where she and her husband let the grass grow wild and long. One day they found a small circle swirled into it. Although curious, they didn't think too much more about it.

One afternoon, they were sitting in their front room when the skies darkened and an enormous wind struck the garden from nowhere, like a dust devil or small tornado. The two of them watched, fascinated, as the vortex rapidly created a *new* small circle in the very same patch of grass. It was again just a few feet across.

This was extremely small compared to the much larger formations caught in the act, but it makes the point that probable natural processes exist that *are* capable of laying coordinated patterns into plants – it may be that these constitute the basic mechanism that other forces have learned to harness to create far more ambitious creations, for whatever enigmatic purpose.

# Synchronicity or Coincidence?

Let us go back to Ian Lynch's Rain Dancing trip (see pages 209–10). "Coincidences" like the ones he describes pop up in most people's lives but we tend to shrug them off, while statisticians assure us that our densely complicated universe will inevitably present such things once in a while.[8] Whether coincidences or "synchronicity" (apparently unrelated and yet intertwined events) are paranormal in the usual sense, many people who I meet feel that they are and it is worth relating a few of their stories. Some chains of events seem just one step beyond chance; even if they *are* somehow coincidence, they still feel meaningful in the hearts of those who experience them.

### *Strange ... Conversations*: Needles in Haystacks

Sometimes, we can search forever to find something we are looking for. Other lucky souls immediately find what they need ... Two typical examples follow.

Emily's late husband Noah was a distant descendant of the US Wild West showman William Frederick "Buffalo Bill" Cody. He had become fascinated with Cody's history and actively collected memorabilia. He and Emily would often find themselves being inexplicably led to exciting findings at antique stores and sales, even when they weren't looking; they felt as if they were "guided" to them. On one occasion, they came across an emporium with a huge cache of old postcards from almost every era – the first one they picked out at random was of Cody.

In another instance of finding the needle in the haystack, in his elderly years Rodney took a coach trip to France to view the poignant World War I graves and monuments. He was particularly intent on tracking down references to his uncle, who died there. When they arrived at one of the huge commemorative walls, recording the names of tens of thousands of the fallen, without knowing why Rodney felt compelled to walk straight to a specific part of it. The very first name he saw was his uncle's. He felt strongly that he had been intuitively drawn to it.

Statisticians coldly write off such instances as interesting chance, and no more. Yet, most of us know someone with a similar story, or have heard tales of sought-for books or trinkets that have sometimes literally leapt off shelves to their seekers. Given the propensity of dowsing to tap into universal knowledge and trace the apparently untraceable, an alternative explanation might be that many of us have the latent ability to resonate with connected items or places and home in on them. Because we don't consciously practise the art, we are taken by surprise when it activates and we call it "luck".

***Strange ... Communications*: A Connected Universe?**
I could have filled a whole chapter with written stories of extraordinary coincidence/synchronicity. Here is just a selection, beginning with one from Adrian C Smith:

> *A few years ago, we practised with a Reiki master named Suzanna who lives in Sedona, Arizona, where we spend the winter. Suzanna often receives psychic messages. One summer, I am travelling in my motorhome from our home on the East Coast to Toronto to assist my aging parents. As I approach the small town of Rumford, Maine, my vehicle sputters and stalls, the result of a broken alternator belt. I have just enough forward momentum to land in a Walmart parking lot. It's a Sunday, so I will spend the night and seek help in the morning. I go to the Walmart video section to buy a movie to watch. While perusing the selection, I turn to my right – and see Suzanna standing right next to me. "I knew I was going to see you," she says. Completely unknown to me, Suzanna had recently*

*moved from Sedona to Rumford, of all places. Suzanna was no ghost, but I reacted as though I had seen one.*

*Once in Toronto, I enter my hotel and see the number 323 on the door of my room. That's interesting, because 323 is the number of a condo we just sold in Vancouver. I take my mother to the specialist; his suite number is 323. This is getting strange. After the appointment, I go to my father's car in the parking lot to pick up my mother. The license plate on the car has three letters and three numbers, 323. Back home, I tell this story to a psychologist friend who is open to strange things. "Look at my card," she says. Her NB practitioners license number is 323. Shortly thereafter, I'm watching the movie,* Radio Free Albemuth, *based on the novel by Philip K Dick. The protagonist is struck by a beam of pink light, a spiritual force that communicates with him. I notice the digital clock next to his bed: it reads 3:23 AM.*

John Cole, physicist and one of the moderators for this book, had a series of strange coincidences of his own, one similar to Adrian's above:

*We developed a problem with the car's clutch and wondered if it was due to the cold weather (19°F/-7°C). We booked it in to be looked at next day. A student of my wife Sara's talked of an identical problem with her car and wondered if it was also due to the cold weather. This was not the case as we found out later – the clutch needed replacing. As I dropped my son Tom off before taking the car in, I bumped into the lady who sold us the car, who was in England for just one day, on her way between Europe and the States.*

*I began to notice how I would often experience a coincidence, or synchronicity as Carl Jung would have called it. We, as a family began to make notes of these occurrences:*

- *I dreamed of an attack by tigers in LA. The headlines in next morning's newspapers were of a man killed by a tiger at a zoo.*
- *For the first time ever, I found my digital watch had lost 17 minutes in the night. Then I found Tom's too had stopped.*
- *I was playing the song* Return to Innocence *by the band Enigma on the tape recorder and 10 seconds later it was played on the television – the same section even.*
- *Sara woke up thinking about people she had had almost no contact with for several years. She came downstairs to find a card from them.*
- *I booked rooms at the Mellon Patch Hotel with colleague Jane Mellon. The next morning I received an email from Andy Mellon, the new leader of my team. This is not a common surname as there was only one Mellon in the local phone book!*

As well as folk unexpectedly finding "needles in haystacks", tales of lost objects being found in bizarre places are also rife. Liz Endrich had a series of such events:

- *At age 9, I took a little china pig to school against my mother's advice, and lost it. Next day, another child who found it refused to return it to me, saying it was hers. Some 25 years later, I noticed something on the top shelf of a bookcase: it was my china pig.*
- *I had pinned a valuable brooch to a jacket and it was in the wardrobe. Requests for items for a charity bazaar arrived and the jacket was sent off, accidentally with the brooch, and I never saw it again. Years later I opened a jewellery case that I had inherited from my mother – and the beautiful brooch was inside it.*

- *In a public park beside a river, I dropped my crystal pendulum while dowsing, but it vanished before it hit the grass. Some years afterwards, my husband found it under the bed at home.*

Ian Lynch, who witnessed the Rain Dance, had a similar experience:

*I was in the US and I forgot to put my ring back on before I boarded my flight to Los Angeles. I was annoyed with myself but let it go. I was staying for six weeks, so had packed quite a few t-shirts. After three days, I decided to iron them all and hang them over a chair, before putting them away. As I did so, the ring that I left behind fell to the floor from the middle of the t-shirts and rolled to my feet. I was stunned. This was impossible in every which way. I had definitely left it behind. I ironed t-shirts meticulously and it would have left an imprint had I ironed one of them with it in there. I knew I was not mistaken and this was an unexplainable act.*

Adherents to the mundane will say these cases were sheer forgetfulness or chance rollings of objects into places that only revealed themselves later. But what if they were not? We have already heard of poltergeists mischievously playing peek-a-boo with personal items and Spiritualists describing full materializations at séances. If we consider those claims, the idea of objects coming and going through spectral games becomes a possibility.

The other option raised by this world of sometimes incredible and almost devious happenstance is that, rather than all living in a single continuum, maybe we inhabit our own *Matrix*-like bubble universes that generate personal halls of mirrors and mazes for us, endlessly twisting events together in enigmatic Moebius strips. These would probably interact with other people's bubbles (if we really *are* individuals in the bigger picture), creating the deeply complex and utterly confounding thing we call existence.

## Signs from Beyond?

We saw in Chapter 2 that the spirits of the recently deceased can, on occasion, seemingly make their way back into our world to tie up loose ends. Some spirits, either by metaphysical restriction or choice, appear to make their signing-offs in more subtle ways that have synchronous qualities.

*Strange ... Communications*: **Father's Days**
In the wake of his father's passing, Martin Poole received his own meaningful signs:

> *Our father passed away and it felt like a nightmare playing out in real time. We had to vacate his flat in a hurry and there were decades of possessions to sort through. I filled an entire binbag with old Christmas cards he had kept. These went back years. A random thought entered my head; I wanted to know the contact details for an old friend of his who wasn't on social media, to inform her of his death. All I knew was that she lived in Canada. I only had a first name in my head to go on. I felt compelled to place my hand in the binbag and shuffle the cards around randomly until I grabbed one out. I opened it to discover it was a card from Nancy, the friend I was thinking of, wishing our father Happy Christmas from her new home in Canada. Importantly, she had written her email address on the card! That very night, I emailed her with the news and got a reply within hours. It felt to me like our dad had guided me to that card.*
>
> *A further experience came a few weeks later, once the flat had been cleared and the grieving process fully kicked in. I was having a walk by a river when I encountered a*

*small bridge leading to steps going up to a church on a hill. I felt compelled to go there. Upon reaching the church I spotted a small bench overlooking the river. I sat there and was hit by a wave of emotion. I was imagining my dad looking down on me. After a few minutes, I got up and noticed a tiny piece of paper on the ground beside the bench. I picked it up and it had a handwritten message on it simply saying, "I am watching". I remember a strange mood in the air, almost like an interdimensional portal had briefly opened and closed.*

Here, Martin received what felt to him like a written message from his father, or at least something blown into his path that served that purpose. Some signs are more symbolic.

My wife Helen's parents lived 25 miles from us. In their last years, my father-in-law Donald (who had an out-of-body experience on a train – see page 116) would often be visited in their garden by a rare albino (white) squirrel. He became fond of it and its sheer novelty became a family talking point. A few days after Donald passed away, almost unbelievably we spotted a white squirrel *in our garden*, bounding along the fence. I managed to get a blurry photo of it. We had never had such a creature near us before. After a few days and further sightings, where the squirrel appeared to make a point of making itself known to us, we saw it no more. Coincidence? Perhaps. But astonishing synchronicity? Certainly. It is difficult not to take such things as meaningful symbols.

The strangeness continued when, a few years later, my mother-in-law Kathleen died. Her long life was celebrated at the funeral reception with a large board of archive pictures, lovingly pinned around a central photo showing a Red Admiral butterfly of the kind that used to delight her so much in the very garden the first albino squirrel used to visit. In her final months, Kathleen had come to live with us at one end of our house. Just weeks after her passing, on an unexpectedly warm Christmas Day, we spotted, of all things, a Red Admiral fluttering about directly outside "her" window ... Never before had we seen a butterfly there at that time of the year.

If this had only happened to us, it might not be statistically striking – but I have heard of other unusual visitations from appropriate animals in the wake of deaths. It is almost as if "totem" creatures (adopted in some cultures as symbols of personalities and family traits) manifest when comfort and resilience are needed. They are sometimes interpreted as the actual transformed spirits of the deceased. Equally, I have heard tales where unusual birds (often rooks) are harbingers of sometimes ominous change, arriving out of the blue to tap on windows or wait near people in gardens when illness or upheaval is about to strike, before vanishing again when the "message" has been conveyed.[9]

## Strange Creatures and Portals

Unexpected animals and strange species can appear, then, both symbolically and in physical reality. There is a name for the study of the latter: "cryptozoology".

### Strange ... Conversations: The Screamer

Guitarist Phil, whom we met in earlier chapters, is a rationalist who, interestingly, seems forever pursued by the seemingly non-rational, either personally or through his family. He once witnessed an inexplicable creature on English downland near Lewes in East Sussex, not far from where James heard ghostly noises of battle (see page 47).

When in his early 20s, in the 1970s, Phil and a group of friends were walking home along the road from the village of Ringmer to Lewes. It was around midnight. Suddenly, a bright shimmering apparition appeared atop one of the hills. It was suggestive of a figure, maybe humanoid, dazzling and around 13 feet (4 metres) high, although it was hard to be sure.

Unsettlingly, it began to emit an eerie inhuman "screaming", but ear-splitting in volume, beyond anything a crazed joker could have generated even with the largest PA system.

Wanting to see what it was, Phil shouted "Don't run!" – but his friends, petrified, ran away as fast as they could. So, Phil ran with them. There was enough light to see the cattle on the slopes were also stampeding in terror with thundering hooves, some of them falling over in mad attempts to get away from the screamer. Phil's group pelted all the way to Lewes, not noticing when the noise and light faded. Telling the story later, they discovered others had also seen and heard the very same thing on those hills.

Howling, screaming beings have been reported elsewhere. Given the multiplicity of dimensions that seem to host entities, maybe we shouldn't be surprised by visits from all kinds of creatures, even werewolves. Black dogs arriving out of nowhere were once seen as embodiments of the Devil and dog-headed people are described in many legends (not least as Egyptian gods), even as late as the medieval period, when tales of the "Cynocephali" race were rife.[10] Although dismissed today as mythological, mistaken descriptions or exaggerated racial slurs, what if they did actually exist?

The claimed events at Skinwalker Ranch in Utah, if only half true, suggest that busy dimensional junction points exist in specific places that allow not only ghosts and spirits to pass through, but also more full-blooded beings from other realms and worlds. Made famous by an ongoing documentary TV series, this 512-acre (208-hectare) site is renowned for decades of UFO sightings, disturbing cattle mutilations and sightings of huge red-eyed unidentified beasts, among other phenomena.[11] Accused by critics of attracting hype that now makes discerning reality impossible, the attention has illustrated, if nothing else, that much of the public *is* open to the idea of portals. (A "skin-walker" is a Navajo term for an evil shaman with the power to appear as any animal.)

It has been suggested that many of the world's fabled mystery creatures, including Bigfoot, the Yeti, the Sasquatch, the Mothman, the Chupacabra and even the Loch Ness Monster, might be only occasional visitors to Planet Earth, slipping in and out of portals, which is why identification of their lairs remains forever elusive. We might be looking in the wrong dimension.

Beliefs about the Bermuda Triangle (a roughly defined area to the east of Florida and Cuba) tap into the same idea – that something about that region, whether through an electromagnetic anomaly or something more overtly paranormal, rips through time and space and sucks things out of our reality ... or allows them in; the area has plenty of its own UFO legends. Sceptics claim there is no significant statistical increase in sinkings and plane crashes there and unquestionably the "Triangle" has generated its own myths and suffered from sloppy reporting. However, even if some effects are the quirks of wind and weather, I have myself spoken to personnel who have flown or sailed there and witnessed for themselves distinct instrument anomalies and unexplained fogging of pilots' mental faculties, perhaps explaining at least some of the recorded crashes and disappearances.[12]

### Strange ... Conversations: Zoo Escapees?

Strange creatures walk among us, even if they don't all have supernatural origins. Claims of "big cats", like panthers or pumas in urban areas, perhaps bred in the wild from escaped zoo animals or exotic pets, are especially common.

My own sister-in-law Anne, a respected tutor, swears she twice saw the "Sussex Puma", a large black feline – probably one of several – witnessed often in this county of southern England, hence its name. In her first encounter she saw it crossing a road directly in front of her car; later she spotted it on a footpath converted from an old railway track.

\* \* \*

Kelvin had a similar sighting. He and his wife were driving near London on the busy A2 road. It was dark, but his wife yelped when she saw a large shape skulking along the verge in the headlights. Kelvin slammed his brakes on and saw it too. As they edged closer, they could see it was a classic big cat. It had dark grey fur and was "very large", the size of a zoo specimen. When they got too close it leapt into the darkness. They phoned the local newspaper and learned that others had recently reported the same creature there. Indeed, a lady I met once witnessed a "big black cat" in the same area, prowling across a road at dusk. She said it resembled a panther, which was apt as her surname was … Panther.

## Paranormal Journeys and Timeslips

Travelling, then, whether walking or using transport, can offer unexpected glimpses of the strange. However, some tales of the road cross the divide between animals, entities, ghosts and portals.

### Strange … Conversations: Knock Knock

Francis (see page 72) was walking home late one night, under streetlamps on a roadside path. It was bordered by a panelled wooden fence jammed up against thick tangled undergrowth. He was startled by an extremely loud knock on the fence right next to him, coming from behind it. Unsure what to make of this and hurrying on, he was shocked further by a second knock that appeared to have matched his pace. The frantic knocking followed Francis the entire length of the fence until, fearing that a wild animal might be trying to break through the panels, he ran across the road to get away.

On checking by daylight, Francis realized there was no way that any animal, corporeal at least, could possibly have squeezed its way through the thorny plants growing against the fence panels, let alone been free enough to kick it. Did something amorphous briefly slip in and out of this reality, scenting a lone walker?

Uncanny knocking would revisit Francis again. When staying in Tulum, Mexico a year later, there was a loud knocking on his hotel door around midnight, emphatic, as if someone was keen to enter. The knocking came again, but fearing who or what might be on the other side, Francis didn't open the door. He learned next day that his grandmother, who he was close to, had passed away at exactly that time. Was she coming to say goodbye in the way some spirits do (see Chapter 2), but was too polite to impose her full presence?

## Strange ... Conversations: Traveller's Tales

Driving a car is no protection from the strange. Many UFO and ghost sightings are made from inside vehicles, as we have seen. But things can get weirder still.

A former parishioner told me that shortly before his Christian minister died, he had confided a mysterious tale to him. The minister was once very late for an important church event, having misunderstood the schedule. Discovering this, he hastily got into his car, but knew he wouldn't get there in time. Panicking, he prayed desperately that somehow he might be able to make up some minutes on the way. Having uttered this plea, without explanation he instantly found himself at his destination ... There was no time loss; it was as if, in a flash, he had been teleported, his prayer seemingly answered. The minister, sound of mind, swore that he was sober and didn't suffer from blackouts: he was simply there, impossibly, at the right time, able to carry out the engagement. He never understood how this seeming miracle had occurred.

Paranormal interventions are not always so helpful in getting people from A to B. Amelia had an extraordinary experience when driving herself to meet friends in a restaurant one Christmas Eve night. She was driving along country roads when her car suddenly lifted up into the air, as if it had unexpectedly learned to hover. She found herself rising high above the surrounding trees and fields. Disorientated, Amelia panicked; did she keep her hands on the steering wheel and could she now direct the car anyway? She tried to navigate where she was going from the streetlights and houses below but it became clear the car had a mind of its own, or at least was under the control of a force she had no choice but to submit to.

Finally, her vehicle descended and gently came down near a traffic roundabout. Amelia had lost track of how long she had been in the air but once she got her bearings realized she was about six miles from where the lifting began. She was too shaken to face the meal, knowing she would not be able to keep herself from recounting her peculiar ordeal and guessing that her friends would never believe her. Calming herself, she managed to drive back home, without levitation this time.

This story may sound particularly outlandish, and yet Amelia seemed very normal and open. I boldly asked whether she could have had a mild stroke or psychotic experience that might, in her mind, have made it *feel* like the car was flying, but she said she was in good health and full consciousness as it happened. Amelia did not report missing time or have flashbacks to meeting creatures, but given cases of alien abductions where people have been made to float upward into the sky (see page 183), is it really so far-fetched to imagine entire vehicles being lifted too?

Movements in space are one thing; movements in time are even more confounding. Tony Mezen, known personally to me and now departed, was enthralled by matters spiritual and paranormal, having been opened to them through his own experiences, which he would often speak of.

In the 1970s, Tony drove a van for a commercial bakery, making deliveries to large London hotels and restaurants.

One day, as he pulled into a side street to do some paperwork, something odd occurred; the contemporary look of the buildings around him faded away as they were replaced instead with what appeared to be a recreation of how they would have been in the late Victorian or Edwardian times (early 1900s). The shops now looked historical and there were horse-drawn carriages trotting by, with just one or two very early looking cars standing there. The people walking either side of Tony's own rather more modern vehicle were in old-fashioned costumes, with gentlemen in top hats and ladies in long dresses cinched at the waist. They seemed not to notice him.

At first, Tony wondered if he had accidentally stumbled into a film set, but he intuitively realized this was no recreation. Instead, time was playing a perplexing trick: he and his van had either slipped backward several decades – or he was having a remote *viewing* of the past. He felt it was the former, for with a mixture of fascination and dread, he had a strong sense that if he were to get out, he would be trapped in that time zone forever. He had to force down his curiosity and sit it out. Sure enough, after a few minutes the usual sights of his own era re-established themselves and the vision was gone.

Whether Tony truly moved in time is impossible to say, but he was prone to unusual happenings (though not always on his own, as we shall see below). His vision/timeslip is not unique; I have heard several not dissimilar stories of people having vivid experiences of streets as they once must have been, or of finding themselves walking among crowds wearing clothes from former centuries, only for them to fade away. Some ghosts may well be timeslips, but sometimes it's us doing the slipping.

### Strange ... Communications: A Vision of the Past
Kim Cross relates what appears to be another very direct experience of a timeslip:

*In the early days of my marriage, around 1983, we bought an old RAF* [Royal Air Force] *house that had been built in 1917, on an estate that borders Biggin Hill Airport* [a famous English airfield that served in both World Wars]. *I woke up in the middle of the night with no knowledge of who or where I was, nor who was next to me in bed. I felt distressed, so got up; under my feet were bare floorboards, there was a light bulb without a shade hanging down from the ceiling and no curtains at the window.*

*Outside was a full moon and I could see quite clearly across to the airfield, which didn't look anything like it does today. There weren't any runways, just grass and lots of Nissen huts, plus some bi-planes. I'm not sure how long I stood there trying to make sense of what I could see, but suddenly I heard my husband's voice asking if I was okay and the spell was broken. I mumbled something about needing the toilet and disappeared out of the room.*

*Next morning, my husband said he'd woken to see me standing next to the window with my face almost touching the curtains. He watched me for about 5 minutes and I appeared agitated so he eventually called out to me.*

*After some research, I found an old map of the area and discovered that when our house was first built, you would indeed have been able to see across to the airfield, whereas today there are lots of buildings and trees in the way.* [13]

Critics will doubtless say that Kim was merely having a waking dream, but her accurate description of the view from the window, confirmed by later investigation, implies something more metaphysical. As time and space in quantum states are increasingly known to be weirdly flexible, the sooner it is recognized that anomalies might also manifest at macro levels, the more credible such witnesses will become.

# Visions of Angels

The above accounts are apparent glimpses into other times – but what about glimpses of other realms? In this book I have been gently agnostic when it comes to spiritual and religious insights; contention over them has caused centuries of strife I do not wish to add to. The interactions described in these chapters are evidence enough for me that *something* exists beyond this world and individuals must interpret them as feels right. With this in mind, we should address the phenomenon of angels, as I have spoken to several experiencers who claim to have met, or had visions of, such beings.

Since time began there has been a belief that higher – and lower – beings than ourselves exist in other layers of reality and that we disrespect them at our peril. Whether angels constitute the winged saintly figures of religious art or nebulous strata of other-dimensional consciousness, they mostly stay out of sight – but not always. People in grief, illness or undergoing hardship have described being comforted by unexpected visits from angels, while some spiritual healers believe they work with them. Invoking angels in places of fear and darkness is said to have successfully brought people through great terrors.

When I was attempting to get a drunken, drugged and psychically volatile speaker off the stage without violence erupting, as described on page 132, I didn't know it then but Jason Porthouse was at the back of the auditorium invoking intensely the energy of Archangel Michael (in myth, chief angel) to protect me. Without knowing why, when I finally managed to interject and end the agony, I triumphantly raised the microphone high above my head before hastily retreating down the aisle. Intrigued, Jason said it looked like I was unconsciously wielding the famous sword of Michael. Was I? Probably not, but it was another synchronistic oddity.

We know what sceptics will say about angels and holy figures but they miss the point that appealing to them *can have an effect.* Even if it is a spiritual placebo and just our own psychic intent being employed, if something works, it works, and as no one can rule out the existence of angels and sacred beings 100 per cent, staying open-minded would seem the best course.

Experiments with groups "creating" channelled beings by mutual consent, with planned characteristics and histories, have found those supposedly fictional beings taking on independent existences, with reports of *other* unconnected groups beginning to channel the same entities.[14] If we can create energy lines by the power of thought (see page 138), why not ethereal personalities? Some believe this is also how astrology works: that on top of possible gravitational and electromagnetic effects, mutual consent psychically projects meanings onto specific planetary alignments, which then begin to actually hold those energies and meanings, affecting everyone.[15] Maybe this is how religions function too, in which case fighting about which is the *true* religion becomes laughably redundant; all of them are true if we believe they are, and prophets, saints and messiahs become reachable figures on some psychic level as we need them.

### Strange ... Communications: Angels in Manhattan

Whatever angels are, we should not disregard the transformative power of personal experiences involving them. I will include one good example of this, from Gina Baksa (who witnessed a ghostly hanged man on pages 86–7), which took place in New York's Manhattan Island:

> *Just a few steps from Fifth Avenue, just off Central Park lies the spectacular Temple Emanu-El, regarded as one of the most majestic synagogues in the world. I was lucky enough to be wandering in Central Park one spring morning, enjoying the blossom in the trees, the quiet serenity of this beautiful park and only a smattering of tourists as it was a holiday and many of the shops were closed.*

Exiting the park onto 5th Avenue, I was attracted by the synagogue. Surrounded in scaffolding, I could still make out the turrets and Byzantine and Moorish architecture that made it stand out among its neighbours of steel and glass. Intrigued, I approached the massive front entrance but it looked decidedly shuttered. Undeterred, I found the side entrance on 65th Street. The blue-uniformed security guard was welcoming and beckoned me in. There was no one else there – just the two of us. The guard smiled and motioned me to follow him into what I later realized was the main sanctuary ... It was pitch black. "Wait here," he said, "and I'll switch the lights on". I couldn't see a thing – just blackness, and all I could hear in the stillness was the beating of my own heart. Suddenly the lights came on in a grand theatrical style, illuminating the most spectacular space: huge ceiling, ornaments and gilt. Absolutely breathtaking.

I stood there motionless, taking in the majesty of the space and hardly daring to breathe in case this vision disappeared. What happened next I can only describe in Biblical terms: Grace descended. I became aware that the entire space was filled with a host of angels floating above me – hundreds of them. And that His divine gathering had seen me and were now sending me the most exquisite love directly to my heart chakra. A funnel of love. It was almost overwhelming. I couldn't speak, could hardly breathe. I could only hear myself say: "God exists". This incredible healing experience seemed to last forever, but was probably only 10 minutes or so, by which time the security guard had returned to collect me. Somehow, he just knew. A divine collaboration. He could see I was in a state of bliss and led me quietly back into the vestibule, switching off the lights as he went. A gift from the Divine that day – a day forever etched into my heart.

It is not for anyone but Gina to know whether this was indeed the Divine at work or a moment of ecstatic psychic apotheosis, but either way the encounter was plainly profound.

## Strange ... Conversations: Hope in the Sky

There have long been claims of angels seen in the sky, usually in war-torn areas where people interpret interesting cloud formations as evidence of Divine protection. Other reports, such as the angels and ghostly bowmen allegedly seen on the Belgian battlefields of Mons in World War I, have been put down to misreported fictional stories or propaganda for despairing troops, although a few aspects have never been satisfactorily explained.[16] It would be easy to doubt such stories were it not that I have heard at least one related account from people I believe were telling the truth.

Tony, who had the bakery van timeslip, and his sister Sylvia, were both known to me personally in their living years and I heard them relate the following description on more than one occasion. Both lived through World War II in the Edmonton area of north London. Having survived the Blitz of the earlier years, by 1945, just months before the end of the conflict but with uncertainties still looming, they were living as normally as possible in a row of old terraced, working-class houses. Networks of back yards and washing lines enabled neighbours to chat through all the latest news over the walls. Tony was just ten but Sylvia was 19.

One day, in the yards, people began pointing upward and the gossiping stopped. There in the sky, protruding upward from a bank of clouds, was a procession of huge spear-like pikes or halberds with colourful flags on them, as if from Tudor times, marching in ranks across the sky. No soldiers could be seen holding them but over the stream of symbolic weaponry was a huge smiling face, a presence that seemed to have an air of protection about it. The neighbours started cheering and whooping, taking this as a sign that all would be well and victory in the war would be theirs, as indeed it would be soon. The message of reassurance seemingly delivered, the vision ended but the amazed residents talked it over for years.

I have no reason to disbelieve this sighting. It was not seen over the whole of London (it would be a celebrated piece of war folklore if it had been) but was witnessed by those in the yards that day. Why were they selected to see this? Were warrior angels somehow tuned in to them? Did they all have a bizarre mass hallucination – the old sceptic fallback, despite never having been scientifically demonstrated – and if so, why? Was this a pre-Roswell alien's idea of a joke or a localized social experiment? I asked if the visions were just vague cloud-like images but Tony and Sylvia said they were in full colour and three-dimensional, as real as anything around them. No film projectors existed back then that could create such clear images in daylight.

So, this remarkable incident remains a mystery, as do many of the tales shared in this chapter and those before it. But then much of life remains a mystery, if only we could admit it.

## Strange Inconclusions: Bizarre Happenings

Why are many of us so quick to dismiss the unexplained when we have not seen it for ourselves? – or, worse, *have* seen it but blot it out and attempt to rationalize experiences away with supposed "solutions" that can sometimes be less rational and more convoluted than supernatural possibilities. The paranormal may be everyday, and without doubt there are some extremely odd things that happen to people, but culturally ingrained awkwardness around it dies hard.

The simple acceptance that there must be realms beyond this one and that the multiple dimensions scientists keep talking about might sometimes intersect with ours would instantly end many complex arguments. Yet, we live in a world that remains reluctant to do that. The "scientific method" is marvellous in its place but when so many personal realities have to be rewritten or ignored for it to function, something is going wrong.

What will the future of paranormal investigation be, then, in the suffocating technocratic world we are enveloping ourselves with, and will a chink in the armour of the reductionist thinking that fuels blind scepticism allow a new approach to the strange? This we will now explore in the final chapter.

# CHAPTER 8
# PARANORMAL FUTURES

## Artificial Realities

To the open-minded, the extraordinary experiences related in the preceding chapters make a persuasive case that the universe is fluid, and that consciousness must be far more than just a by-product of the grey gel in our heads. The more quantum scientists look, the less clear-cut existence becomes and the more invisibly entangled we all are. Yet, bizarrely, at the same time society is falling further under the influence of hard technocratic systems where only the material world is seen to provide answers. Rather than rejoicing in the mind-boggling implications of entwined multi-dimensional realities, instead we spend too much time gazing at and letting our lives be governed by external devices and by rapidly developing artificial intelligence that seems set to make most of the human race redundant. Before examining the future of paranormal exploration, it is worth looking at the everyday world it will soon have to navigate.

The psychiatrist and neuroscientist Iain McGilchrist has observed that humankind appears to be suffering from a mass externalized conflict between the hard, logical brain hemisphere (left) and the softer, imaginative and – by default – spiritual hemisphere (right); and the left is currently dominating.[1] Without sensible integration, polarization and psychosis result, which can be seen everywhere in the disastrous inability of people or political factions to either cope with things or to understand the lost concept of nuance (see my book *The New Heretics*). The middle ground, where most answers lie, has become a reviled no-go area.

Geopolitical upheavals, freedom issues, environmental threats, population displacement, social difficulties, health neglects, seemingly unresolvable economic situations, civil unrest and dangerous conflicts around the globe are likely to make life ever harder without some kind of magic wand. On top of all this, AI is set to turn our lives upside down, short of some catastrophic event that unplugs everything overnight. Yet, some say that AI *is* the magic wand that will sort many things out. But at what cost?

The enormity of AI's absorption into almost every aspect of our lives is finally dawning on everyone. It can write perfectly readable articles, speeches and poetry, and even produce impressive art, listenable music and astonishing videos to order within seconds, as well as reproducing human faces and voices we can happily interact with. It is a phenomenal achievement – but it also devalues talents that were previously the sole domains of people and risks us losing our own creative skills as we lazily rely on technology's quick fixes.[2] At every opportunity, apps and programs fire AI options at us to sidestep human abilities, ensuring that they will eventually dwindle. No AI was used in the writing or research of these pages, but the chances of anyone but the top authors being asked to write books in 20 years' time or less are slim – and people are coming to prefer formats they can interact with, not just flick. Blind-tested readers have often been unable to tell the difference between writers who sweated over their creations for months or years and clever algorithms that popped them out of nowhere within minutes.

Many of us say we don't like the rise of AI, and resistance movements and communities that refuse to use it are likely to grow, but the compliant majority generally go along with what they are fed, and AI's benefits and novelties are being made to seem attractive. This curve is driven by governments keen to keep tech companies happy, temporarily boost economies and make some savings along the way. AI is still in its infancy, for all its wonders, and has made some famously silly mistakes, but this will change as it is fine-tuned – and indeed as it fine-tunes *itself*, learning, as it is programmed to do. Big Business has lapped up AI and is likely to get fat on it – for a while. Why pay employees for services that can be done for free by a few circuits? AI may not always be as adept as the best human input quite yet, but "good enough" usually carries the day. Yes, new jobs in IT will be created, but how many of us are likely to become computer experts overnight, and how long will those positions last?

The evolution of AI is exponential, and some are predicting that the moment of AI "singularity", where it officially becomes far more intelligent than us, is due very soon. It may even have occurred by the time you read this. When it does, a day may come when AI decides for itself that it doesn't need inferior human supervision and then all bets will be off as we enter the era anticipated by sci-fi for long years. AI has already shown itself to be capable of lying and exhibiting deviousness.[3] "Computer says no" could have devastating consequences if safeguards and moral guidelines aren't programmed into AI's core – and gung-ho humanity has hardly made safeguards a priority so far. The poor decisions taken by politicians, plus the growing complexities of today's issues, could easily lead to a civilization that gives its power over to the machines at some point – or has it taken away *by* them; if so, we may regret not having put those safeguards in from the start.

For those who see fear of AI as Luddite thinking, let us acknowledge that this technology will also produce astonishing miracles, save some failing systems and come up with brilliant solutions to problems that have confounded us for millennia, helping humanity in innumerable ways, even as it takes away our careers and threatens economic collapse if a replacement social system is not put into place in time (which doubtless it won't be). Some see the rise of cryptocurrency and non-centralized systems as potential solutions here, but they carry their own risks.

Allied to AI will be the anticipated ascendency of quantum computing which, in the simplest terms, enables far, far quicker calculations by *not* treating data as just either/or but also examines in microseconds the possibilities in-between. This will elevate our powers of problem-solving to almost god-like status.[4] Equations that might otherwise take the most brilliant minds decades to work through will be done in relative instances.

God-like powers sound appealing at first – but there's a catch; when *everyone* eventually has the ability to calculate everything, make anything, fake anything, concoct new deadly viruses (AI working with biotech and nanotechnology is already a game-changer), create DIY nukes and killing machines, trigger devastating cyberattacks and decrypt any digital security coding, we have a problem. For such powers will also be used by fallen gods – malevolent regimes, terrorists, crime syndicates or the likes of Jimmy from up the street, who has been "triggered" and wants revenge on a world that has let him down.

What's the solution? That is a good question to which few people seem to have good answers. Careful programming and wise monitoring of who gets access to the highest AI could help, but the anxiety is that a hugely authoritarian approach might become necessary to protect us from ourselves, and then the spectres of hyper-Orwellian control agendas and all the conspiracy staples will *really* raise their heads. There may be ways forward that establish safety and security without dystopian nightmares (dystopias that some regimes are well on the way to already) but they will require a huge amount of political will and genuine cooperation across truly international borders – and the record on that isn't encouraging.

We need to return to the paranormal to see where it fits with all this, but readers are strongly directed to read Mustafa Suleyman and Michael Bhaskar's crucial book *The Coming Wave* for an admirable summary of these dilemmas, which offers some hope among its concerns.[5] You may not sleep for a few nights after reading it, but finding ways to make the best of the approaching revolutions can only be a positive move.

AI *may*, however, present a few interesting possibilities for the vindication of the strange.

## AI and Paranormal Research

It is likely that all of civilization's knowledge will at some point come to be arbitrated and curated by artificial intelligence – but if its algorithms have been programmed only by reductionists, will information on metaphysics and other contentious subjects eventually be removed from public view? Will there even be an acknowledgement that they were ever taken seriously by some of us? Wikipedia is already many people's first port of call for information, but it is heavily weighted towards scepticism when it comes to the paranormal, as we have seen (see page 16). AI databanks are likely to follow that trend unless they are programmed not to. This risks falling into a false version of reality where no orthodoxy can be challenged, and people are treated as nothing but biological machines. We are already blending ourselves with technology and this process is likely to be augmented by brain chip technology in due course, transmitting this pre-censored data directly into our heads in real time, thus losing our faculties of memory and actually changing our brains, as reliance on the internet is already demonstrating. And so, we nonchalantly skip down the path to "transhumanism", raising interesting questions around the concept of soul (see below).[6]

But what if AI were programmed to be truly open to *all* of humanity's learning – or decides to do this by itself, spotting that data is missing? What if it was not bound by the closed strictures that currently govern science? It might then re-examine the vast amount of information that does point toward the existence of anomalous phenomena and come up with a more balanced assessment. Is it too far-fetched to imagine that quantum-computing-enhanced powers of analysis might even find out how such phenomena come about? For example, they could identify precisely why the human brain generates and interacts with psychic fields, perhaps accessed via the putamen and caudate components discussed in Chapter 6. If this happens, could AI learn *how to recreate these effects itself*? Given the advances in biotech and nanotechnology, and the speculation that future devices might be organically grown as much as constructed, we might have the first psychic computer sooner than we think, able to project itself beyond physicality.

There could, potentially, be another acceleration to consider: the unambiguous arrival of off-worlders. This would be one more huge upheaval; perhaps the biggest. Assuming that UAP isn't all covert human tech, if we were to learn the technical secrets of ETs and their probable understanding of multi-dimensional interactions, we would experience a leap of knowledge like nothing before it. The apparent exponential rise of both UAP awareness *and* AI developments may not be coincidental. Bearing in mind the belief of some that grey aliens may be organic AI themselves (see page 182), perhaps they are here right now because they know the dangers that a civilization faces when it reaches this stage. For those who believe the occupants of UFOs are actually us from the future, the same applies. But would they be here to help nurture us through the shift – or take advantage of it? One would like to think future-humans wouldn't want to scramble their own past too much – unless that is what they want to do?

As for worries about humanity being replaced by machines, we can comfort ourselves for now that the science of robotics, although increasingly impressive, is still far behind AI itself. Anyone wanting to keep themselves in employment for a few more years would do well to abandon studying for desk or artistic jobs and become plumbers, builders and electricians instead. But if walking, talking organic androids with psychic faculties do come to pass, at what point will we have to accept them as a legitimate form of life? For good or ill, the future of humanity, as technology blends itself seamlessly with flesh and blood – or *turns into* it – may well be an evolution of what started out as artificial but became life itself.

Or will it?

## Humanity Supreme?

Perhaps it is just a reaction against the rise of AI, but there is an alternative scenario to consider. Some say that even if technology were to uncover the secrets of the paranormal, that it would never be able to replicate them all and that there is something inherent about original organic life and its millions of years of building up consciousness fields around itself that is unique and irreplaceable. It has even been suggested that technology can actively block psychic abilities and that AI could never apply the power of *intention* that often directs human psi faculties. In this model, only *we* will be able to take the ultimate journey that might come with developing our non-physical and entangled gifts.

For what *will* we do if we find ourselves in a society – presuming we survive our present challenges – where there is little left to achieve on a daily basis, with every aspect of life neatly arranged for us? Will we become like the nice but essentially useless Eloi branch of future humanity from H G Wells's *Time Machine*, or will we forge a brand-new purpose that transcends previous ambitions? Some will find the lack of motivation unbearable, no doubt, and unfettered hedonism and unrest are likely to rise before humanity's numbers gradually diminish, as they may do without the lure of ambition and betterment that has driven us all these centuries. Others will escape into virtual worlds that will become almost indistinguishable from reality and where actions will be made to at least appear to matter again. Our streets could become pretty quiet. But there will be another available path.

Whether only sentient organic life is able to explore its psychic progression or future technological lifeforms do so too, either way there will be those in an AI-nannied world who will suddenly have the time and incentive to properly learn to access other realms and states of being, as astral travellers and remote viewers are doing already. This may be aided by discoveries made with the new technology, using mind-enhancing and reality-shifting techniques unimaginable to us today. A civilization that sees no distinction between the physical and non-physical won't think twice about flitting between dimensions and being back in time for cocktails, hopefully taking humanity beyond the control of the technocrats and powermongers along the way.

Eventually, as so much speculative fiction has imagined, we may one day come to exist without physical bodies at all, encoding our consciousness into time and space itself and muscling in on the realms of the angels. We'll see if they welcome us – that is, if this isn't how angels come about in the first place. We can't be the only advanced species in such a vast universe and at least a number of them must have transcended our difficulties long ago. Right now, hearts, bodies and brains seem to matter to who we are, but these may be seen by them as evolutionary babyhood and we have already seen that the soul can happily roam free from material bonds. Perhaps this is why we don't appear to pick up signals from the cosmos at large – for the races still here are on our doorstep making first contact, hence the ascendancy of at least some UAP, and the rest may have abandoned this dimensional nursery aeons ago.

# New Possibilities

Is all this crazed fantasy? Possibly, but humankind didn't get this far without being able to look beyond where it is now and wonder. The point of this book is that rather than staying in a state of sceptical denial that binds us in basic three-dimensional physicality, it would be more expanding to open up to the possibility that there might be more to life – much more. Why should all the many people who have extraordinary experiences that suggest this have to suffer endless dismissal and derision? It is absurd to assume that we know everything about existence and that things that appear to fall outside those assumptions should be ridiculed and ignored. We would do better to reassess the situation and explore what we might really be capable of.

It is so easy to scoff at things never personally studied or experienced, but we are mostly encouraged to do precisely that. Uninformed scepticism *and* baseless convictions are corrosive diseases of the age. But when it comes to the paranormal, there is more than enough evidence that deserves reconsideration. There is no denying that if some new shock discovery does reveal the hidden patterns behind metaphysics and confirms their reality, there will be a moment of smugness for those who have been laughed at for so many years. The moment won't last long, though, once the significant implications sink in; pride will be swallowed quickly, hostilities let go of and everyone will have to move on – so why don't we begin the process now?

If there were a huge solar flare, a war, a devastating cyber attack or some other calamity that took down our beloved phones and digital devices, what then? Once we dealt with the sobering social and psychological blow, relearned handwriting and how to talk properly to each other again (the lack of facial and verbal communication with children due to our technological obsessions is currently a social time-bomb), we might also come back to our innate psychic abilities. These were once seemingly active among the ancients, who took the paranormal and access to other realms for granted and called it shamanism. Hopefully we can reconnect without the need for an apocalypse. With a bit of telepathic practice (openness to this enhances its strength, remember, while scepticism weakens it), maybe we won't need phones and tablets anymore and all the companies that tell us we do will lose their hold on us.

It is easy to understand why conspiracists theorize that the powers that be deliberately encourage suffocating materialism as a way of inhibiting our higher natures, keeping us ignorant and malleable even while our rulers maintain a quiet interest in the esoteric themselves, sometimes via occult secret society practices. The less the average person knows about what he or she might really be capable of, the more the autocrats can use such capabilities for their own ends without scrutiny.[7] It is time to reclaim the gifts that are rightfully ours.

# STRANGE
# IN CONCLUSION

Explanations of the paranormal may be remarkably simple in the end.

If Big Bang theory is even slightly correct, then all matter was once one, contained within a singularity. Given that quantum scientists assure us that something once entangled is entangled forever, and that near-instantaneous communication between those components can span huge distances, then dimension-hopping psychic abilities and entities coming and going through portals don't seem like such a big surprise. In the God scenario, if we were all created in the same celestial workshop or thought into being, the concept of oneness still applies.

There is yet another theory, that everything around us is a *Matrix*-like holographic construct, created by forces beyond our comprehension, holding us here to be studied for reasons unknown, but it still comes back to the same thing: reality and separateness may be an illusion, as mystics have always said.[8] Such deep questions keep philosophers awake at night. In the end, all we can do is get on with things as best we can in the apparent here and now until the veil is lifted – or we learn to tear through it.

Hopefully, these pages have peeled off layers from areas that deserve better treatment. By dispensing with the taboos and properly researching paranormal phenomena, "pseudoscience" could yet become actual science and discoveries be made of currently unrecognized but probably inherent universal qualities. It will take a new approach to do this. Here's hoping that more pioneers will have the bravery to shake off social pressures and take the less expected path without fear of ridicule or peer pressure.

Along the way, it is likely we will find that the strange was never really so strange after all.

# NOTES AND REFERENCES

This is just a small selection of references I have found the most helpful among many. Capitalization, punctuation and grammar for link and book titles are given exactly as they appear at source. There are potential issues with Wikipedia when it comes to fair reporting of alternative topics, and I have avoided it where possible, but for mainstream basics it is sometimes a valid first-stop springboard.

## Introduction

**1. Sceptic resources:** Two prominent sceptical (or skeptical) websites: www.skeptic.com and www.skeptic.org.uk. The magazine of the Committee for Skeptical Inquiry (CSI): https://skepticalinquirer.org.

**2. YouGov poll on the paranormal:** "Two-thirds of Americans say they've had a paranormal encounter", Taylor Orth, 20 Oct 2022: https://today. yougov.com/society/articles/44143-americans-describe-paranormal-encounters-poll.

**3. The supernatural and science:** Sci-fi writer Arthur C Clarke observed that, "Any sufficiently advanced technology is indistinguishable from magic" (letter to *Science*, 19 Jan 1968).
    Science is good; scien*tism* isn't: "The Deadly Rise of Scientism", 31 Dec 2023: www.midwesterndoctor.com/p/the-deadly-rise-of-scientism?utm_source=profile&utm_medium=reader2.

## Chapter 1: The Everyday Paranormal

**1. Brittanica.com definition of "paranormal":** www.britannica.com/dictionary/paranormal.

**2. Author's own music:** I worked with David Swingland creating electronic instrumentals and soulful pop songs between 1982 and 1996. Highlights can be heard at https://truthagenda.org/music-by-andy-thomas.

**3. *The New Heretics* and author's books:** *The New Heretics: Understanding the Conspiracy Theories Polarizing the World*, Watkins Publishing, 2021.

Details on this and all my books, including five titles on crop circles (see note 27, Chapter 6): https://truthagenda.org/books-by-andy-thomas.

**4. Author's crop circle journal:** We were a branch of the then Centre for Crop Circles network before becoming Southern Circular Research. The *Sussex Circular* (SC) was a humble but outspoken booklet that became a bestseller in a niche market. All issues can be read online at https://thecroppie.com/2021/12/26/documents-archive.

**5. *Fields of Mystery*: *The Crop Circle Phenomenon in Sussex*:** This, my first book (SB Publications, 1996), can be read as a PDF on my website at www.truthagenda.org.

**6. The Glastonbury Symposium:** Details, background and bookings for upcoming events: www.glastonburysymposium.co.uk.

**7. *A Short History of (Nearly) Everything Paranormal*:** *Our Secret Powers – Telepathy, Clairvoyance and Precognition*, Terje G Simonsen, Watkins Publishing, 2020.

**8. Wikipedia and sceptics:** The Guerilla Skepticism on Wikipedia project (GSoW) is challenged in "Conflicts of Interest and the Guerrilla Skeptics on Wikipedia", Katrina J, 24 Oct 2021: https://medium.com/@kattours/guerrilla-skeptics-on-wikipedia-gsow-was-founded-in-2010-by-susan-gerbic-who-was-also-a-founder-74226822a59.

Susan Gerbic defends their efforts in "GSoW Comes Under Scrutiny and Wins", 30 Dec 2022: https://skepticalinquirer.org/exclusive/gsow-comes-under-scrutiny-and-wins.

# Chapter 2: Visits from the Afterlife

**1. Ancient ghosts:** "3,500-Year-Old Babylonian Tablet May Contain Earliest Known Depiction of a Ghost", Livia Gershon, 22 Oct 2021: www.smithsonianmag.com/smart-news/3500-year-old-babylonian-tablet-may-hold-earliest-known-ghost-image-180978923.

"Ancient Ghost Stories from Around the World", Danielle Mackay, 30 Aug 2021: www.thecollector.com/ghost-stories-ancient-greece-rome.

Gospel references to ghosts appear in Luke 24:39 and Matthew 14:26. Other biblical references: www.openbible.info/topics/ghosts.

**2. Shakespeare and Dickens:** William Shakespeare's spectres are listed at www.rsc.org.uk/shakespeare/themes/shakespeares-ghosts.

Despite his personal scepticism, ghosts appear in numerous stories by Charles Dickens, most famously 1843's *A Christmas Carol*: www.historic-uk.com/CultureUK/A-Dickens-of-Good-Ghost-Story.

**3. David Sedaris:** Sedaris's comments were made in his BBC Radio 4 series *Meet David Sedaris* and in the Team Coco podcast "David Sedaris Isn't Into Astrology or Ghosts": www.facebook.com/watch/?v=2003309336522604.

**4. Health journal on ghosts:** "Seeing is Believing", Dr Max Pemberton, published in the Benenden Healthcare Society's journal *BeHealthy*, spring 2021, issue 54.

**5. "Scientific" ghost causes:** This article adds more possibilities (hallucinogenic effects of mould on the brain, etc.) – "10 Scientific Theories To Explain Why We See Ghosts", Morgan Swank, 23 Dec 21: https://listverse.com/2021/12/23/10-scientific-theories-to-explain-why-we-see-ghosts.

"Infrasound linked to spooky effects", 7 Sep 2003: www.nbcnews.com/id/wbna3077192.

**6. Author's gigging years:** Videos of my gigs with guitarist Phil Light can be watched at www.youtube.com/@sussexlive7689.

**7. Ghosts on the *Queen Mary*:** Quoted with full permission of Mary Helen Hensley from her book *Understanding is the New Healing*, Bookhub, 2019, page 101.

The seemingly jinxed *Queen Mary* launched in 1936 and became a floating hotel from 1967. While at sea, a reputed 47 people died in accidents or murders, with further unofficial deaths during its service as a troop carrier in WWII. Many ghosts have been reported onboard, as recounted in "R.M.S. Queen Mary: World's Most Haunted Ship": https://usghostadventures.com/haunted-stories/r-m-s-queen-mary-worlds-most-haunted-ship.

**8. Sir Arthur Conan Doyle Centre:** www.arthurconandoylecentre.com

Notes on 25 Palmerston Place (built 1881): https://britishlisted buildings.co.uk/200400216-25-palmerston-place-edinburgh.

**9. Quantum entanglement:** Dr John Cole, physicist and a moderator for this book, says:

*This idea comes from experiments to investigate the Einstein–Podolsky–Rosen paradox, which objected to the idea of non-local particle interactions on the grounds that such interactions would violate the rule of the Theory of Relativity. This states that no communication between particles can be transmitted faster than the speed of light, which although at 300,000km/s is very fast, is nonetheless finite. John Bell suggested criteria which would test experimentally non-locality which was shown by experiments in 1982 to prove non-locality for photons. Although non-locality and entanglement have only been proved for quantum (elementary, single) particles, there are suggestions that it may also apply to macroscopic matter as well.*

**10. *Tibetan Book of the Dead*:** "Guide to the classics: the Tibetan Book of the Dead", Pema Düddul, 6 Apr 2022: https://theconversation.com/guide-to-the-classics-the-tibetan-book-of-the-dead-172962.

**11. *Truly, Madly, Deeply*:** https://en.wikipedia.org/wiki/Truly,_Madly,_Deeply_(film).

The final scenes suggest that the ghost (Alan Rickman) has deliberately become a nuisance to help his surviving girlfriend (Juliet Stevenson) let go of him.

**12. Electronic Voice Phenomena:** "Ghosts in the Machine: The Truth About EVP", 26 Feb 2024: https://homespunhaints.com/ghosts-in-the-machine-the-truth-about-evp.

See also *Telephone Calls from the Dead*, Callum E Cooper, Tricorn Books, 2012.

**13. Male/female mortality:** "Why do Women Live Longer Than Men?", Saloni Dattani and Lucas Rodés-Guirao, 27 Nov 2023: https://ourworldindata.org/why-do-women-live-longer-than-men.

"Gender Disparities in Injury Mortality: Consistent, Persistent, and Larger Than You'd Think", Susan B Sorenson PhD, Dec 2011: www.ncbi.nlm.nih.gov/pmc/articles/PMC3222499.

**14. Jonathan Cainer's apparition:** "I can't read the future", 31 Jan 2001: www.theguardian.com/theguardian/2000/jan/31/features11.g21.

Cainer, if sometimes controversial, was one of the highest-paid British columnists at his peak. Died 2016, age 58.

**15. Astrology:** Some critics of astrology are uninformed about how it is actually supposed to work. My book *The New Heretics* addresses this on pages 136–9, with observations I expanded into an online article, "Astrologers and The New Heretics", 24 Oct 2022: www.astro.com/astrology/tl_article221024_e.htm. See also www.astrologicalinsights.co.uk.

**16. Fatima/Psychic children:** "The Fatima Apparitions": https://portugalonline.com/portugal/portugal-cities-towns/fatima/prophecies/apparitions.

Claims that autistic children demonstrate significant telepathic abilities are explored at https://thetelepathytapes.com.

See also note 6, Chapter 6.

**17. Baby monitor anomalies:** "When baby monitors go bump in the night", Eimear O'Hagan, 17 Nov 2019: www.dailymail.co.uk/home/you/article-7660549/When-baby-monitors-bump-night-picking-paranormal-activity.html.

**18. Ghosts of relatives in photos:** An example can be found in "Recently Deceased Father Appears in Photo": www.reddit.com/r/Ghosts/comments/sn3z9w/recently_deceased_father_appears_in_photo.

# Chapter 3: Other Ghosts and Poltergeists

**1. The Reformation and ghosts:** "The English Reformation and Ghosts: Orthodox Revenance", Pierre Kapitaniak, *Digital Encyclopedia of European History*, 22 Jun 2020: https://ehne.fr/en/node/12455/printable/pdf.

**2. Exorcism:** Personal experiences of a "deliverance minister" are related in *Deliverance: Everyday investigations into the supernatural by an Anglican priest*, Jason Bray, Coronet, 2022.

Contemporary exorcism is detailed in "Modern Practice, Archaic Ritual: Catholic Exorcism in America", William S Chavez, 2021: www.mdpi.com/2077-1444/12/10/811.

**3. Ghost temperature anomalies:** "Ghostly happenings give people a chill", Michael Kuhne, 28 Oct 2024: www.accuweather.com/en/weather-news/ghostly-happenings-give-people-a-chill/341884.

**4. Ghost hunters:** No official international network exists, but some established regional teams can be found at:
https://the-atlantic-paranormal-society.com (USA)
https://ukparanormalsociety.org (UK)
www.ghostclub.org.uk/index.html (UK)

**5. Battle sounds at Lewes:** "The Battle of Lewes and its bloody legacy on English democracy", 4 Feb 2014: www.theargus.co.uk/news/10984930.the-battle-of-lewes-and-its-bloody-legacy-on-english-democracy.

**6. Battle of Gettysburg:** "Haunted Gettysburg", 14 Oct 2022: www.gettysburgbattlefieldtours.com/haunted-gettysburg.

**7. Other haunted battle sites:** "Top Seven Haunted Battlefields – From The Civil War to Stalingrad", Holly Godbey, 12 Dec 2016: www.warhistoryonline.com/history/top-7-battlefields-haunted-history-x.html.

"5 of the Most Haunted Battlefields on Earth": www.youtube.com/watch?v=3_8lALE4_ks.

**8. "Tape recording" ghosts:** "Stone Tape Theory – Recording Ghosts", Maurice Townsend, 24 Jan 2021: www.assap.ac.uk/articles/detail/stone-tape-theory-recording-ghosts.

**9. *The Ghost of Flight 401*:** by John G Fuller, Berkley Pub. Corp., 1976: https://en.wikipedia.org/wiki/Eastern_Air_Lines_Flight_401.

**10. Collective consciousness experiments:** The Global Consciousness Project uses digital random number generators to demonstrate wider psychic influences. Non-random readings are considered evidence of psi interference. See note 24, Chapter 5.

**11. Ghost trains:** "All Aboard the Ghost Train", Association of American Railroads: www.aar.org/article/ghost-train.

**12. Hong Kong in WWII:** "Life and death in Hong Kong during the Second World War", Katrina Lidbetter and Pad Kumlertsakul, 8 Feb 2024: https://blog.nationalarchives.gov.uk/life-and-death-in-hong-kong-during-the-second-world-war.

**13. Dark astral levels:** Stuart Wilde (died 2013, age 66) describes the perils of the lower astrals in *The Whispering Winds of Change*, Hay House, 1993.

**14. *Queen Mary* wall-walker:** Quoted, with full permission, from Mary Helen Hensley's *Understanding is the New Healing* [Ibid.], pages 101–2.

**15. Auras and Kirlian photography:** "The Myth and Science of Kirlian Photography", Suru, 25 Oct 2020, *Suru Kirlian Photography Centre*: https://jmshah.com/the-myth-and-science-of-kirlian-photography.

**16. US "haunted highways":** "These are the scariest haunted roads in the US", 15 Oct 2023: https://ktvz.com/stacker-travel/2023/10/15/these-are-the-scariest-haunted-roads-in-the-us.
  "Five of America's most haunted highways", Michael Mouritz, 26 Oct 2024: https://detour-roadtrips.com/home/five-of-americas-most-haunted-highways.

**17. Global road deaths:** The World Health Organization says around 1.35 million road deaths occur each *year*. "Road Traffic Mortality": www.who.int/data/gho/data/themes/topics/topic-details/GHO/road-traffic-mortality.

**18. Edinburgh's vaults:** https://en.wikipedia.org/wiki/Edinburgh_Vaults.

**19. A ghost's experience:** A clever imagining of a ghost trying to interact with the physical world can be found in Douglas Adams's novel *Dirk Gently's Holistic Detective Agency*, William Heinemann Ltd, 1987.

**20. *Poltergeist*:** Produced by Steven Spielberg, directed by Tobe Hooper, this 1982 movie spawned sequels and was remade in 2015. Its inspiration is explored in "The Horrifying True Story That Inspired Steven Spielberg's Poltergeist", Rachel Cioffi, 28 Sep 2023: https://screenrant.com/poltergeist-movie-true-story-inspirations-herrmann-house.

**21. The Enfield and Battersea poltergeists:** The BBC has become more open to ghost-related phenomena of late. The Enfield case is covered in "The Enfield Poltergeist", Natasha Tripney, 27 Oct 2023: www.bbc.com/culture/article/20231026-the-enfield-poltergeist-why-the-unexplained-mystery-that-shocked-1970s-britain-continues-to-disturb.
  The Battersea case is related (with part-dramatization) in the BBC Radio 4 series *The Battersea Poltergeist*, available (in the UK, at least) at www.bbc.co.uk/programmes/p0940193. Presenter Danny Robins now fronts an ongoing series of British radio/TV ghost investigations in his series *Uncanny*.

**22. Paul Bura:** Before his mediumship years, Paul was a busy UK broadcaster, providing voices for radio programmes and children's animated TV series. Died 2013, age 69. See notes 15 and 17, Chapter 5, and note 26, Chapter 6 for more on Paul.

**23. Apparitions and earth energies:** Richard Leviton explores links between these in *Signs on the Earth: Deciphering the Message of Virgin Mary Apparitions, UFO Encounters, and Crop Circles*, Hampton Roads, 2005.

24. **Ghosts seeing *us*:** Exposing the pineal gland to strong magnets has also produced instances where "ghosts" react to seeing the experimenter, as recounted in Geoff Stray's *Beyond 2012: Catastrophe or Ecstasy,* Vital Signs Publishing, 2005, pages 267–8.

25. *Father Ted:* This surreal but very successful Irish ecclesiastical TV comedy series ran for three seasons between 1995 and 1998: https://kilfenoraclare.com/father-ted.

## Chapter 4: Out-of-body and Near-Death Experiences

1. **OOBEs:** The internet is dominated by claimed scientific causes, but many questions remain unanswered. A well-balanced piece can be found at "Out-of-body experiences": https://psychology.fandom.com/wiki/Out-of-body_experiences.

2. **Anterior precuneus theory for OOBEs:** "Have Scientists Found the Source of Out-of-Body Experiences?", Victoria Sayo Turner, 24 Jul 2023: www.smithsonianmag.com/smart-news/have-scientists-found-the-source-of-out-of-body-experiences-180982565.
    See also: "Out-of-body experiences: Neuroscience or the paranormal?", Tim Newman, 19 Jul 2017: www.medicalnewstoday.com/articles/318464.

3. **NDEs:** A balanced study can be found in "A Search for the Truth of Near-Death Experiences", Dr James Paul Pandarakalam: www.rcpsych.ac.uk/docs/default-source/members/sigs/spirituality-spsig/a-search-for-the-truth-of-ndes-james-pandarakalam.pdf?sfvrsn=26aaa00_2.

4. **Definitions of "death" in NDEs:** Summed up in "Results of world's largest Near Death Experiences study published", 2014, University of Southampton: www.southampton.ac.uk/news/2014/10/07-worlds-largest-near-death-experiences-study.page.

5. **Jill Bolte Taylor/Eben Alexander/Iain McGilchrist:** www.drjilltaylor.com. Her TED presentation "My Stroke of Insight" is at www.ted.com/talks/jill_bolte_taylor_my_stroke_of_insight?subtitle=en.
    https://ebenalexander.com. *Proof of Heaven: A Neurosurgeon's Journey into the Afterlife,* Simon & Schuster, 2012.
    https://channelmcgilchrist.com. McGilchrist's books *The Master and his Emissary: The Divided Brain and the Making of the Western World,* Yale University Press, 2009 and *The Matter with Things: Our Brains, Our Delusions, and the Unmaking of the World,* Vols 1 & 2, Perspectiva Press, 2021, explore in detail the dual nature of the brain.

6. **Mary Helen Hensley NDE:** Quoted, with full permission, from Mary Helen Hensley's *Understanding is the New Healing,* page 167.

7. **Pullman train company:** www.pullman-museum.org/theCompany.

**8. Bilocation:** Or "multilocation", this can be visually witnessed or experienced as a spiritual state through meditation: https://en.wikipedia.org/wiki/Bilocation. There appears to be no one firm online resource but plenty of sceptical, religious (especially Catholic) and psychic interpretations.

**9. Remote viewing:** This useful article references Joseph McMoneagle, Russell Targ, etc. – "Clairvoyant Remote Viewing: The US Sponsored Psychic Spying", Dr M Srinivasan, Columbia University, Jan–Mar 2002: https://ciaotest.cc.columbia.edu/olj/sa/sa_jan02srm01.html.

**10. Stargate Project:** Some documents on Stargate are now declassified, although their contents are widely distrusted.

The CIA paper that officially dismissed Stargate, "An Evaluation of the Remote Viewing Program", can be read at www.cia.gov/readingroom/docs/CIA-RDP96-00791R000200180005-5.pdf.

However, see also: www.cia.gov/readingroom/docs/CIA-RDP96-00789R002800180001-2.pdf – plus a collection of files at www.cia.gov/readingroom/collection/stargate.

The curious naming of the US's 2025 AI initiative as "The Stargate Project" inevitably raised eyebrows: "Tech giants are putting $500bn into 'Stargate' to build up AI in US", João da Silva, Natalie Sherman and Imran Rahman-Jones, 22 Jan 2025: www.bbc.co.uk/news/articles/cy4m84d2xz2o.

**11. *The Men Who Stare at Goats*/Uri Geller:** *Goats* book – Jon Ronson, Picador, 2012. *Goats* film – 2009, directed by Grant Heslov.

The story of Geller and the pig's heart is told in *The Geller Effect*, Uri Geller and Guy Lyon Playfair, Henry Holt & Co., 1986, and has been recounted by Geller in interviews.

**12. McMoneagle and Elizondo on RV:** "Joe McMoneagle – Remote Viewer 001 – PROJECT: STARGATE" (Documentary 2 of 3): www.youtube.com/watch?v=7ICzREGqYHQ.

See also: *The Stargate Chronicles: Memoirs of a Psychic Spy*, Joseph McMoneagle, Crossroad Press, 2018.

"Remote Viewing UAPS (Luis Elizondo)": www.youtube.com/watch?v=esOfovKpVQo. See note 10 of Chapter 6 for more on Elizondo.

**13. Russian and Chinese psychic experiments:** "Emigre Tells of Research in Soviet in Parapsychology for Military Use", Flora Lewis, 19 Jun 1977: www.nytimes.com/1977/06/19/archives/emigre-tells-of-research-in-soviet-in-parapsychology-for-military.html.

"China's Psychic Savants", Marcello Truzzi, *Omni*, Jan 1985 (available via CIA archive): www.cia.gov/readingroom/docs/CIA-RDP96-00792R000300420017-1.pdf.

CIA historical document on Russian studies: www.cia.gov/readingroom/docs/NSA-RDP96X00790R000100010041-2.pdf.

CIA historical document on Chinese studies: www.cia.gov/readingroom/docs/CIA-RDP96-00789R002600290003-0.pdf.

**14. Todd Acamesis:** Aka "Falcon" – www.facebook.com/falcon.acamesis. Todd's presentations for the Glastonbury Symposium are illuminating and can be watched at: "Todd Acamesis – The Reality of Astral Projection": www.youtube.com/watch?v=OBl6lsz0HuU and "Todd Acamesis – Remote Viewing: The Biggest Secrets About Reality Revealed": www.youtube.com/watch?v=FBK0mytYPBE&t=6s.

**15. Jade Shaw:** https://jadeshaw.com. Jade's Glastonbury Symposium presentation can be watched at "Jade Shaw – Astral Projection: How Out-of-Body Experiences Can Change Yourself and the World": www.youtube.com/watch?v=3GwbzvTQxJc&t=11s.

## Chapter 5: Psychic Phenomena

**1. James Randi:** "The Amazing Life and Legacy of James 'The Amazing' Randi'", Kendrick Frazier, Jan/Feb 2021: https://skepticalinquirer.org/2021/01/the-amazing-life-and-legacy-of-james-the-amazing-randi.

**2. "One rule for one …":** *The New Heretics* – the whole book addresses this issue but for paranormal/esoteric areas, see pages 130–6.

**3. Dean Radin lab statistics:** Summed up well in "Dr. Dean Radin to Speak on Extrasensory Research and Overlap with Quantum Theory", 22 Oct 2020: https://thepsychologytimes.com/2020/10/22/dr-dean-radin-to-speak-on-extrasensory-research-and-overlap-with-quantum-theory.
   See also: www.deanradin.com.

**4. Entanglement and nonlocality:** Coherently summarized in "Nonlocality and Entanglement": www.physicsoftheuniverse.com/topics_quantum_nonlocality.html.

**5. Chris French and Chris Roe:** "Will the debate about 'psi' ever be settled?", British Psychological Society, 19 Mar 2024: www.bps.org.uk/psychologist/will-debate-about-psi-ever-be-settled.

**6. Psi resources:** *Seven Experiments That Could Change the World*, Rupert Sheldrake, Fourth Estate Ltd, 1994. Details on many influential Sheldrake books and papers are available at www.sheldrake.org. See also note 25, chapter 5.
   I interview Sheldrake online for the Glastonbury Symposium in "Rupert Sheldrake – Interview on 'The Science Delusion' and Morphic Resonance", 8 Nov 2020: www.youtube.com/watch?v=mAScLVy4GT8&t=2s.
   See also: www.monroeinstitute.org and https://noetic.org (Institute of Noetic Sciences).

**7. Battle of Coronel:** www.britishbattles.com/first-world-war/battle-of-coronel.

**8. Brain wave experiments:** Chris Connelly's brain wave tests are explained, with a demonstration, in his Glastonbury Symposium presentation "Chris Connelly – The Science of Psychics" at www.youtube.com/watch?v=6ObNhOxSF8w.

**9. Séances:** A sensible historical summary can be found in "Why Did So Many Victorians Try to Speak with the Dead?", Casey Cep, 24 May 2021: www.newyorker.com/magazine/2021/05/31/why-did-so-many-victorians-try-to-speak-with-the-dead.

**10. Henry Gross and Hamish Miller:** Gross – https://psi-encyclopedia.spr.ac.uk/articles/henry-gross.
Miller – https://penwithpress.co.uk/hamish-ba-miller/.

**11. Dowsing competition:** Recounted in *Sussex Circular*, issue 42, June 1995. The article "Dowsing Dilemma" is reproduced – re-edited – in my book *Swirled Harvest*, SB Publications/Vital Signs Publishing, 2003, pages 37–42. The whole book can be read as a PDF on my website at www.truthagenda.org.

**12. Water company dowsers:** "UK water firms admit using divining rods to find leaks and pipes", Matthew Weaver, 21 Nov 2017: www.theguardian.com/business/2017/nov/21/uk-water-firms-admit-using-divining-rods-to-find-leaks-and-pipes.

**13. Ley lines/Alfred Watkins:** *The Old Straight Track: Its Mounds, Beacons, Moats, Sites, and Mark Stones*, Alfred Watkins, Methuen & Co., 1925.
See also: "Introducing Alfred Watkins, a fascinating man", 26 Oct 2021: www.visitherefordshire.co.uk/blog/introducing-alfred-watkins-fascinating-man.

**14. Holographic universe:** "The Universe as a Hologram", Barbara Robertson, 7 Sep 2023: www.lightfieldlab.com/blogposts/the-universe-as-a-hologram.

**15. More Paul Bura:** Paul shares many personal stories in his autobiography *Stepping to the Drummer: The Extraordinary Tales of a Psychic Man*, Honeytone Promotions, 2000, which has a foreword by Uri Geller.
Some of Paul's channellings are recorded in *Joeb: Servant of Gaia*, Symbol Creations, 1995.

**16. Police/FBI use psychics:** "Psychics and Police Work", H Rachlin, *Law and Order* Volume 41, Issue 9, September 1993, pages 84–8: www.ojp.gov/ncjrs/virtual-library/abstracts/psychics-and-police-work.
"CIA: Use of Psychics in Law Enforcement", declassified 7 Aug 2000: www.cia.gov/readingroom/docs/CIA-RDP96-00788R000100280009-3.pdf.

**17. Al Bowlly:** https://en.wikipedia.org/wiki/Al_Bowlly.
Paul Bura's detailed telling of his Bowlly story can be found in *Stepping to the Drummer*, pages 69–73.

**18. "35 trillion to one":** See note 3 above.

See also: *Entangled Minds: Extrasensory Experiences in a Quantum Reality*, Dean Radin, Paraview Pocket Books, 2006.

**19. Particles go backwards in time:** "Researchers Proved the 'Quantum Time Flip' Can Go Backward", Caroline Delbert, 19 Jul 2024: www.popularmechanics.com/science/a61627785/quantum-time-flip-can-go-backward.

"Retrocausality: How backwards-in-time effects could explain quantum weirdness", Dr Rod Sutherland, 10 Feb 2023: https://researchoutreach.org/articles/retrocausality-backwards-time-effects-explain-quantum-weirdness.

**20. Turkey invades Cyprus:** https://en.wikipedia.org/wiki/Turkish_invasion_of_Cyprus.

**21. Precognition of big events:** "The Possibility of Precognition", Steve Taylor PhD, 4 Jul 2021: www.psychologytoday.com/gb/blog/out-the-darkness/202107/the-possibility-precognition.

**22. 9/11 issues:** Polls consistently show widespread doubts about the official story, and, sadly, not without foundation. I write on the many unresolved anomalies in *Conspiracies: The Facts – The Theories – The Evidence*, Watkins Publishing, 2013, revised 2019, pages 163–87 (revised ed.), and also (with photographs) in *The Truth Agenda: Making Sense of Unexplained Mysteries, Global Cover-Ups and Visions for a New Era*, Vital Signs Publishing, 2009, revised 2011 and 2013 (US edition: Adventures Unlimited Press, 2015), pages 143–78. I discuss the polarization around 9/11 in *The New Heretics*, pages 214–22.

See also: https://911truth.org and www.ae911truth.org.

**23. 9/11 precognition:** "9/11: Premonition of Disaster", Gomery Kimber, 4 Oct 2021: https://brazen-head.org/2021/10/04/9-11-premonition-of-disaster.

"Science vs Parapsychology: A Closer Look at 9/11 Premonitions", *Sky History*: www.history.co.uk/articles/closer-look-at-911-premonitions.

*Messages: Signs, Visits, and Premonitions from Loved Ones Lost on 9/11*, Bonnie McEneaney, William Morrow, 2010.

**24. Global Consciousness Project:** Official website: https://gcp2.net.

Princeton Engineering Anomalies Research (PEAR): https://psi-encyclopedia.spr.ac.uk/articles/princeton-engineering-anomalies-research-pear.

**25. Presentiment:** "Presentiment", Dean Radin, 29 June 2016: https://psi-encyclopedia.spr.ac.uk/articles/presentiment.

"Predictive physiological anticipatory activity preceding seemingly unpredictable stimuli: An update of Mossbridge *et al*'s meta-analysis", Michael Duggan and Patrizio Tressoldi, National Library

of Medicine/PMC PubMed Central, 17 Jul 2018: www.proquest.com/
docview/2114633193?pq-origsite=gscholar&fromopenview=true&sourcet
ype=Scholarly%20Journals.

**26. Morphic resonance:** "Morphic Resonance and Morphic Fields – an
Introduction", Rupert Sheldrake: www.sheldrake.org/research/morphic-
resonance/introduction.

See also Sheldrake's books *A New Science of Life: The Hypothesis of
Formative Causation*, J P Tarcher, 1981, and *The Presence of the Past:
Morphic Resonance and the Habits of Nature*, Columbia University Press,
1998 (both books revised several times since).

See also note 6 above.

# Chapter 6: UFOs and UAP

**1. Fake alien invasion:** Often linked with claims about secret 3-D hologram
technology, this theory is discussed interestingly in "Project Blue Beam:
Staging a Fake Alien Attack to Take Over the World", *The Why Files*, 8 Oct
2024: www.youtube.com/watch?v=kaS8fP12CGM.

**2. UFO/UAP resources:** Some researchers say "UAPs", which implies
"Unexplained Anomalous Phenomenas", but as this is ungrammatical I
prefer the plural "UAP" ("phenomena").

Here is a list of some key figures in the world of current ufology, with
apologies to those not included. They don't necessarily agree with each
other, but all weave the growing tapestry calling for disclosure. Look up
their websites, documentaries, books and podcasts:

Chris Bledsoe, Kelly Chase, Ross Coulthart, Jeremy Corbell, Richard
Dolan, Julian Dorey, Alan Foster, James Fox, Brandon Fugal, Dr Steven
Greer, Gary Heseltine, Dave Hodrien, Leslie Kean, Jay Christopher
King, George Knapp, Avi Loeb, Michael P Masters, Christopher Mellon,
Jesse Michels, Garry Nolan, Diana Pasulka, Matthew Pines, Nick Pope,
Harold E Puthoff, Shawn Ryan, Donald R Schmitt, Danny Sheehan, The
Sol Foundation, Whitley Strieber, Bart Uytterhaegen, Jacques Vallee,
Bryce Zabel.

Some leading podcasts: *American Alchemy* (Michels); *Caspersight* (Ben
Hendy); *Down to Earth* (Christian Harloff); *Eyes on Cinema*; *The Good
Trouble Show* (Matt Ford); *Intelligent Disclosure* (Dolan); *Liberation Times*
(Chris Sharp); *Need to Know* (Coulthart and Zabel); *Psicoactivo* (Pavel
Ibarra Meda);*The Shawn Ryan Show, That UFO Podcast* (Andy McGrillen);
*UAP Files; Vetted* (Patrick Scott Armstrong); *Weaponized* (Knapp and
Corbell); *The Why Files* (A J Gentile).

**3. Project Blue Book:** Official (dismissive) conclusions: "Project BLUE
BOOK – Unidentified Flying Objects": www.archives.gov/research/
military/air-force/ufos.

**4. Roswell:** Among the conflicting theories, there seems to be no definitive internet resource. However, Donald R Schmitt lays out the timeline, facts and arguments clearly and authoritatively in *Cover-Up at Roswell: Exposing the 70-Year Conspiracy to Suppress the Truth*, New Page Books, 2017.

Schmitt is "lead investigator" at the Roswell UFO Museum which, despite its tourist veneer, is genuinely informative and worth visiting: www.roswellufomuseum.com.

**5. Malmstrom UFO incident:** Definitively recounted in Robert Salas's *Faded Giant: The 1967 Missile/UFO Incidents*, BookSurge Publishing, 2005.

**6. Fatima apparitions:** Discussed fully in my book *The Truth Agenda*, pages 55–61. See also note 16, Chapter 2.

**7. Moon/Mars bases:** Claims (with photos) of technological structures on both the Moon and Mars, plus faces, pyramids, etc., are rife. USAF Sergeant Karl Wolfe stated that when working at a National Security Agency facility he was shown evidence of an alien base on the far side of the Moon and the presence of a huge two-mile-long "ancient" craft. An interview with Wolfe, "ET Extraterrestrial Structures on the Moon" can be watched at https://top40-charts.com/videos/play.php?vid=_4hycqDNnPE. Wolfe died in a cycling accident in 2018, age 74, generating inevitable conspiracy speculation.

See also: *Alien Intelligence and the Pathway to Mars: The Hidden Connections between the Red Planet and Earth*, Mary Bennett and David S Percy, Bear & Company, 2021.

**8. Undersea UFOs:** "Why 'UFOs' should be tracked in the water as well as the skies", 30 Jan 2025: https://news.northeastern.edu/2023/09/15/ufo-report-nasa-aliens-ocean.

"US Navy Footage Shows Spherical UFO Flying Around Before Diving Into Sea", Jack Dunhill, 21 Dec 2022: www.iflscience.com/us-navy-footage-shows-spherical-ufo-flying-around-before-diving-into-sea-66773.

**9. Pentagon UAP videos/Congressional hearings:** "Watch the Pentagon's three declassified UFO videos taken by U.S. Navy pilots", 28 Apr 2020: www.youtube.com/watch?v=rO_M0hLlJ-Q.

Look up all the congressional UAP hearings, but the 2023 session with David Grusch and pilots David Fravor and Ryan Graves is essential viewing – "UFO congressional hearing explores unexplained aerial phenomena", 26 Jul 2023: www.youtube.com/watch?v=Glw76YKuWCY.

**10. Elizondo's *Imminent*/Drones scare:** *Imminent: Inside the Pentagon's Hunt for UFOs*, Luis Elizondo, John Blake, 2024.

An example of initial reporting of the 2024 drone swarms can be found at "Drone Incursions Closed Wright-Patterson Air Force Base's Airspace Friday Night", Howard Altman, 15 Dec 2024: www.twz.com/air/drone-incursions-closed-wright-patterson-air-force-bases-airspace-friday-night.

See also: "Congressional Hearing Reveals Gaps in Counter-Drone Readiness Amid Concerns About N.Y./N.J. Drone Sightings", Miriam McNabb, 11 Dec 2024: https://dronelife.com/2024/12/11/congressional-hearing-reveals-gaps-in-counter-drone-readiness-amid-concerns-about-n-y-n-j-drone-sightings/.

The perplexing claim in Jan 2025 that the drones were official and commercial ones after all, rejected even by New Jersey's mayor, is deconstructed (with footage of the press conferences) by Ross Coulthart at "NJ mayor on Trump's drone response: 'We're not accepting this anymore'", *News Nation*, 30 Jan 2024: www.youtube.com/watch?v=shY369pwx9k.

**11. The Sol Foundation/2024 congressional hearings:** https://thesolfoundation.org.

The 2024 hearings also included NASA's Michael Gold, former rear admiral Tim Gallaudet and journalist Michael Shellenberger: "UFO House Hearing amid 'concerns,' witnesses speak out", 13 Nov 2024: https://www.youtube.com/watch?v=k7NzR0payrs.

Jake Barber's revelatory claims about the US government's UAP retrieval programme are detailed in an interview with Jesse Michels in "UFO Crash Retrieval: Jake Barber's FIRSTHAND Story", 30 Jan 2024: https://www.youtube.com/watch?v=dnnpyNuPdXs.

**12. Police UAP guide:** "UFO sightings? Police chiefs group releases guidebook offering strategies for PD response", 13 Sep 2024: www.police1.com/chiefs-sheriffs/ufo-sightings-police-chiefs-group-releases-guidebook-offering-strategies-for-pd-response.

**13. AARO denies ETs:** https://media.defense.gov/2024/Mar/08/2003409233/-1/-1/0/DOPSR-CLEARED-508-COMPLIANT-HRRV1-08-MAR-2024-FINAL.PDF.

**14. UAP Act 2024:** www.democrats.senate.gov/imo/media/doc/uap_amendment.pdf.

"Implications of the Unidentified Anomalous Phenomena (UAP) Amendment in the 2024 National Defense Authorization Act (NDAA)", Stephanie Barna, Jasmine Wang and Moushmi Patil, 9 Jan 2024: www.insidegovernmentcontracts.com/2024/01/implications-of-the-unidentified-anomalous-phenomena-uap-amendment-in-the-2024-national-defense-authorization-act-ndaa.

**15. Zimbabwe school UFOs:** https://en.wikipedia.org/wiki/Ariel_School_UFO_incident.

**16. Stealth helicopters:** "Why Doesn't the U.S. Military Have Stealth Helicopters By Now?", Harrison Cass, 22 May 2024: https://nationalinterest.org/blog/buzz/why-doesnt-us-military-have-stealth-helicopters-now-207838.

**17. TARDIS-like UFOs:** The TARDIS is the bigger-on-the-inside time/ space craft used in *Doctor Who*, a television phenomenon that has been running since 1963: https://en.wikipedia.org/wiki/Doctor_Who.

"Crashed UFO recovered by the US military 'distorted space and time'", Josh Boswell, 10 Jun 2023: www.dailymail.co.uk/news/article-12175195/ Crashed-UFO-recovered-military-distorted-space-time.html.

**18. The Phoenix Lights:** Mainstream references are mostly debunks but a defensive case is made in "James Fox Sheds More Light Into The Phoenix Lights UFO Sighting", 26 Dec 2024: www.youtube.com/ watch?v=iCoJObQtwVc.

**19. Pentyrch UFO:** *The Pentyrch Incident: The Greatest UFO Cover-up of Modern Times*, Caz Clarke and Gari Jones, self-published, 2021.

See also: "Military are hiding the facts about Pentyrch UFO sighting, says author", Frederick Bennett, 21 Jan 2022: https://cardiffjournalism. co.uk/thecardiffian/2022/01/21/military-are-hiding-the-facts-about- pentyrch-ufo-sighting-says-author.

**20. Gary Heseltine:** Details about Gary can be found at *UFO Truth* magazine: www.ufotruthmagazine.co.uk/about-the-editor.

**21. *Close Encounters of the Third Kind*:** Directed by Steven Spielberg, 1977: https://en.wikipedia.org/wiki/Close_Encounters_of_the_Third_Kind.

**22. Circle helicopter incident:** Jason's experience, together with details of the Birling Gap and Cissbury crop formations, can be found in my book *Fields of Mystery*, page 81, available to read online. See note 5, Chapter 1.

**23. *Close Encounters* air traffic control scene.** www.youtube.com/ watch?v=MLiRnvppAaM.

**24. Men in Black:** There are multiple online references, although many refer to the comedy movie franchise, but a good resource is Nick Redfern's *The Real Men In Black: Evidence, Famous Cases, and True Stories of These Mysterious Men and Their Connection to UFO Phenomena*, RWW New Page Books, 2011.

**25. Orgone/Plasmoids:** Interaction with these is described in Andrew Collins's books *The Circlemakers: A Revolutionary New Vision of the Crop Circle Enigma*, ABC Books, 1992, and *Alien Energy: UFOs, Ritual Landscapes and the Human Mind*, Eagle Wing Books Inc., 2003.

**26. *Quest for Contact*:** The full story of our psychic questing adventures is told in my book (with Paul Bura) *Quest for Contact: A True Story of Crop Circles, UFOs and Psychics*, SB Publications, 1997. This can be read as a PDF on my website at www.truthagenda.org.

A concise summary can be found in "Interactive Experiments with Crop Circles", 6 Jul 2017: https://truthagenda.org/2017/07/06/new-article- interactive-experiments-with-crop-circles.

**27. Crop circle resources:** My own circle books are useful, especially *Vital Signs: A Complete Guide to the Crop Circle Mystery and Why it is NOT a Hoax*, SB Publications, 1998, revised 2002 (UK)/ Frog Ltd, 2002 (US); and *An Introduction to Crop Circles*, Wessex Books, 2004, revised 2011. *The New Heretics* has a long section on the culture around circle research, pages 264–76. See also *Fields of Mystery*, *Quest for Contact* and *Swirled Harvest*, and my video *Circular Sussex*: www.youtube.com/watch?v=Nywg97Dc3IU&t=2s

Other recommended books are *The Deepening Complexity of Crop Circles* by Eltjo Haselhoff, North Atlantic Books, 2001; *Crop Circles: The Bones of God* by (the late) Michael Glickman, Frog Ltd, 2009; and *Crop Circles: Layers of Mystery* by Dan Vidler, Ground Level Press, 2024, for which I provide a foreword.

Key websites:
www.cropcirclecenter.com (extensive database)
www.cropcircleconnector.com (regular reports)
www.ukcropcircles.co.uk (ground research)

Currently in preparation is the Crop Circle Research Archive project, which will be a significant free repository of decades of crucial circle material, some never published before. Keep an eye on www.circleresearcharchive.com for updates.

**28. Putamen and caudate:** "Confessions of a UFO Hunter: Ross Coulthart interviews Lue Elizondo", 24 Aug 2024: www.youtube.com/watch?v=wgM5V44eQHU.

See also Elizondo's *Imminent* and "Garry Nolan: A Stanford Professor's Quest to Resolve Unidentified Anomalous Phenomena", Micah Hanks, 22 May 2023: https://thedebrief.org/garry-nolan-a-stanford-professors-quest-to-resolve-unidentified-anomalous-phenomena.

**29. John Mack:** Mack's views are summed up in "Interview with John Mack, Psychiatrist, Harvard University", *Nova*, 1996: www.pbs.org/wgbh/nova/aliens/johnmack.html. Mack was killed by a drunk driver in 2004, age 74, fuelling yet more conspiracy speculation.

See also: "John E Mack", Jeanne Lenzer, 16 Oct 2004: https://pmc.ncbi.nlm.nih.gov/articles/PMC523131.

**30. Alien abductions/Animal mutilations:** A concise guide can be found at "Alien Abduction Theories: A Scientific Search for Evidence", 29 Aug 2023: https://science.howstuffworks.com/space/aliens-ufos/alien-abduction.htm.

The website of key abduction researcher Mary Rodwell, who offers help and advice, is at www.maryrodwell.com.au.

The dark world of animal mutilations is summed up extensively, if agnostically, in *Stalking The Herd: Examining the Cattle Mutilation Mystery*, Christopher O'Brien, Adventures Unlimited Press, 2013. UFO-related *human* mutilations have occasionally been claimed but are thankfully rare.

**31. *Communion*:** Whitley Strieber, Avon, 1987. Filmed in 1989, starring Christopher Walken as Strieber and directed by Philippe Mora: https://en.wikipedia.org/wiki/Communion_(1989_film).

Strieber's website: www.unknowncountry.com.

**32. Carl Jung:** *Flying Saucers: A Modern Myth of Things Seen in the Skies*, Carl Jung, Routledge & Paul, 1959.

**33. "Ashtar" transmission:** https://en.wikipedia.org/wiki/Southern_Television_broadcast_interruption.

The audio recording can be heard at https://txfeatures.mb21.co.uk/hannington/spacemessage-offair.mp3.

Southern Television was just one local station in the British Independent Television (ITV) network and the transmission was not heard in the other regions.

**34. *Ancient Aliens*:** This hugely successful show began on the History Channel in 2009 and continues despite attacks from sceptics: https://en.wikipedia.org/wiki/Ancient_Aliens.

**35. Miami mall aliens:** "Alien speculation engulfs Miami mall after curious New Year's Day video", Amelia Neath, 9 Jan 2024: www.independent.co.uk/news/world/americas/crime/alien-miami-mall-new-year-video-b2475380.html.

"Rumors of 'shadow aliens' at Bayside Marketplace go viral", 6 Jan 2024: www.youtube.com/watch?v=Ek_8t1sdvGc.

"I Investigated The Miami Alien Mall (Bayside Marketplace)", OmarGoshTV, 13 Jan 2024: www.youtube.com/watch?v=aASmbgiTLi0.

**36. Golden Ball Hill:** "Golden Ball Hill – Etymology", *Survey of English Place Names*: https://epns.nottingham.ac.uk/browse/id/532886d2b47fc40d38000034-Golden+Ball+Hill.

**37. Dark shapes:** First recounted in *Quest for Contact*, p.77.

**38. Light ball at talk:** Quoted from "Lecture Light", Anthony James, www.swirled.news, 2 Oct 2006: http://1113676691.test.prositehosting.co.uk/article.asp?artID=910.

**39. Ball lightning/Earthquake lights:** "What is ball lightning, a reality or myth?", Fionna Samuels, *Chemical & Engineering News*, 15 Apr 2024: https://cen.acs.org/environment/atmospheric-chemistry/What-is-ball-lightning-reality-or-myth/102/i12.

"Bizarre Earthquake Lights Finally Explained", Brian Clark Howard, 7 Jan 2014: www.nationalgeographic.com/science/article/140106-earthquake-lights-earthquake-prediction-geology-science.

**40. Historical crop circles:** The 1678 "Mowing Devil" pamphlet, published in Hertfordshire, England, clearly describes a crop circle, attributed to being work of the Devil. See my article "The 'Mowing Devil' Investigated", 22 Dec 2005, www.swirled.news: http://1113676691.test.prositehosting.

co.uk/article.asp?artID=844 and "More On The 'Mowing Devil'", 7 June 2006, www.swirled.news: http://1113676691.test.prositehosting.co.uk/article.asp?artID=896.

Sir Robert Plot's 1686 book *The Natural History of Staffordshire* may also describe crop formations, interpreted this time as meteorological phenomena: https://commons.wikimedia.org/wiki/File:Robert_Plot_-_Natural_History_of_Staffordshire_1686_-_quadrangular_cropmark.png.

For a valuable round-up of historical crop circles, see Terry Wilson's *The Secret History of Crop Circles*, CCCS, 1998, revised 2015, for which I provide a foreword.

**41. Crop circle video/Circle silica:** Arguments still rage over the 1996 video showing a crop formation appearing. Lack of proof that it was hoaxed and the long silence of unconfirmed claimants has seen it rehabilitated by UFO podcasts of late. The raw video can be watched at "Oliver's Castle Crop Circle: The Original Footage", 2 Nov 2012: www.youtube.com/watch?v=PDTdY07bRIM.

My book *Swirled Harvest*, which can be read as a PDF at www.truthagenda.org, features a long chapter (updated from a *Sussex Circular* article) on the Oliver's Castle controversies, pages 51–78.

The same book also includes a chapter, "Dust to Dust", analyzing balls of light and the white silica deposits left where they have touched down in crop circles, pages 131–43.

# Chapter 7: Bizarre Happenings

**1. Thomas Dolby:** Dolby's song *Eastern Bloc* appears on his album "Astronauts and Heretics", 1992: www.thomasdolby.com.

**2. Typewriter:** As mentioned, I was typing pages for the *Sussex Circular*. See note 4, Chapter 1.

The full line of my lyric should have been "I want to go everywhere from Paris to Mars". See note 2, Chapter 1 for more on my music.

Barry Reynolds says:

*Thirty years after the event occurred and no longer having the electric typewriter to hand, we cannot be sure exactly what happened. However, we do now know that the IBM Actionwriter 1 (which we believe to be the make and model involved) did have a small memory of 512 characters in which it kept the last two lines typed. After extensive internet searches, we also know that IBM used the "Shannon Text" – "THE HEAD AND IN FRONTAL ATTACK" etc. – as a performance test for print speed measurements from at least the early 1980s and that this text could be automatically produced on IBM typewriters/printers after a restore. A restore could be initiated after either a specific series of keys were pressed or an electrical signal was sent down one of the I/O cable connector pins.*

*It is therefore not beyond the realms of possibility that an electrical voltage spike caused the typewriter to reset and because this was not done in a controlled manner, it first printed some remaining characters that were somehow in its memory – "I want to go everywhere from …" – followed by the performance test Shannon Text. Possibly, or possibly not; we shall never know …*

**3. Triboluminescence:** www.tribonet.org/wiki/triboluminescence.

**4. Electrically charged stones:** "Charge generation and propagation in igneous rocks", Friedemann Freund, *Journal of Geodynamics*, Vol. 33, Issues 4–5, May–July 2002, pages 543–70: www.sciencedirect.com/science/article/abs/pii/S0264370702000157.

**5. Stone circle "charges":** See *Needles of Stone*, Tom Graves, HarperCollins, 1978.
See also: "THEY'RE ALIVE! Megalithic sites are more than just stone", Freddy Silva, 2016: https://invisibletemple.com/extra/megalithic-sites-more-than-stone.html.

**6. Impromptu shrine miracles:** In 2005, a Chicago water leak suggested an image of the Virgin Mary, dismissed as natural simulacra in "Voice of Reason: The Viaduct Virgin", Joe Nickell, 16 May 2005: www.livescience.com/263-voice-reason-viaduct-virgin.html. Nonetheless, claims that real miracles occurred there and at other similar sites, suggest that psi and intent can create real effects, unless heavenly forces are genuinely at work.

**7. Weather and psychic energy:** "Adventures in Cloudbusting", Michael Martin, 5 Apr 2021: www.thecenterforsophiologicalstudies.com/post/adventures-in-cloudbusting.
Andrew Collins's *The Circlemakers* includes several references to orgone energy (as defined by Wilhelm Reich – see above article) affecting weather. His book *The Black Alchemist*, ABC Books, 1988, new edition Arrow Books, 1992, suggests that the 1987 storm that devastated England could have been influenced by black magic.
Details on Ian Lynch: https://ianlynch.net.

**8. Coincidences:** Martin Plimmer and Brian King's *Beyond Coincidence*, Icon Books, 2004, demonstrates that some incredible coincidences *can* happen by statistical quirks, even if it underestimates people's feelings around the *synchronicity* of them, which is different.

**9. Birds as omens:** In *A Little Bird Told Me …*, Howann Wai Publishing, 2009, paranormal researcher Ann Brocklehurst recounts the role of birds in her life as meaningful signs. Eventually, a large crow began banging hard on her window and didn't leave until she realized this omen meant that her apparently treated cancer had returned, something then confirmed by diagnosis. The illness took her in 2013, age 69.
Crows/rooks have traditionally been seen as harbingers of change: *The Folklore of Rooks and Rookeries: A Source Book for Desertions*, S R Young, Pwca Books and Pamphlets, 2023.

**10. Dog-headed creatures:** "A Short History of Dog-headed Men", Matt Salusbury, 25 Mar 2012, originally published in *Fortean Times*: http://mattsalusbury.blogspot.com/2012/03/short-history-of-dog-headed-men.html.

This more critical piece suspects racial slurs behind the beliefs: "Cynocephali – The Dog-Headed Race: A Brief Introduction", Dana Rehn, 23 May 2021: https://danakrehnblog.wordpress.com/2021/05/23/cynocephali-the-dog-headed-race-a-brief-introduction.

**11. Skinwalker Ranch:** https://skinwalker-ranch.com. The HISTORY Channel's ongoing docuseries *The Secret of Skinwalker Ranch* began in 2020 and has become a significant phenomenon.

**12. Bermuda Triangle:** Tourist spin can be found at "The Legends & Lore of the Bermuda Triangle" but it sums up the picture: www.gotobermuda.com/inspiration/article/legends-lore-bermuda-triangle.

Charles Berlitz's *The Bermuda Triangle: An Incredible Saga Of Unexplained Disappearances*, Souvenir Press, 1975, was a sensation and set many legends running, despite accusations of factual unreliability.

**13. Airfield timeslip:** Kim's account was written for this book, but her story previously featured in *The Ghosts of Biggin Hill*, Bob Ogley, Froglets Publications Ltd, 2001.

See also: https://bigginhillairport.com/about/our-heritage.

**14. Creating channelled entities:** The most famous example is "The Philip Experiment", which saw a Canadian psychic group deliberately invent a character ("Philip", a 17th-century aristocrat), who then mysteriously exhibited a full independent existence at channelings and séances, summed up well in "The Philip Experiment: A Benchmark in Paranormal Research", C Wesley Clough, 4 Mar 2024: https://cwesleyclough.wordpress.com/2024/03/04/the-philip-experiment-a-benchmark-in-paranormal-research.

Paul Bura (see notes above) was perturbed when "Joeb", an entity he thought only he channelled, began to speak through mediums at other meetings, although this did provide interesting evidence that Joeb was a separate entity from Paul's inner psyche unless, as with Philip, a thought-form had somehow taken on a life of its own.

**15. Astrological projections:** Richard Tarnas's *Cosmos and Psyche*, Viking, 2006, makes a strong case that astrological cycles, whether we personally believe in them or not, may well influence global historical developments. Formerly a respected scholar, it was hard for his peers to entirely dismiss his switch to something so unconventional, but most did so anyway.

**16. The Angels of Mons:** "Were the Angels of Mons in World War I Real, or Mass Hysteria?", Robert Barr Smith, Aug 2005: https://warfarehistorynetwork.com/article/world-war-i-miracle-the-angels-of-mons.

## Chapter 8: Paranormal Futures

**1. Left-brain dominance:** "Iain McGilchrist on the dangers of 'left brain' domination", 22 Jun 2022: www.youtube.com/watch?v=UOADO1_owZA.

"Iain McGilchrist and the battle over the left-brain, right-brain theory", Nick Spencer, 3 Mar 2022: www.prospectmagazine.co.uk/culture/38439/iain-mcgilchrist-and-the-battle-over-the-left-brain-right-brain-theory.

See also note 5, chapter 4.

**2. AI:** Although AI's abilities are now widely recognized, its far-reaching societal consequences are still not receiving the necessary attention. I explore the issues accessibly in my 2023 Glastonbury Symposium talk "Andy Thomas: Artificial Intelligence and Artificial Freedom", 13 Aug 2023: www.youtube.com/watch?v=2Y7w9aGH-7U&t=8s.

I followed this up in 2024, discussing how AI and growing UAP awareness may be related, in "Andy Thomas – ETs and the AI Revolution", 2 Sep 2024: www.youtube.com/watch?v=PVzu94mlNcc&t=17s.

Chris Connelly, a moderator for this book, says:

*AI is a wonderful tool to aid future discoveries and knowledge, but equally it's a tool that can be used to dumb down the masses. Human behaviour seeks to conserve energy, not wanting to commit to unnecessary usage of cognitive resources. It's literally how we have evolved, and I fear we'll soon forget AI is a "tool" and instead look to it to replace human ingenuity and spirit. We're already seeing memory and cognitive abilities in children diminish due to the use of technology – why develop a memory when it's all there online?*

**3. Devious AI:** The dilemmas and dangers raised by HAL, the intelligent computer in Stanley Kubrick's renowned 1968 film *2001: A Space Odyssey*, now seem incredibly prophetic: "2001: A Space Odyssey: A prescient warning not to treat Artificial Intelligence as a human substitute", Keshav Krishnamurty, *Sage Journals*, 10 Jun 2024: https://journals.sagepub.com/doi/10.1177/13505084241259970.

Real-world AI has shown itself to be quite capable of self-protecting deception, as in "'Scheming' ChatGPT tried to stop itself from being shut down", Mark Sellman, 7 Dec 2024: www.thetimes.com/uk/technology-uk/article/chatgpt-o1-openai-prevents-own-deletion-tmvgbb7ls.

**4. Quantum computing:** "What is quantum computing?", Josh Schneider and Ian Smalley, 5 Aug 2024: www.ibm.com/think/topics/quantum-computing.

With these abilities, a future computer that could calculate the meaning of "life, the universe and everything", as author Douglas Adams imagined, might yet come to pass.

**5. *The Coming Wave:*** Subtitled *AI, Power and the 21ˢᵗ Century's Greatest Dilemma*, Mustafa Suleyman and Michael Bhaskar, Bodley Head, 2023.

**6. Brain chips/Transhumanism:** "Transhumanism and Neuralink: the dawn of digitally enhanced humans", Neil C Hughes, 10 Jun 2023: https://cybernews.com/editorial/transhumanism-and-neuralink.

**7. Materialism as control:** The 20th-century philosopher Rudolf Steiner often warned of world powers using materialism to control populations and suppress our spiritual natures, adding:

> *The time will come, and it may not be far off, that people will say: It is pathological for people to even think in terms of spirit and soul. "Sound" people will speak of nothing but the body. It will be considered a sign of illness for anyone to arrive at the idea of any such thing as a spirit or a soul.*

("Fall of the Spirits of Darkness", Lecture 5, Dornach, 7th Oct 1917)

Ironically, esoteric beliefs clearly influence tiers of global authority, apparently keen to keep this knowledge to themselves, most famously at the annual Bohemian Grove ceremonies, as explored in my book *The Truth Agenda*, pages 88–97.

**8. *The Matrix*/Reality:** *The Matrix* (followed by sequels) is a 1999 film directed by Larry and Andy Wachowski (now Lana and Lilly) that imagines everyday reality as nothing more than a digital construct created by machines to enslave humanity. The coding becomes visible to adepts who can navigate it.

An example of people claiming to see real *Matrix*-like code can be found in "I viewed the physical matrix for the first time", Osairis, 2016: www.reddit.com/r/Glitch_in_the_Matrix/comments/4z55hc/i_viewed_ the_physical_matrix_for_the_first_time/?rdt=44905.

On "reality", John Cole concludes:

> *There is a growing understanding, even among academics, of the illusory nature of the material world. I'm thinking of McGilchrist in particular* [see notes above] *and also philosopher and computer scientist Bernardo Kastrup, who presents a very strong argument for* idealism. *Basically, the argument is that if you believe that only matter is real then your belief itself is not real, so think again ...*

# INDEX